# The Lexicon

# OXFORD TEXTBOOKS IN LINGUISTICS

# The Lexicon

## An Introduction

**Elisabetta Ježek**

OXFORD

UNIVERSITY PRESS

# OXFORD
UNIVERSITY PRESS

Great Clarendon Street, Oxford, OX2 6DP,
United Kingdom

Oxford University Press is a department of the University of Oxford.
It furthers the University's objective of excellence in research, scholarship,
and education by publishing worldwide. Oxford is a registered trade mark of
Oxford University Press in the UK and in certain other countries

© Italian edition *Lessico. Classi di parole, strutture, combinazioni*
first published by Il Mulino in 2005
© 2005 by Società editrice Il Mulino, Bologna
English revised translation © Elisabetta Ježek 2016

The moral rights of the author have been asserted

This edition first published in 2016
Impression: 1

Published in the United States of America by Oxford University Press
198 Madison Avenue, New York, NY 10016, United States of America

British Library Cataloguing in Publication Data
Data available

Library of Congress Control Number: 2015940140

ISBN 978–0–19–960153–0 (hbk.)
ISBN 978–0–19–960154–7 (pbk.)

Printed in Great Britain by
Clays Ltd, St Ives plc

# Contents

# Preface to the English edition

The aim of this book is to provide the reader with the basic tools to approach the study of the lexicon. This is achieved by illustrating its structural organization and its behavior in actual use.

The lexicon of a language can be described as the set of its words. It will quickly become evident that to determine what constitutes a word in a language, to describe its meaning, how it is used, and how it can be combined with other words is no simple matter. On closer inspection, words prove to be a bundle of information of different sorts, and their meaning reveals multiple facets in context, inextricably linked with the syntax in which they appear.

We currently have a number of tools to scientifically describe the lexicon. Linguistic research, especially in the last 20 years, has devoted a lot of attention to this component of human language. This has occurred for several reasons, which we will not examine in detail—this book is intended to provide an introduction to the topic. Nevertheless, we should bear in mind that when we first learn a language we do so by initially using single words or unstructured sequences of words, and only later do we develop other skills, such as syntactic ones, often through the recognition and generalization of syntactic patterns associated with words. Moreover, if one engages in the study of human language from the point of view of the lexicon, one is forced to consider all aspects of language simultaneously (phonology, morphology, semantics, syntax and pragmatics), and to clarify how they interact. Words, in the end, are a direct mirror of how we conceptualize the world and our experience of it.

Since the study of the lexicon can be approached from several different perspectives, it is necessary to clarify the prespective taken in this book. This volume does not aim to present a theory of the lexicon from the point of view of its mental organization (i.e. the lexicon as it is stored and processed in our minds), nor does it aim to examine the way in which the lexical competence of speakers develops through time in language learning. More basically, its goal is to provide a description of the main properties of words and the organizational principles of the lexicon that can be derived by examining the use we make of words on a daily basis; it introduces the categories that are useful to classify the various phenomena that can be observed by querying digitalized corpora and gathering speakers' judgments, and proposes viable representations for each of them, using the formalisms developed in the field of general and theoretical linguistics.

The book conforms to the tradition of structuralist and formal approaches to the study of language, and reexamines themes that have been a matter of debate since antiquity, such as the notion of word class, themes that found a systematization in the 1970s in the works of leading scholars such as J. Lyons and D. Dowty. In view of the lively debate surrounding current studies of the lexicon, the text provides an overview of central topics that are still highly controversial rather than a statement of a received doctrine.

The book is organized in two parts. The first part consists of the first three chapters. Chapter 1 presents the basics, introduces different lexicalization types, discusses what counts as a word in a language, and illustrates the types of words that exist in the languages of the world. Chapter 2 discusses the different types of information contained in words, and illustrates the interplay between lexical information and encyclopedic knowledge in the interpretation of words in their context of use. Chapter 3 is devoted to the meaning of words, and clarifies how words contribute to form the meaning of sentences, assuming a multi-dimensional model of lexical meaning.

The second part of the book consists of Chapters 4, 5, and 6. In this part, the focus shifts from the properties of individual words to an analysis of the structures that can be identified in the global lexicon. Chapter 4 discusses word classes. The focus is on nouns and verbs, for both of which several classes are proposed, identified on the basis of both syntactic and semantic criteria (valency structure, *Aktionsart*, type of entity, etc.). The last part of the chapter focuses on typological variation, and presents the main systems of word classes that are attested in the world's languages, based on Hengeveld's model. Chapter 5 discusses paradigmatic relations between words based on their meaning (synonymy, hyponymy, etc.), whereas Chapter 6 introduces the main constraints operating on the combination of words, and describes the main types of possible combinations.

I would like to thank the following colleagues who read the original manuscript or parts of it for their valuable comments: Giorgio Arcodia, Nicola Grandi, Claudio Iacobini, Alessandro Lenci, Michele Prandi, Paolo Ramat, Raffaele Simone. Raffaele Simone deserves a special thanks for his advice on the content and structure of the book. I am also grateful to James Pustejovsky, whose work on lexical and compositional semantics has greatly inspired my interest in the study of the lexicon, and to Patrick Hanks for introducing me to the use of corpora in lexical analysis. A special thanks also goes to the students of the Syntax and Semantics class of the Master Program of Theoretical and Applied Linguistics I run at Pavia University, whose comments helped me refine the presentation of several concepts for pedagogical purposes. Finally, I acknowledge Jaap Hillmann for his constant support during the preparation of the English edition and Peter Lofthouse for his most valuable feedback on the English language. Family, friends, and acquaintances deserve my warm thanks for supporting the effort required to complete this project. Thanks also to four anonymous reviewers for their comments and to the editorial staff of OUP for their help in production. All errors are, of course, my own.

I would like to dedicate this book to the memory of my father, Giorgio Ježek.

# Typographic conventions

Asterisks

For expressions that are semantically incongruent and/or grammatically incorrect, e.g. *a well meal, *an evening black dress.

Question marks

For expressions whose semantic or grammatical acceptability is uncertain, e.g. ? The man looked *quickly* up.

Small capitals

For concepts and ontological categories, e.g. PERSON, THING, PLACE.

For semantic primitives, e.g. DO, CAUSE, BECOME.

For lexical relations, e.g. HAS_AS_PART, HAS_AS_PREREQUISITE.

Capitals

For semantic primes in Wierzbicka's model, e.g. PEOPLE, UNDER, NOW, VERY.

Round Brackets

For semantic and aspectual features, e.g. (male), (abstract), (homogeneity).

Angle brackets

For selectional restrictions, e.g. <animate>, <eatable>.

Bold Type

For technical terms when first defined, e.g. **frame, qualia**.

Italics

For technical terms introduced but not defined, e.g. we will examine the notion of *lexicalization* in section 2.

For lexemes and expressions when used in the text, e.g. *simple, be late, wine glass*.

For emphasis on specific lexemes in examples of use, e.g. "a *do-it-yourself* culture."

Single quotation marks

For meanings, e.g. Chinese *bing* may mean 'get sick' (verb) but also 'illness' (noun).

Double quotation marks

For examples of use, e.g. "a comfortable chair."

For examples from corpora, e.g. "The species' classification evolved during time from static to dynamic."

For emphasis on terms, e.g. the "legitimate" parts of an object.

For quotations from other authors, e.g. "the categories and types that we isolate from the world of phenomena we do not find there because they *stare every observer in the face*" (Whorf 1956).

Square brackets

For phonetic representation, e.g. [i:] for *bee*.

# Abbreviations

| | |
|---|---|
| adj. | adjective |
| adv. | adverb |
| art. | article |
| CLF | classifier |
| det. | determiner |
| Engl. | English |
| f. | feminine |
| Fr. | French |
| Gen. | genitive |
| Germ. | German |
| Gr. | Greek |
| ingr. | ingressive |
| It. | Italian |
| Lat. | Latin |
| m. | masculine |
| n. | neuter |
| Nor. | Norwegian |
| obj. | object |
| perf. | perfect |
| plur. | plural |
| prep. | preposition |
| sing. | singular |
| subj. | subject |

# 1

# Basic notions

To address the study of the lexicon a list of basic notions are needed; these are provided in the first part of this chapter. In the second part, we examine the notion of *lexicalization,* and discuss the many ways in which information content may be associated with a word. Finally, we address the question of what counts as a *word* in a language and illustrate the different types of words that can be found in languages throughout the world.

## 1.1. Lexicon and dictionary

The **lexicon** is the set of words of a language, while the **dictionary** is the work of reference that describes that word set. Lexicon and dictionary do not correspond. A dictionary is a concrete object, typically a book, in either printed or electronic format, whereas the lexicon is an abstract object, that is, a set of words with associated information, stored in our mind and described in the dictionary. The relationship between these two entities is approximately the same as the relationship that exists between the grammar of a language, understood as the set of its syntactic and morphological rules, and the book that lists these rules and illustrates how they apply (a grammar of English, of Italian, of Hindi, and so on).

The structure of the lexicon does not correspond to the structure of the dictionary. In dictionaries, the information is organized according to practical considerations; for example, words are listed in alphabetical order for ease of consultation. The lexicon, instead, is not organized alphabetically but rather in word groupings whose members share similarities from the point of view of their form and/or their meaning. Typical lexical structures are, for example: morphological word families, such as *book, booking, booklet, bookstore,* based on the presence of the word *book*; semantic networks such as *buy, acquire, purchase, sell, negotiate, pay, own,* based on meaning associations; and groups of words with similar syntactic behavior, for example *nouns, verbs,* or *adjectives.* The dictionaries that mimic more closely the structure of the lexicon are the so-called "semantic" dictionaries, which organize words on the basis of the proximity of their meaning and put for example *nail* near *hammer, concert* near *music, paint* near *paint brush, table* near *chair, kitchen* near *eat, park* near *garage,* and so forth. Since Roget's work (*Thesaurus of English Words and Phrases,* 1852), these "semantic" dictionaries are called **thesauri,** using a word borrowed from Greek via Latin. Standard thesauri list only words which are similar with respect to a given heading (for example *ship, vessel, boat, craft*) while extended versions also include word groupings which are based on different kinds of relations, such as those holding between the words mentioned above (a *paint brush* is used for *painting,* what you typically do in the *kitchen* is *eat,* and so forth).

Finally, the term **vocabulary** may be used to refer to both the body of words in use in a particular language (hence, its lexicon), and the reference work that collects and describes this heritage (therefore, its dictionary).

We have said that a dictionary is the description of a lexicon. In fact, it is more appropriate to say that it is an attempt to describe the lexicon, just as a grammar book is an attempt to describe the syntactic and morphological rules of a language, which we often experience as lacking or imprecise in many respects. The very fact that multiple dictionaries or grammars are available for the same language shows that both the lexicon and the rules of grammar can be described according to various principles and from different perspectives. The dictionary never constitutes an exhaustive source of all the words, meanings and attested or possible usages of words in a language.

In many cases, the incompleteness of dictionaries is a deliberate choice. For example, a dictionary of contemporary usage might intentionally exclude rare, literary, archaic, or specialized words. In other cases, however, incompleteness is the unintended consequence of the fact that the number of words in a language is hard to determine (section 1.4.1) and the properties of the individual words are not so easily identifiable (Chapter 2). Finally, we must consider that the information to be found in dictionaries, despite being incomplete, is usually larger than the average lexical competence of an individual speaker. Indeed, a native speaker never knows all the words, the meanings, and the uses documented in a dictionary, much less specific information such as, for example, the etymology of a word and its first documentation in texts. Conversely, the lexical competence of a native speaker is not merely a sub-set of the information contained in dictionaries. Missing from dictionaries are complex words with highly predictable meaning, such as Dutch *winkeltje* 'small shop,' formed on the basis of *winkel* 'shop' through the addition of *-tje* 'small.' Such forms are often not included in dictionaries based on the idea that they do not reside permanently in the speaker's lexicon, especially if they are not frequent in use, but are constructed "online" by speakers by directly combining items in the context of use.

The disciplines that study the lexicon and the dictionary also have different names and purposes. **Lexicology** investigates the lexicon of a language with the goal of identifying the inherent properties of words and illustrating how, by virtue of their meaning, words relate to one another and may be successfully combined into larger expressions that are both meaningful and grammatical. In its most recent developments, lexicology aims at emphasizing that both the information associated with words (Chapter 2) and the lexicon in its entirety (Chapters 4–6) are highly structured. This view contrasts with the idea that the lexicon, unlike grammar, is a loosely structured collection of information—an idea that has circulated in the linguistic community for a long time, according to which the lexicon is "a list of basic irregularities." Given the composite nature of lexical knowledge (which can be said to include phonologic, morphological, semantic, and syntactic knowledge, cf. Chapter 2), lexicology is a discipline that exploits methodologies and formalisms developed in related fields of study. These include **lexical semantics**, concerned with defining the meaning of words, explaining its flexibility in context, and accounting for how it contributes to the meaning of sentences, or syntax, concerned with how words may or may not be combined, their relations of dependence, etc. The final goal of lexicology is to develop a **theory of the lexicon**, that is, a hypothesis about how the lexicon is structured, and to design a **lexical model**, namely a formal system that represents this structure.

**Lexicography** consists in the practical work of compiling dictionaries for human users. Its main goal is to identify the most effective ways to present the linguistic properties of words in dictionaries according to specific criteria such as the type of dictionary, the intended user group, etc. In common opinion, a secondary aim often associated with dictionaries is prescriptive, i.e. to establish the norm of the language. People consult dictionaries to know how a word "must" be spelled, what it means, and how it is supposed to be used.

Within lexicography, a distinction can be made between **traditional** and **computational lexicography**. The difference lies in the tools and techniques adopted by lexicographers in their work, as well as in the goal of the lexicographic task. For example, while traditional lexicographers tend to rely on their individual linguistic competence to write a dictionary entry, computational lexicographers use instead linguistic evidence found in large collections of digitalized texts (corpora). Also, computational lexicographers use software tools that are designed to manage the entire process of producing a dictionary, from the compilation of entries to final publication.

Besides applying computer technology to dictionary-making, computational lexicography is devoted to building computational lexicons. **Computational lexicons** are repositories of information associated with words (such as word senses, grammatical class, typical combinations, idiomatic expressions), that are usually designed not for human users but as components of computational systems intended to process natural language with the goal of enhancing human–machine interaction. The best-known computational lexicon today is WordNet (Fellbaum 1998), focused on the representation of semantic relations between words (e.g. between *dog* and *animal*, *hot* and *cold*, *take in* and *digest*), to which we shall return in Chapter 5.

Despite the fact that both lexicology and lexicography focus on words, until recently there has been no significant interaction between the two fields. Scholars such as J. Apresjan, S. Atkins, and L. Zgusta have repeatedly expressed the opinion that linguistic research can be useful to practical dictionary-making; nevertheless, lexicologists have often regarded lexicography as a practice rather than a real science, and lexicographers have claimed that theoretical insight about the structure and composition of the lexicon are of limited use from an applied perspective. Recent work carried out in computational lexicography has helped to bridge this gap and fostered interaction between the two fields.

## 1.2. Lexicon and semantics

When we think of the lexicon, we think first about the meaning of words. Lexicon and semantics, however, intersect but do not coincide. In the following, we will clarify this point. We will first look at the ways in which information content may be associated with a word. Then, we will examine how information content may also be associated with a syntactic structure or a morphological category. The discussion of how sentence meaning is built by combining the bits of meaning coming from all these layers will be postponed until Chapter 3.

### 1.2.1. Concepts and lexicalization

A word's primary characteristic is its information content, commonly called "meaning." The questions of what counts as the meaning of a word and how word meanings may be defined and represented have engaged linguists, philosophers, and scholars of many other disciplines since ancient times. In this chapter, we will focus on how information content may be associated with words. This aspect can be looked at independently from the epistemological question on the nature of meaning, which will be addressed in Chapter 3.

Let us start from the basic consideration that in language, as well as in any other semiotic system, it is possible to identify two dimensions—form and content—and that in both dimensions one may isolate single elements; thus, lexical forms such as *earth* on the one hand, and meanings such as 'planet in the solar system,' 'substance on the land surface,' etc. on the other hand. Suppose now that meanings, when they are not yet associated with a lexical form, may be thought of generically as *concepts*, intended as mental categories carrying some information content, which can be said to exist independently from language. In this view, the direct association of a concept with a lexical form that results in the existence of a word may be defined as **lexicalization** (for this use of the term, see Talmy 1985). This is represented in Figure 1.1.

The notion of lexicalization may be interpreted in several ways. A first interpretation coincides with the one above, according to which lexicalization is any process based on which, in a given language, a certain information content is associated with a lexical form. We may then say that every word in a language is the outcome of a lexicalization process.

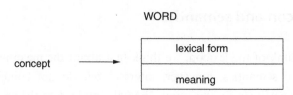

**Figure 1.1** Lexical encoding or lexicalization

For example, the English word *aunt* lexicalizes the concept of 'father's or mother's sister'—in other words, it is the product of the lexicalization of this concept. This use of the term lexicalization prevails for example in Lyons (1968), where Fr. *montrer* is described as the lexicalization of the concept 'faire voir' [ibid. 369]. In this sense, the term *lexicalized* should be understood as 'encoded in the lexicon' (instead of in the grammar).

In a narrower interpretation the term lexicalization refers to the specific process according to which a sequence of words that frequently recur together in texts acquires the status of lexical unit with an autonomous meaning. For example, the sequence *per haps* in fifteenth-century English, with the plural of a disappeared noun *hap* which we may still recognize in *happening*, has become lexicalized and has produced a new lexical item in Modern English, that is, *perhaps*. Similarly, the Italian equivalent *forse* comes from Lat. *fors sit* 'be the chance'; Dutch *misschien* is the lexicalization of *mag schien* '(it) may happen'; finally, Nor. *kanskje* lexicalizes *kan skje* 'can happen' (cf. Ježek and Ramat 2009). This phenomenon is often referred to also as **univerbation** or **lexification** in the literature (Cruse 2011: 82–91; Booij 2007: 19). Univerbation may involve different types of word sequences, exhibiting structures which may be quite close to the structure of full sentences: see for example Engl. "a *do-it-yourself* culture" (adj.); "a *happy-go-lucky* attitude" (adj.); Fr. "un *je-ne-sais-quoi*" (noun) lit. 'I don't know' 'what quality that cannot be described easily.' The sequences of words that undergo lexicalization usually develop a meaning that cannot be directly derived from the meaning of the individual words, as in the case of *happy-go-lucky*, meaning 'unconcerned about the future.' Also, they display a certain rigidity from a syntactic point of view in the sense that modification and substitution of their constituent parts is constrained. For example "a *do-it-themselves* culture," where *yourself* is substituted by *themselves*, sounds odd.

Yet another example of lexicalization concerns word forms that acquire the status of autonomous words such as Fr. *pendant*, originally the present participle of the verb *pendre* 'to hang,' used today primarily as a preposition (i.e. "pendant le dîner" 'during dinner') or It. *cantante* originally the present participle of *cantare* 'to sing,' used today primarily as a noun (i.e. "un cantante lirico" 'an opera singer').

Finally, lexicalization occurs when two usages of a word become semantically distinct to the point that the link between the two is no longer available to the speaker, and they are perceived as two separate words. The following are examples of this type: Engl. *chair* 'seat' ("a comfortable chair") and *chair* 'position of authority' ("the department chair"); It. *penna* 'feather' ("una penna d'oca" 'a goose feather') and *penna* 'pen' ("una penna d'oro" 'a golden pen').

A last interpretation of the concept of lexicalization is static. In this view, lexicalization is not seen from the point of view of the process but from the point of view of its outcome, that is, from the perspective of the resulting new word. In this interpretation, every word in a language can be said to constitute a lexicalization. For example, we may say that English has two lexicalizations to express the state of being able or allowed to do what one wants to do, i.e. *liberty* and *freedom*.

## 1.2.2. Lexicalization patterns

The process of associating concepts with words introduced in section 1.2.1 is complex because there is rarely a one-to-one correspondence between concepts and words, that is, a relation according to which every concept is connected to exactly one word, and vice versa (Murphy 2002: 389). In most cases, the lexicalizations we find in languages are of a different type, that is, not biunivocal.

Consider, to start with, the case where a combination of concepts is expressed by a single word. A good example is provided by the systems of motion verbs in various languages, as noted by Talmy (1985). For example, while the English verb *move* can be said to encode only the general concept of MOTION, *go* combines (generic) MOTION with DIRECTION (away from the speaker); *run*, on the other hand, does not express DIRECTION nor a GOAL but rather the MANNER in which the motion takes place (at high speed), and the INSTRUMENT (feet, legs). In a similar fashion, *walk* combines MOTION *and* INSTRUMENT (feet, legs), whereas *limp* and *march* combine MOTION, INSTRUMENT, and MANNER (they are basically manners of *walking*). Unlike English, German has no generic verb expressing directed motion corresponding to

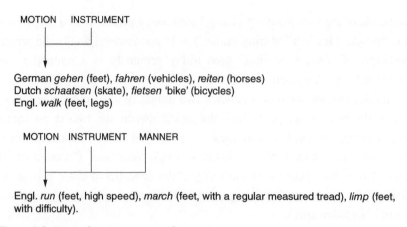

German *gehen* (feet), *fahren* (vehicles), *reiten* (horses)
Dutch *schaatsen* (skate), *fietsen* 'bike' (bicycles)
Engl. *walk* (feet, legs)

Engl. *run* (feet, high speed), *march* (feet, with a regular measured tread), *limp* (feet, with difficulty).

**Figure 1.2** *Lexicalization patterns for motion*

*go* but has many verbs that lexicalize MOTION with INSTRUMENT, such as *gehen* 'go by foot,' *fahren* 'ride a vehicle,' and *reiten* 'ride a horse.' Similarly to English, Dutch has many denominal verbs (i.e. verbs derived from nouns) referring to specific manner of motion, such as *schaatsen* 'to skate,' from *schaats* 'skate' and *fietsen* 'ride a bicycle' (or 'bike'), from *fiets* 'bicycle.' We shall call these types of lexicalizations **synthetic lexicalizations**. In such cases in the association between content and form a process of synthesis takes place according to which several "pieces" of content are incorporated into a single lexical form. Talmy 1985 uses the term ***conflation*** to refer to this process. This is illustrated in Figure 1.2.

Consider now the case where a concept that can be analyzed as unitary is expressed by multiple words, as in the case of verbal expressions describing activities such as Engl. *have dinner, make an effort,* and *get ready,* happenings such as *get sick, become aware,* and *fall asleep,* and states of being such as *be late* or *be ashamed.* Evidence in support of a unitary analysis of the concepts lexicalized by these expressions is provided *inter alia* by cross-linguistic pairs such as Engl. *be late* / It. *tardare.* We shall call these cases **analytic lexicalizations** to underline how the form/content association is achieved in this case by means of analysis, that is, by distributing a unitary content over several lexical forms.

As a rule, languages have both lexicalization techniques available to them. At times, both techniques are exploited to lexicalize the same concept, as in the case of the Engl. pairs *dine/have dinner, stimulate/provide a stimulus, consider/take into consideration, distinguish/make a distinction, exit/go out,* and so forth.

In other cases, only one of the available procedures is employed. For example, in Italian, as well as in English, there is no single word to express the concept of 'bring in a particular direction': see It. *portare dentro* 'to bring inside'; *portare su* 'to bring up'; *portare giù* 'to bring down.' In Dutch, many verbs expressing a change of state are construed analytically by means of a series of semi-copulative verbs (roughly comparable to English *become* or *get*), i.e. *worden, raken, gaan*: *rijk worden* 'to get rich'; *kwijt raken* 'to lose'; *kapot gaan* 'to break.' In German, despite the vast array of verbs describing specific manners of motion, there is no single word for the following activities: *Schi laufen* 'to ski,' *Rollschuh laufen* 'to roller skate,' etc. Note that in both German and Dutch, analytic forms tend to change their spelling over time, and be written with no internal spacing, or a hyphen.

---

As noted in Schwarze (1997), it is difficult to determine whether a concept is simple or complex (i.e. whether it can be broken down into simpler concepts or not), and by what criterion a concept can be said to be of one kind or the other. It is also possible that a speaker perceives a concept as simple precisely because it is expressed by a single word in her language, regardless of whether it is complex from a cognitive perspective.

Scholarly thought varies considerably in this respect. For example, according to the American scientist Jerry Fodor, concepts have no internal structure, i.e. they are unitary entities that cannot be decomposed in more elementary ones (Fodor 1998). The theory of concepts proposed by Fodor is known as **conceptual atomism**. This theory represents a substantial criticism of the prevailing view among cognitive scientists today, according to which concepts are complex arrays of properties or features.

The key element in our reasoning, however, is not the number of concepts involved, but rather the fact that one and the same conceptual content (whether it be constituted by an atomic entity or a bundle of properties) may be expressed either as a single word or as a sequence of words in the language. Put differently, a concept may be simple or complex, but this appears to be at least partly independent of how it is encoded in the lexicon, because there is no necessary one-to-one relationship between concepts and words.

A distinction that intersects with the one introduced above between synthetic and analytic lexicalizations is that between *descriptive* and *labeling lexicalizations*, due to the German linguist H.J. Seiler, who used the terms *deskriptive* and *etikettierende Benennung* in the original text (cf. Seiler 1975). This distinction points to the different ways in which an object may be given a name. Specifically, the two types of lexicalization identified by Seiler differ with respect to the semantic relation that holds between the *designatum* (that to which the word refers) and the word itself. In the case of **descriptive lexicalization**, the *designatum* is associated with the word by means of a description; in the case of **labeling lexicalization**, it is associated with the word by being attributed a label.

The first type of lexicalization is frequent in several languages of North and Central America. Good examples are provided by Cahuilla, a Uto-Aztec language of Southern California, where, for example, *stone* is lexicalized approximately as 'that which has become hard' and *basket* is lexicalized as 'that which is woven' (examples are taken from Seiler 1975). The German linguist H.J. Sasse found similar examples in Cayuga, an Iroquois language of Canada (Sasse 1993), in which many nominal concepts are lexicalized with complex expressions: for example, *table* 'she (impersonal pronoun) prepares food on it'; *horse* 'he drags logs,' and so forth.

The distinction between descriptive and labeling lexicalization is present, albeit less evidently so, in Indo-European languages. For example the English term *worker* may be analyzed as a descriptive noun, because it includes a morpheme (*-er*) signalling that the referent of the word is an individual engaged in an activity, either habitually or occasionally (on a par with *writer*, *driver*, and so on). *Doctor*, on the other hand, is a labeling noun, because it does not contain any such element. Similarly, the noun *building* (as in "a three-storey building") alludes to the activity that brought about the built object, while this is not the case for *palace*. Note that some terms that we interpret as labeling today were, originally, descriptive (Ramat 2005: 71): for example, It. *orologio*, Lat. *horŏlŏgĭu(m)*, Gr. *hōrológion* originally '(that which) indicates the hour.'

Let us return now to the distinction between analytic and synthetic lexicalization for some additional considerations. First, the choice of analytic instead of synthetic procedures heavily influences the structure of the lexicon. This can be seen clearly if we compare data from different languages: Engl. analytic expressions *get sick*, *be ashamed*, and *fall asleep* correspond to It. synthetic *ammalarsi*, *vergognarsi*, and *addormentarsi*; It. analytic *stare sdraiato* 'to lie down on a surface, such as a bed or the ground' corresponds to Dutch synthetic *liggen*, and so forth.

Second, the cross-linguistic comparison enables us to notice two other phenomena. The first is that some languages appear not to have single words to name certain concepts. Traditionally, this phenomenon is interpreted as a deficiency of the language in question (so-called **lexical gap**), but the perspective changes radically if we extend the notion of lexicalization to analytic expressions. In this perspective, there is always a way to express a concept; what changes is the way the concept is mapped onto linguistic items (synthetic vs. analytic). Very often, concepts that are not universally lexicalized as single words reflect the cultural particularities of the language communities and are related to specific domains, such as, for example, cookware, gastronomy, or national sports. The example in (1) illustrates this point:

(1)   Frisian *klunen* 'to walk on skates avoiding those spots along the route where the ice is dangerous.'

---

The reasons for the lack of one-to-one mapping between words and concepts are not well understood. At the root of the problem there is the debate as to whether all human beings share an analogous conceptual apparatus and, therefore, the same set of concepts, due to the similarity in the biological structure of their brain. A typical set of shared conceptual categories at the highest level of generality is the following: THING, QUALITY, QUANTITY, PLACE, TIME, STATE, PROCESS, EVENT, ACTION, RELATION, MANNER. These represent fundamental modes of conception (Bossong 1992) that the human mind is innately predisposed to adopt in classifying things and occurrences in the world. This similarity in conceptual structure is assumed to be the reason why, despite the superficial differences, all languages share a common core in their deepest organization (the so-called Universal Grammar, UG). The innatist theory of language—a theory that has circulated for hundreds of years but has had new life breathed into it by the American linguist Noam Chomsky—does not deny the existence of a cultural influence on the way we categorize the world, but holds that this only affects the superficial layers of language, such as vocabulary (and then only in a few conceptual domains of importance to the community), and not the deeper ones, such as syntax.

The opposing view is the **relativist hypothesis**, according to which conceptual categories are instead profoundly determined and shaped by culture and by language. In this respect, the American linguist B.L.Whorf, who has been credited as the father of this approach, observes that "the categories and types that we isolate from the world of phenomena we do not find there because they *stare every observer in the face*: on the contrary, the world is presented in a kaleidoscopic flux of impressions which has to be organized by our minds—and this means largely by the linguistic system in our minds" (Whorf 1956: 212–14). From these words, we can see the role that this approach attributes to language in the process of conceptualization.

The second phenomenon to be noted is that, through their lexicon, languages appear to dissect the same concepts differently. For example, It. *orologio* covers the concept that is covered in French and English by two distinct words, each identifying a different type of time-measuring tool, i.e. Fr. *montre* / Engl. *watch* and Fr. *horloge* / Engl *clock*. In a similar fashion, It. *tempo* covers the concept covered in English by four different terms: *time* (chronological), *tense* (grammatical), *weather* (meteorological), *tempo* (musical). Other familiar examples are the following: It. *portare* and Engl. equivalents *bring* (towards the speaker) and *take* (away from the speaker); It. adverb and conjunction *perché* and Fr. equivalents *pourquoi* (adverb) and *parce que* (conjunction). Historically, we observe the same phenomenon in the distinction between Lat. *albus* 'opaque white' and *candidus* 'bright white.'

The cases above give us the opportunity for a final comment on the process of lexicalization, which helps us understand how assuming the distinction between analytic and synthetic procedures in mapping concepts onto linguistic expressions contributes a radical change in viewing the structure of the lexicon. A closer look at the data reveals in fact that Italian has two analytic expressions corresponding to Engl. *watch* and *clock* and Fr. *montre* and *horloge*, namely *orologio da polso* (lit. 'watch for wrist') and *orologio da parete* (lit. 'watch for wall'). These are expressions we would be unlikely to classify as "words." However, they are somewhat special combinations, as is shown by the fact that they cannot, for example, be modified as ordinary combinations can; i.e. in Italian, where the adjective regularly follows the noun it modifies, one would say "un *nuovo* orologio da polso" (lit. 'a new watch for wrist') or 'un orologio da polso *nuovo*' (lit. 'a watch for wrist new') instead of 'un orologio *nuovo* da polso' (lit. 'a watch new for wrist').

It becomes clear that the interpretation of the phenomena we described in this section depends on our assumptions about what counts as a "word" in a language. Traditionally the term word is reserved for graphically isolated forms (i.e. the stretches of letters that occur between blank spaces in text), but this view is insufficient to account for several phenomena occurring in the lexicon, such as those discussed so far.

In sum, languages differ both in how they subdivide concepts by means of words and in how they associate one and the same conceptual content with lexical forms. The tension between analysis and synthesis is a typological characteristic of languages which stands out particularly in the organization of their lexicon (some languages are more analytic, others are more synthetic). Finally, languages may be more analytic or synthetic in relation to certain conceptual fields (for example, with regard to the expression of MOTION).

## 1.3. Lexical meaning and grammatical meaning

Although the most distinctive characteristic of words is their meaning, words are the not only elements in language capable of carrying meaning; syntactic structures such as the *passive*, and morphological categories such as *gender* and *number* also bear meanings. In fact, meaning is "distributed" over all the elements that make up a language, including intonation. What distinguishes a word's meaning from the meaning carried by syntactic and morphological units is that a word's meaning can be perceived and described by the speaker in a more immediate way. To illustrate this point, in this section we shall first introduce the distinction between content words and function words in the lexicon (section 1.3.1), and show how it correlates with the distinction between two different meaning types: lexical meaning and grammatical meaning. We shall then look in detail at some major types of grammatical meanings, focusing on how they are encoded in the languages throughout the world (section 1.3.2).

## *1.3.1. Content words and function words*

From the point of view of their meaning, the words that make up a language's lexicon fall into two large groups: **content words** and **function words** (Lyons 1968: 435) (see Table 1.1). Other established terms for referring to these groupings are **lexical words** and **grammatical words,** or, less frequently, **full words** and **empty words.** Within the formal semantic tradition (cf. Chapter 3), the opposition between **substantive** and **functional lexicon** is also widely used today to refer to the two groups of words.

In the literature, the distinction most usually is introduced by saying that words belonging to the major lexical categories—that is, verbs, nouns, adjectives, and, according to some, also adverbs—fall into the first group, while those belonging to the minor lexical categories—such as determiners, pronouns, conjunctions, and prepositions—fall into the second group. As we shall see below, the comparison with word classes is imperfect but useful, because it highlights the different way in which these two word types contribute to the meaning of the sentences in which they appear; while content words supply the content, function words perform the function of clarifying the relations that hold between the pieces of content that content words introduce.

Consider the sentence: "I like to have a cup of coffee in the morning." If we take out the function words (therefore being left with "like have cup coffee morning") the resulting sequence is still able to convey a meaning (that is, we can still somewhat interpret it), despite the fact that the relations between the elements are now opaque. If, instead, we omit the content words (therefore being left with "I to a of in the"), the remaining elements alone are

**Table 1.1.** Content words and function words

| Content words | Function words |
|---|---|
| Verbs: *go, run, call* | Pronouns: *our, I, you* |
| Nouns: *Lynda, pen, beauty* | Articles: *the, an* |
| Adjectives: *high, bright, steady* | Demonstratives: *that* |
| Prepositions: *over, with* | Prepositions: *to* |
| Adverbs: *quickly, late* | Adverbs: *not* |
| | Verbs: *have* (aux.) |

not able to evoke any meaning, because the words that supply the semantic basis to the sentence, with respect to which *I, to, a, of, in, the* specify something, are missing. The meaning of content words is called **lexical meaning** and that of function words is called **grammatical meaning**. While content words are semantically autonomous—at least up to a certain degree (see the discussion in sections 3.3.2 and 3.3.4)—the meaning of function words is more readily dependent on the content words to which they are related. For example, the word "in" in the example above means 'during' because it occurs in the context of the noun *morning*, which denotes a time period; should it be combined with the noun *building*, it would mean 'inside.'

A further difference between content words and function words is that the former constitute an **open set** of items, that is, a set that gains and loses members relatively rapidly, while the latter constitute a **closed set** that tends to remain constant through time. In fact, while the acquisition of new content words in the lexicon is a recurrent phenomenon (a person can easily invent new ones, for example *landline, emoticon,* or *netbook*), the emergence of a new function word is an isolated phenomenon which occurs less frequently and requires more time. Interestingly, when it does occur, the new function word may be the outcome of the transformation of a pre-existing word form with lexical meaning into a function word: for example Engl. *while*, originally a noun meaning 'moment, period of time' (as in "a little while"), later came to be used as a conjunction meaning 'during the time that' (as in "while she was writing . . . ").

As referenced above, the criterion that establishes a correspondence between word class (verbs, nouns, etc.) and type of meaning (lexical or grammatical) is imperfect. Verbs such as *auxiliaries* are typical examples of function words; the term itself (from a Latin word meaning 'help') points to the fact that they are verbs that help conjugate other verbs, particularly in forming compound tenses (for example, Engl. "I go / I *have* gone," "I write / I *have* written"; Fr. "Je vais / Je *suis* allé," "J'écris / J'*ai* écrit"). Prepositions, too, are unequal: next to prepositions with a strong relational (and, thus, functional) meaning, such as Engl. *to*, we have prepositions with a more defined (i.e. context-independent) lexical content, such as *over*. And finally, adverbs: content ones, such as *quickly*, and function ones, such as the negation *not* (more on this point in Aronoff and Fudeman 2005: 40–1).

## 1.3.2. Types of grammatical meanings

In the discussion above we argued that, besides function words, other elements in the language might express a grammatical meaning; these are for example syntactic structures and grammatical morphemes.

Consider the case of the passive, illustrated by sentences such as "The flight was canceled," which is an instantiation of the "be + past participle" construction in English. In this case, a specific syntactic structure enables the speaker to talk about an event, removing from the focus of attention the entity that brings it about (*the airline* in our example) and focusing instead on the entity to which something occurs (*the flight*, which is canceled). The passive can thus be defined as a syntactic structure that has the (grammatical) meaning of presenting a situation from the point of view of the participant who is not active in what is reported.

As for morphology, consider the case of the morpheme *–a*, as it occurs as last letter in It. *ragazza* 'girl' (the term *morpheme* will be discussed at appropriate places in this work; pending such discussion, morpheme will be used in the restricted sense of 'non-autonomous part of a word'). This morpheme combines two types of semantic information, namely *gender* (feminine) and *number* (singular). These are two distinct grammatical meanings; they do not provide the lexical meaning of the word—which is expressed instead by the morpheme *ragazz-* 'young person'—but they specify it, in the sense that they characterize it providing gender and number information; compare *ragazza* 'girl' with *ragazzo* 'boy' and *ragazze* 'girls.'

In both cases, it is convenient to distinguish between the semantic feature at play (thus, the meaning of passive, gender, number, and so forth) and its formal realization (respectively, the passive construction, the gender morpheme, and the number morpheme—which, as we have seen, in languages such as Italian may be fused into a single morpheme). This distinction is convenient because even within the same language the same meaning may be expressed by different formal means. As it happens, this key feature of languages renders the distinction between lexical and grammatical meaning very complex. Consider for example the Engl. verb *receive*. *Receive* can be said to denote an event seen from the point of view of the individual who experiences it somewhat passively, in the sense that the subject of a sentence whose main verb is *receive* is not the individual who intentionally initiates the event described by the verb but rather the entity who undergoes it, to his/her benefit, as in "John received an award," or to his/her disadvantage, as in "Mark received a fine." On this basis, we may conclude that in the case of *receive*, the meaning of passive understood broadly as 'absence of an active role,' is encoded in the lexicon, particularly in the role that the verb assigns to its subject (experiencer instead of agent).

Also the gender distinction may be achieved by lexical rather than morphological means. Compare for example the opposition between *ragazzo/ragazza* in Italian, where the gender distinction is realized by the morphemes *-o/-a*, with the opposition between *jongen* (boy) and *meisje* (girl) in Dutch, *boy* and *girl* in English, *garçon* and *fille* in French, where the gender opposition is expressed by two distinct lexical items.

We can compile a list of meanings that are usually expressed by grammatical means (especially in those languages that display a rich morphology). The most relevant ones are listed in Table 1.2.

The first two meanings (number and gender) are frequently associated with nouns, while the last three (time, aspect, and voice) are frequently marked on the verb. In the following, we look at these meanings in some detail, with the specific intent of highlighting how, despite being typically expressed by grammatical means, they can also be expressed by words. Following a well-established tradition, we shall call these meanings **categories**.

The category of **number** makes it possible to distinguish between "one" and "more than one" (more subtle distinctions are present in the world's languages, such as the so-called *dual*; we will not, however, consider them here). In the languages that lexicalize this distinction, number is frequently expressed by means of grammatical morphemes (plural affixes of various types), mostly attached to the noun: for example Engl. *book/books*, German

**Table 1.2.** Types of grammatical meanings

| Grammatical Meanings |
| --- |
| Number |
| Gender |
| Time |
| Aspect |
| Voice |

*Schuh/Schuhe* 'shoe/shoes,' etc. The distinction in number can, however, also be expressed by duplication of the lexical item (see for example Indonesian *buku-buku* 'books,' *pohon-pohon* 'trees,' *kwee kwee* 'sweets'), by its internal modification (as in English *goose/geese, man/men*), or by contextual cues, for example by addition of a separate word indicating number in the context; compare for example Engl. "There was one fish in the water" (sing.) with "We saw two fish in the water' (plur.). Note that the number category, as understood from the semantic point of view, is encoded in other forms in the language, for example in the distinction between countable nouns (*book*), mass nouns (*sand*), and collective nouns (*family, people, traffic*), or in the lexicalization of nouns expressing portions and quantities (*period* of time, *pinch* of salt, *bag* of potatoes, *slice* of bread) and quantifiers (*much* noise, *many* people, *any* student, *some* chairs, and so forth).

Languages apply the **gender** distinction between masculine (m.), feminine (f.), and occasionally neuter (n.) broadly (but not identically) not only to words that refer to persons and animals (as in the case of pairs such as *lion/ lioness*) but also to those that denote concrete objects (It. la *forchetta* 'fork' (f.), il *coltello* 'knife' (m.); *Fr.* le *bureau* 'desk' (m.), la *table* 'table' (f.)) and abstract entities (It. il *coraggio* 'courage' (m.), la *paura* 'fear' (f.)), where no distinction can be drawn as far as the biological characteristics of the entity in question are concerned. At times, languages apply the gender distinction even in contrast with such characteristics, as in the case of Germ. neuter *das Mädchen 'the (little) girl.'* It is therefore necessary to distinguish between *natural* (or *biological*) *gender* and *grammatical gender*. Grammatical gender constitutes a linguistic category, which may coincide with the category of natural gender, or may group entities on the basis of criteria that have nothing to do with those based on natural grounds. For example in Arabic, the nouns *umm* (mother), *nār* (fire), *ǧaḥīm* (hell), and *harb* (war) all belong to the class of feminine nouns. A similar situation is found in Dyirbal, an aboriginal language of Australia, where the nouns for *woman, fire*, and *fight* receive the same feminine classifier, *balan* (Lakoff 1987: 92–6). Grammatical gender is frequently expressed by morphological means; for example, by specific endings (It -*a* for feminine, -*o* for masculine, Engl. -*ess* for feminine), but can also be expressed by lexical means, especially in the case of oppositions based on natural gender. We have already mentioned the case of Dutch *jonge/meisje* and Engl. *boy/girl*; other familiar cases are Engl. *father/ mother, brother/sister*, and so forth. Finally, when it coincides with biological gender, grammatical gender is occasionally signaled by adding the word *masculine* or *feminine* to the word being inflected, as in It. *tigre maschio/tigre femmina* (lit. 'male tiger'/'female tiger' (Simone 1990: 315–16).

The category of **time** refers to how the chronological distinction between *past*, *present*, and *future* is encoded in language. For example, languages have temporal systems (the verbal **tenses**) that allow the speakers to place the events they talk about before, after, or around the time of speaking, as in "I left Rome 11 years ago" or some other reference time, as in "Tom had a drink before he boarded the plane." These temporal systems vary from language to language. For example, there are languages that have multiple forms to express the future time, depending on the temporal proximity to the moment of speaking, the intention of the speaker, and so on. English for instance uses the auxiliary *will* to express a future with a certain degree of intentionality ("He will not go"), while *go* (as in the *be going to* construction) is used to convey the additional idea that the intention is premeditated ("I'm going to stop now"); Italian expresses an event that will occur in the very near future and is already arranged by using the present tense: It. "Domani sera vado a teatro," lit. 'Tomorrow night I go to the theater.' Notice that the future may at times be expressed lexically, for example by means of temporal adverbs rather than through the verbal morphology or the syntax. An example can be found in the Italian context we have just introduced, where the future meaning is conveyed by the adverbial expression *domani sera* 'tomorrow night.' Finally, temporal information may occasionally be marked on nouns instead of verbs. This appears not to be uncommon in certain native languages of North America. For example, in Yup'ik, a language spoken in Central Alaska, both past and future tense can be indicated by nouns; compare *nuliaqa* 'my wife,' *nulialka* 'my late/-ex wife,' *nuliarkaqa* 'my wife-to-be' or 'my fiancée' (cf. Mithun 1999). Similarly, Guaraní, an indigenous language of South America, has two temporal markers (*-kue* and *-rã*) which attach to nouns and appear to express past and future tense. Examples are: *òga-kwé* 'former house' and *tendota-rã* 'presidential candidate' (the data are from Tonhauser 2007).

The category of **aspect** refers to the way in which an event is presented in the language, in relation to the temporal phases that constitute it. For example, an event can be presented in its initial (*inceptive*) moment ("it is about to rain") or in its progress ("it is raining"). There are several ways of expressing the category of aspect in language. First, the category of aspect may be encoded in the lexicon (*lexical aspect*), for example in the distinction between *to swim*, durative, and *to wake up*, punctual. Second, aspect can be expressed by means of morphology, for example in the distinction between *perfect* (*I sang*) and *imperfect* tenses (*I was singing*) (*grammatical aspect*). Third, aspectual meaning can emerge in the syntax (*syntactic aspect*). For example, "Julia sang for us" denotes an event which is not delimited in time while "Julia sang *a song* for us" denotes one which is, because the *song* introduces an end point to the event.

Finally, the category of **voice** has to do with the perspective from which an event is presented in the language. If the individual who initiates the event is expressed as subject in the sentence, the voice is said to be *active*; if, instead, the subject expresses the individual who undergoes or experiences the event, the voice is considered *passive*; compare "John scared Mary" (active) with "Mary was scared (by John)" (passive). As we noted earlier, in the languages that encode this distinction the passive is frequently expressed by a dedicated syntactic structure (the passive construction). Nevertheless, passive may also be expressed by a morpheme attached to the verb, as in Lat. *amor* 'I am loved (vs. *amō* 'I love'), or it may be inherent in the verb, as with Engl. *undergo* ("undergo an operation") or *suffer* ("suffer a damage"), whose subject is not a volitional agent but the entity which is affected by the event. In addition to verbs that have an inherent "passive" meaning, there exist verbs which may be considered *middle* (that is, intermediate between active and passive from the point of view of the *voice*), because their subject is at the same time the site of the event's onset and that of its experience. An example is Engl. *regret*. Many languages have a special morpheme to mark the middle voice on the verb. For example, Romance languages use the reflexive pronoun to mark "middle" situations. Examples are: It. *commuoversi* 'be, get moved,' *pentirsi* 'regret, repent,' *arrabbiarsi* 'get angry,' *vergognarsi* 'be ashamed.' Fr. *s'émouvoir*; *regretter/se repentir*; *se mettre en colère/se fâcher*; *avoir honte*. In English, on the other hand, middle verbs are not marked by a specific morpheme, as we can see from the translations above.

> Along with middle verbs, many languages display a so-called middle construction, which is exemplified in English by examples such as "This message reads well," "This car drives smoothly," and so forth. This construction differs from the passive construction in various ways; the most evident being that it expresses a generic statement instead of a

dynamic situation, and does not allow the expression of an under-lying agent: see the ungrammaticality of "*This message reads well by John."

To sum up, we have seen how, in addition to words, syntactic construc-tions and grammatical morphemes also have a meaning. It is usually claimed that the meaning conveyed by syntax and morphology (grammat-ical meaning) is different from the meaning conveyed by words (lexical meaning) in that it is functional. We have seen, however, that it is impossible to draw a sharp distinction between the two; on the contrary, there is considerable evidence that it is a common feature of languages to allow one and the same concept to be expressed by different linguistic means (specifically by a word, a grammatical morpheme, or a syntactic construction—for the sake of simplicity, we do not take into consideration other aspects which are equally significant: intonation, word order, and so forth). One can at best speak in terms of tendency, and argue that particu-larly in languages with a rich morphology, such as Romance languages, **functional meanings**, i.e. meanings which are highly dependent on other meanings for their interpretation, such as *gender* or *voice*, tend to be expressed by grammatical categories, while **substantive** (i.e. autonomous) **meanings** tend to be expressed by words.

## 1.4. The notion *word*

The notion *word* is immediate and intuitive for the speaker but difficult for the linguist to define. For non-specialists, a word expresses a unitary mean-ing, is included between two white spaces in a text, and can be pronounced in isolation. This definition does not satisfy the linguist, who knows that not all languages have a written tradition (and yet have words) and for whom "unitary meaning" is too vague a definition. Upon closer examination, not even the ordinary speaker would consider sequences such as It. *scrivimi* (lit. 'write-me' as in "Scrivimi presto" 'It. write-me soon') to be single words, despite the fact that graphically they do not contain any white spaces. On the other end, many English speakers would probably agree in analyzing *air bag* as one word, no matter how it is spelled (hyphenated, joined, or not joined, as in the variant above). In what follows, we try to define what a word is, starting from addressing the question of how many words a language has.

## 1.4.1. Counting the words of a language

Counting the words of a language is not a simple task. To illustrate this point, let us start by looking at the English verb *talk*. We know that next to *talk*, there is a family of "*talk* forms," such as *talks, talked, will talk, has been talking*, and so forth. In languages with rich inflectional morphology such as Italian, there are even more forms for the equivalent verb *parlare*, practically one for each verb usage: *parlo* '(I) talk,' *parla* '(he) talks,' *parlano* '(they) talk,' *parlerete* '(you) will talk,' *parlarono* '(they) talked,' *parlerebbero* '(they) would talk,' *abbiamo parlato* '(we) have talked,' etc. The same variability occurs, although to a lesser extent, with words belonging to other word classes, particularly nouns (Engl. *class, classes*), and adjectives (German *schön* 'beautiful,' *schöne*—as in "*schöne Aussicht*" 'beautiful view'—, and *schönes*—as in "*schönes* Haus" 'beautiful house'). All these variants, as is known, constitute the so-called inflected forms. The question is: how should inflected forms be analyzed? Intuitively, the answer is: as different forms of the same word, and, thus, as forms that can be ascribed to a single word. This is a point one can easily agree on.

But what form represents the word? The answer to this last question is less straightforward. The form that stands for a word (known as the **citation form**) is determined by convention: the infinitive for verbs, the singular for nouns and adjectives, and so on. However, nothing would prevent us from choosing a different form. For Italian verbs, for example, the citation form might be the third person singular of the present tense (*parla* '(he) talks'), which is enough to predict the inflectional class and, according to Giacalone Ramat 1993, constitutes the basic form employed by language learners in the early stages of acquisition (i.e. the form that is initially extended to all the uses of the verb). It is evident that the citation form is a matter of convention and does not necessarily reflect the organization of the lexicon.

This line of reasoning leads us to introduce two concepts, and thus two terms, to account for the phenomenon described above, that is, the presence of families of forms for single words: the *lexeme* on the one hand and the *lemma* (or *lexical entry*) on the other. In lexical analysis, **lexeme** identifies the unit of lexicon that constitutes the base form to which all the inflected forms are ascribed (for example, the conjugated forms of verbs or the inflected forms of nouns) and **lemma** corresponds to the lexeme seen as an entry in a dictionary.

> The concept of lexeme is more abstract than that of word, especially in languages that have inflection; in fact, in those languages in actual usage the most frequent forms are precisely the inflected ones.

A lexeme often unites not only a family of forms but also a family of categories (verbs, nouns, etc.). Consider again the English word *fish*, used to denote both the animal living in water and by *conversion* the action of catching it. Are *fish* (noun) and *fish* (verb) the same lexeme or two separate ones? It is commonly assumed that two usages of a word that exhibit clear relatedness of meaning, as in the case of *fish* above, belong to the same lexeme. In lexicography, the phenomenon is dealt with by saying that *fish* (noun) and *fish* (verb) are two lemmas of the single *headword fish*. In this interpretation, the term lemma defines the sum of inflected forms of a headword that belong to the same category.

Now let us proceed with our line of reasoning, aimed at establishing the number of words of a language, and consider the case of derived words, such as Engl. *art/artist, respect/disrespect*, and so forth. From a lexical point of view, despite the fact that the words in the pairs share the same lexical morpheme (*art, respect*), we are dealing in this case with two distinct words. The reason we consider these words to be distinct is that besides having a different form (which is not per se a sufficient reason, as we saw in the case of the inflected forms) they also carry a different meaning.

Let us now look at **compounds**, in particular such typical ones as Engl. *sunglasses, newspaper*, or *bookstore*. In this case, too, we are dealing with words that are distinct from the base words (*sun, glass; news, paper; book, store*). The difference is evident not only from the point of view of their form but also from the point of view of their meaning. In English, compounds spelled jointly or with a hyphen (*check-in, long-term*) are always classified as autonomous lexical entries in dictionaries (headwords, in lexicographic terms); they are granted full status as words. Dictionaries list as entries also compounds spelled with internal spaces, provided that they have an idiosyncratic meaning, i.e. a meaning that cannot be fully predicted from the meaning of the individual words (as in *traffic light, air bag, credit card*) or, despite having a predictable meaning, they are the established term to refer to a particular thing (*waiting room, nursing home*). Productive compounds, such as *apple/chocolate/carrot/plum cake, plastic/paper/leather bag*, etc., are instead not registered as lemmas.

Let us finally consider nominal expressions such as Engl. *round table, work in progress, part of speech, state of the art*; or verbal expressions such as Engl. *look up, have a walk/rest, give a speech, take a stab (at something)*. If our criterion for identifying words is mainly semantic, these expressions, in spite of the fact that they consist of multiple words, somehow resemble lexemes, because they express a concept that is salient when taken as a whole, and therefore unitary. In Cruse's terms, they are, albeit with very different modalities, a **semantic constituent** (Cruse 1986). The fact that such an expression as *round table* is a semantic constituent is easily proven. If we say that "a third round table was held on August 25," we are not referring to a table, let alone a round one, but to an event during which people discuss specific topics with other people. For other nominal expressions in the list above, the status of semantic constituent is less obvious, as they often mean what is expected from the sum of their meanings; nevertheless, we must recognize that these, too, are special sequences when compared with ordinary phrases. In the case of *work in progress*, for example, we cannot insert a modifier like *good* between the two elements to specify the stage/quality of the work: *\*a work in good progress* is not a well-formed expression in English.

Globally, the linguistic expressions that are made up of multiple words and yet exhibit a word-like behavior are called **multi-word lexical units** (Zgusta 1967 and 1971), **multi-word expressions** (MWEs) (Calzolari et al. 2002), or **lexicalized phrases** (Sag et al. 2002). Sometimes, the term **complex word** is also found; this, however, is in fact a more general term as it refers to all the words consisting of multiple morphemes, as we will see shortly. When the meaning is non-compositional (as in the case of *round table*), the preferred terminology is **idiom** or **idiomatic expression**; if the idiomatic expression exhibits internal variability in the sense that it has one or more open slots that may be filled by different words to produce several variations of the same expressions (as in Engl. *bring an issue / a concern / a fact into light*), the preferred term is **constructional idiom** (Jackendoff 2002) or **idiomatic construction** (Nunberg et al. 2004). It is worth remembering, however, that despite being called by a different name, the lexical status of these forms can be likened to that of simple words.

## Box 1.1. Tests for "wordhood"

There are several empirical tests that can be used to identify whether a sequence of words in a text works the same way as a simple word. These tests verify the presence of certain properties that are assumed to constitute the essential requirements of a word. But what are these properties? The many studies dedicated to defining the notion "word" converge in arguing that words, to be considered such, must exhibit at least the following two properties: **cohesiveness** and **fixed order of the constituent parts**. Both properties are based on the assumption that words have an internal structure (that is, that they can be broken down into constituent parts: phonemes, syllables, and morphemes) but that they nevertheless constitute atoms, monads, or single units at some level of linguistic analysis. Also, it is sometimes proposed that words possess a third property, namely **autonomy**, that is, the ability of standing alone and of carrying a meaning in and of themselves. Note that this ability is not shared by the so-called *bound morphemes*, such as Engl. *-ly, -ness, -ize, un-*.

One of the tests that can be used to verify whether a sequence of words has the property of cohesiveness is the *separation test*. This test consists of separating the parts that are supposed to be the constituents of a (complex) word by putting lexical material between them, and then evaluating whether the result is acceptable. The material that is inserted may be an adjective that modifies a noun, if there is one. If the result of the insertion is not acceptable, the parts can be said to constitute a word. Indeed words are, by definition, units that cannot be separated nor modified partially. The following are examples of this type. The forms on the left are the word sequences for which we are verifying the status of complex words, and those on the right are the result of the test; we include in the list standard noun–noun compounds (as in (a)), to show how their word-like status is confirmed by the separation test.

(a)  Engl. waiting room       *a waiting *little* room
     Engl. credit card        *a credit *new* card
     Engl. evening dress       *an evening *black* dress

(b)  Engl. blind spot         *a blind and *tiny* spot
     Engl. round table        *a round and *big* table
     Engl. work in progress    *a work *of art* and in progress

*(continued)*

(c)  Engl. take care (of)          take *good* care (of)
     Engl. catch fire              *catch *big* fire
     Engl. take advantage (of)     take *full* advantage (of)

(d)  Engl. take a stab (at)        take a *serious* stab (at)

In general, it appears that the nominal expressions in (a) and (b) cannot be broken up by insertion of an adjective that modifies one of its parts. The expressions can be modified only globally; a *little waiting room* is acceptable, while *a waiting little room is not. This comes across as a sign that these combinations have a word-like status. Note that insertion of an adjective appears to be disallowed in the case of both idiomatic expressions (*round table*) and expressions whose meaning can be at least partially predicted (*blind spot*). This shows that the impossibility of separating and modifying the parts of a complex word is not exclusively determined by its idiomaticity but may derive from the conventionality of the expression. On the other hand, the expressions in (c) give different results to the test: *take care* and *take advantage* allow the insertion of a modifier while *catch fire* does not. Finally, despite its idiomatic character, *take a stab* (*at*) in (d) allows modification of *stab* in its 'attempt' sense. This means that the expression is not totally blocked as regards insertion/modification.

With expressions which function as verbs, separation may also be performed by inserting a modifying adverb between the verb and the rest of the expression. Examples are:

(e)  Engl. take place               *The event will take *soon* place.
     Engl. catch fire               *The roof caught *quickly* fire.
     Engl. take advantage (of)      *He took *immediately*
                                     advantage of the situation.

(f)  Engl. turn up                  *The guests turned *late* up.
     Engl. look up                  ?The man looked *quickly* up.
     Engl. go out                   We went *straight* out for dinner.

In such cases, the insertion of an adverb between the verb and rest of the expression is not allowed, except when the meaning of the whole expression is highly predictable, as in the case of *go out*.

*(continued)*

With expressions functioning as verbs separation may finally be performed by placing the object (if there is one) between the verb and the
rest of the expression, while maintaining the order of the constituents
unchanged, as in the examples in (e) and (f).

| | | |
|---|---|---|
| (g) | Engl. look after | *We looked *the baby* after. |
| | Engl. look up | We looked *the word* up (in the dictionary). |
| | Engl. take into consideration | We took *every single factor* into consideration. |

It appears that only some of the combinations in (g) can be interrupted.
This comes across as a sign that they do not all have a word-like status.

A second test which can be used to verify whether a sequence of words
has word-like properties consists of modifying the order of the constituents, for example by putting into focus a single part of the expression.
If the result of this operation is not acceptable, the sequence of words
under examination can be said to constitute a complex word. To repeat,
a word is a unit whose constituents cannot be separated, or modified
individually—only the whole unit can be manipulated. This is called
(lexical) *integrity*. The following are two examples:

| | | |
|---|---|---|
| (h) | (Mary is in the *waiting room*) | Which *room* is Mary in? |
| | (Mary is attending a *round table*) | *Which *table* is Mary attending? |
| (i) | go out | *Out* he went. |
| | turn up | *Up* they turned. |

The sequences yield different results with respect to the test; certain
modifications are not acceptable, others are acceptable provided that
certain conditions are satisfied (as for example a specific intonation
pattern), and yet others give us no problem at all.

A third test (substitution test) that may be used to verify whether a
sequence of words acts as a single unit is that of substituting one of its
constituents for a synonym or near-synonym, an operation which is
generally allowed by ordinary phrases. This can be illustrated as
follows:

*(continued)*

> (j)   Engl. blind spot            *blind *place*
>        Engl. take place           *take *location*
>
> In the contexts above, *spot*, *place*, and *location*, despite being near-synonyms, are not substitutable for each other. It appears that in the examples in (j), paradigmatic variation with near-synonyms is blocked. If the sequence has a word status, as in the example above, synonym substitution destroys the semantic integrity of the complex word and produces a sequence devoid of sense.

To conclude, it is evident that counting the number of words in a language is not a simple task, because we need to take into account inflected forms (*walk*, *walks*), converted forms (*fish*, *to fish*), derived words (*art*, *artist*), compounds (*air bag*), and the very large number of (idiomatic and non-idiomatic) multi-word expressions which substantially increase the number of items that populate the lexicon.

Moreover, upon closer examination, if semantics is taken as the main criterion for identifying words, there is a further problem. In fact, single lexical forms often display multiple meanings; for example, *character* denotes the typical psychological qualities of someone (which we shall temporarily call *character₁*), but also the graphic sign (*character₂*). How should *character₁* and *character₂* be analyzed? As two **homonyms** (that is, two forms that happen to share the sound and/or spelling but have unrelated meanings) or as a **polysemous** lexeme (i.e. a single form associated with several related meanings)?

It is often difficult to decide one way or the other. Nevertheless, there are some criteria that can be used to distinguish **homonymy** from **polysemy**. These criteria have to do with the development of language over time; very often, the ambiguity between the two cases can, in fact, be resolved only in diachrony, which means that ordinary speakers, who have reduced access to knowledge about the history and development of their own language, are not in a position to distinguish clearly between the two (although they may have judgments about it).

Two related criteria will be considered here. The first is etymology, which predicts that if two meanings associated with the same lexical form have different etymologies, they are very likely to be homonyms.

For example, the French noun *livre* 'book' is a homonym of the measure term *livre* 'pound' because the two meanings derive from historically unrelated words: 'pound' comes from Latin *libra*, 'book' from Latin *liber*. The second criterion is relatedness between meanings. According to this criterion, if the different meanings associated with a lexical form can be related to one another conceptually (as in the case of extended or figurative uses based on literal ones), we can be reasonably certain that we are dealing with a polysemous lexeme. This is the case, for example, with the word *neck*, which refers to a part of the human body ("She was wearing a scarf around her neck"), and, by sense extension, to the part of a garment that is around or near the neck ("the neck of the shirt"), by similarity to that of a long and narrow object near the mouth of a container ("a bottleneck"), and so forth. The same holds for Engl. *character*, originally 'distinctive mark,' later 'distinguishing qualities, especially of a person.'

While homonymy is a rare and accidental phenomenon, polysemy is pervasive in language and follows regular patterns, which will be discussed at length in 3.3.2.

## 1.4.2. Word types

We have so far approched the concept of word primarily from the point of view of establishing the number of words in a language. In this section we examine words from the point of view of their internal structure, with the aim of providing an overview of the most common word structure types that exist in the world's languages.

Before we begin listing these types, it is worth recalling that from the point of view of their genesis, words that are present in a language at a given moment of time fall into two main groups. Group (i) consists of words which have been formed through application of the available word-formation rules of the language. Traditionally, these are described as rules of derivation, compounding, and conversion, to which we will add **template specification**, that we will illustrate in a moment. Words in group (ii), on the other hand, originate in the gradual strengthening of the syntactic and semantic links existing between two or more words that frequently co-occur in text, a process we referred to as univerbation in section 1.2.1.

In what follows, we provide an overview of the type of words that can be found in languages, focusing on words of group (i). We systematically give examples of two languages, English and Italian, which differ considerably as far as their morphological structure is concerned. A detailed consideration of words of group (ii) will be postponed to Chapter 6, devoted to the analysis of word combination phenomena and their development through time.

A third group of words we shall leave aside consists of *loanwords*, which may be numerous and impact the word-formation rules in the target language. Think of all the English words derived from Latin, often with French as the intermediary language, such as *liberty* (vs. *freedom*), *vacation* (vs. *holiday*), and so forth.

From the point of view of their form, words can be conveniently classified into two distinct types: **simple** (or *simplex*) and **complex words.** Simple words consist of a single morpheme (so-called *free morpheme*) such as Engl. *table, up, happy, the*; It. *ieri* 'yesterday' or a morpheme which requires an inflectional ending; this is the case of most simple words in languages such as Italian: see for example It. *borsa* 'bag,' which is composed of *bors-* (lexical morpheme) and *-a* (inflectional ending marking feminine gender and singular number).

Complex words consist of more than one morpheme (besides inflectional endings). Therefore, they can be said to have an internal structure that simple words lack. The internal structure of a complex word can be either morphological or syntactic. Prototypical examples of **complex words with morphological structure** are **derived words**, that is, words formed by a lexical morpheme and by one or more affixes, such as Engl. *printer* (composed of *print* and *-er*). Other examples of complex words with morphological structure are **compounds**, that is, words formed by (at least) two morphemes with lexical meaning (such as Engl. *bookstore*) and words that are at the same time compounded and derived, such as Engl. *New Yorker*, which consists of two lexical morphemes—*New* and *York*—and the affix *-er*).

**Complex words with syntactic structure** look like phrases on the surface, but when tested for "wordhood" (see Box 1.1), they exhibit an internal cohesiveness that ordinary phrases lack (*parts of speech* and not *\*parts of the speech* etc.). For our current purposes we shall call such fixed phrases **phrasal words** (a term inspired by Lyons' 1977 *phrasal lexeme* and Simone's 1997 *parola sintagmatica*). Phrasal words are multi-word expressions that function as words in text (e.g. phrasal verbs, phrasal nouns, phrasal adjectives, and so on). They cannot be straightforwardly analyzed as the product of word formation rules, because their properties (for example, their meaning) are not fully predictable; nevertheless, it appears that certain syntactic structures "crystallize" and serve as models for the coinage of new complex words, therefore beginning to compete, in part, with standard morphological rules of derivation and compounding. We shall call these structures **templates** and the process of coining new words based on templates we shall call **template specification**. Templates are syntactic structures associated with an abstract meaning, which function as a scheme for creating new words.

In Box 1.2 we provide a list of templates for phrasal nouns and verbs in English and Italian, which appear to be productive from the point of view of word formation.

---

### Box 1.2. Templates with word-like status

Nominal templates

| | |
|---|---|
| (a) adj + noun | Engl. *nervous* disease (= *located in* nerves) |
| | Engl. *solar* panel (= *uses* sun's rays) |
| | Engl. *postal* service ( = *delivers* post) |
| | It. macchina *fotografica* (= *used for* fotografare 'take a picture') |
| | It. carta *telefonica* (= *used for* telefonare 'call by phone') |
| | It. intossicazione *alimentare* (= *caused by* alimento 'food') |
| (b) noun + prep + noun | Engl. bird *of* prey (= *eats* prey) |
| | Engl. son-*in*-law (= *acquired through* law) |
| | Engl. work *of* art ( = *created by* art) |
| | It. mal *di* macchina lit. sickness of car (= *caused by the movement of the car*) |
| | It. piatto *di* pasta lit. *dish of pasta* (= *holding* pasta) |
| | It. piatto *di* plastica lit. *dish of plastic* ( = *made of* plastic) |

*(continued)*

Verbal templates

(c) verb + particle   Engl. *eat up* 'eat completely'
                      Engl. *work out* 'have a good result'
                      Engl. *give up* 'cease'

                      It. *avere addosso* lit. have on 'wear'
                      It. *lavare via* lit. wash away 'remove by washing'
                      It. *mettere giù* lit. put down 'hang up (the phone)'

(d) verb + noun       Engl *have breakfast*
                      Engl. *give birth*
                      Engl. *ask permission*

                      It. *fare festa* lit. make party 'to party'
                      It. *prendere sonno* lit. take sleep 'to fall asleep'
                      It. *sporgere denuncia* 'press charges'

The templates in Box 1.2 are very abstract and specify only the parts of speech (noun, verb, preposition, etc.) that make up the pattern. The examples can be seen as instantiations of less abstract variations of such templates. For example, It. *piatto di pasta* 'dish of pasta' is a more specific instantiation of the template in (2):

**(2)**    noun$_{CONTAINER}$ *di*$_{HOLD}$ noun$_{CONTAINEE}$

which specifies the semantic classes of the nouns that can fill the template (CONTAINER and CONTAINEE), the preposition at play (*di*), and the semantic relation holding between the two nouns (HOLD). The template in (2) is less abstract than the template in (b) because it poses constraints on the type of lexical items that may fill the template.

What has been said so far can be summarized in Figure 1.3. Here, the various word types introduced above are located inside the grey box that

Lexicon

| | | |
|---|---|---|
| | morphologically simple words | free morphemes Engl. *table* bound morphemes and inflection It. *borsa* |
| Morphology → | morphologically complex words | derivations Engl. *printer* compounds Engl. *bookstore* |
| Syntax → | phrasal words | fixed phrases Engl. *part of speech* |

**Figure 1.3** Word formation

represents the lexicon, while the arrows on the left point to the language component where they are assumed to be formed. Compounds consisting in the combination of two or more lexical morphemes are analyzed as the most syntactic morphological constructions.

It is possible to focus on specific portions of the box in Figure 1.3. For example, if we zoom in on the border between morphology and syntax, we may identify different types of compounds; for our present purposes, the distinction between incorporated and juxtaposed compounds will serve, because they are the closest to syntactic constructions (see Figure 1.4).

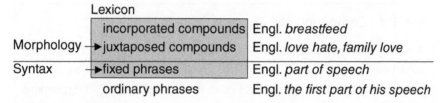

**Figure 1.4** Compounds

**Incorporated compounds** are complex words formed by means of a mechanism called incorporation. This mechanism is very widespread in the Indian languages of North America and Siberia. The most common type of incorporation consists in the conflation of a noun in a verbal root to create a new verb whose meaning is more specific than the original one. An example comes from the *Koryak* language: *qoya-* 'reindeer' + *-nm* 'kill' → *qoyanm* 'to reindeer-slaughter' (the example is from Mithun 1984). The phenomenon is present in words such as Engl. *breastfeed* and It. *manomettere* lit. 'to hand-put', of Latin origin, meaning 'tamper (with).'

**Juxtaposed compounds** is a label that unites all word sequences that consist of multiple words placed next to one another along the chain of speaking so as to express a unitary concept that is of relevance to a given linguistic community. Structurally, the relation between the words that form a juxtaposed compound may be a relation of coordination, as in Engl. *love hate* = 'love and hate,' as in "a love–hate relationship" or It. *ristorante pizzeria*, in which the elements are structurally parallel, or a relation of dependence, as in Engl. *family love* = 'love felt for the family' or It. *treno merci* 'freight train' = 'train that transports freight.' In both cases, the relation is opaque because of the absence of an element that makes it explicit, for example, a preposition or a case marker (more on compound classification in Box 1.3).

**Fixed phrases** are word sequences that exhibit an internal (syntactic) cohesiveness that ordinary phrases lack. They are located at the crossroads between morphology and syntax and even linguists have a hard time proposing clear criteria to distinguish between compounds and fixed phrases on the one hand, and between fixed phrases and ordinary phrases on the other. Empirical evidence suggests that a satisfactory account of such phenomena should incorporate at least the following two assumptions. First, word-formation processes may be fed both by morphology and by syntax. Second, when applied to complex linguistic expressions, the notion of "wordhood" should be seen as a scalar property, i.e. one that comes in degrees, ranging from zero (prototypical phrases) to maximal values (prototypical words).

---

## Box 1.3. Compound classification

A principled criterion to classify compounds is the sort of relation that can hold between the constituents. This relation can be looked at from a grammatical or a semantic point of view. Bisetto and Scalise (2005) propose a classification on grammatical grounds (see also Scalise and Bisetto 2009). According to their account, the grammatical relations holding between the constituents of a compound are basically the relations that hold in syntactic constructions: *subordination, attribution*, and *coordination*. Based on these relations, they propose to distinguish three major types of compounds, namely *subordinate, attributive*, and *coordinate compounds*.

In **subordinate compounds** one of the constituents is the complement of the other. For example, in the English compound *book seller*, *book* is the complement of the head *seller*; more precisely, it is the complement of the verb *sell*, from which the noun *seller* is derived. According to Bisetto and Scalise, a subordinate relation may be found also in compounds such as *apple cake* and *sunglasses*, where the head is not a noun derived from a verb as in *book seller*. In this case, the relation that links the two constituents and determines which of them is the subordinate term remains implicit; for example, an *apple cake* is a cake that contains apple as one of its ingredients (apple is subordinate), *sunglasses* are glasses which protect the eyes from the light of the sun (*sun* is subordinate), and so on. **Attributive compounds**, on the other hand, consist of a noun modified by an adjective that expresses a property or quality of the noun, as in *red wine*, where the adjective *red* conveys a property of the head noun *wine*. The modifier may also be a noun and/or have a figurative interpretation, as in *hot topic*. Also in these latter cases, the constituent being modified conveys a property attributed to the head.

*(continued)*

Finally, in **coordinate compounds**, the first element of the compound does not modify the second. According to Bisetto and Scalise, the constituents are linked by a simple coordinate relation, without a dependency holding between them. The entity can be said to be both one and the other; recall the examples above: Engl. *love hate*, It. *ristorante pizzeria*.

An alternative way of classifying compounds is based on the semantic rather than the grammatical relation holding between the constituents. For example, the classification proposed in Johnston and Busa (1999) distinguishes three major types of semantic relations holding between the constituents of a compound, which for current purposes can be conveniently called the MADE_OF relation, the USED_FOR relation, and the CAUSED_BY relation. Examples are as follows: *glass door* 'door made of glass' (MADE_OF relation), *bread knife* 'knife used to cut bread' (USED_FOR relation), and *lemon juice* 'juice that is brought about by squeezing a lemon' (CAUSED_BY relation).

An interesting aspect of Johnston and Busa's work is that they examine parallel data from English and Italian. Specifically, they compare English compounds such as *glass door* with their Italian equivalents. This shows that the most common Italian equivalents of English binominal compounds are not standard compounds but rather phrasal expressions of the noun-prep-noun type. For example, the corresponding Italian forms of the English compounds above are *glass door* = It. *porta a vetri* (lit. door-at-glass), *bread knife* = It. *coltello da pane* (lit. knife-from-bread), and *lemon juice* = It. *succo di limone* (lit. juice-of-lemon). From the examples we can see that while the semantic relation holding between the nouns is left implicit in the English compounds, in the corresponding Italian expressions it is partially specified by the preposition that introduces the second noun. This feature of Italian provides the motivation for Johnston and Busa's semantic analysis, which aims at predicting the interpretation of the compounds on the basis of the type of preposition. For example, the appropriate preposition for the MADE_OF relation is claimed to be *a*.

## 1.4.3. Word typology

Let us now finally turn to the types of words that can be found in the languages throughout the world. From a typological perspective, one can identify at least five main types of words: these are the words of the **isolating**, **polysynthetic**, **agglutinating**, **fusional**, and **introflexive** languages. These types intersect with those previously described (simplex and complex words) and pertain more directly to the overall morphological structure of the language in question, rather than the morphological structure of the single words. Let us look at them in order.

The words of **isolating** languages, such as Mandarin Chinese or Vietnamese, tend to consist of a single free lexical morpheme (they are, therefore, morphologically simple words) that carries one and only one meaning and is invariable in its form. For example, in Mandarin Chinese (the example is taken from Li and Thompson 1981):

(3)  *tā*          *zài*  *túshūgǔn*  *kàn*    *bào*
     3ᴿᴰ SING   in     library      read    newspaper
     'he reads the newspaper in the library'

In these languages also grammatical categories, such as plural, past tense, etc., when they are realized, are conveyed by means of monomorphemic words. For example the plural of *mǎ* 'horse' is formed in Mandarin Chinese by adding a separate morpheme expressing the number, obligatorily accompanied by the classifier *pǐ* (note that *mǎ* 'horse' does not vary):

(4)  *yi*      *pǐ*   *mǎ*
     one     CLF-horse
     *liang*  *pǐ*   *mǎ*
     two     CLF-horse

If the noun is not followed by a number morpheme, it can be interpreted as either singular or plural:

(5)  *mǎ*        *xǐhuan*  *chī*   *cǎo*
     horse      like       eat     grass
     'The horse/horses like(s) to eat grass'

We have many examples of words of this type in English (*boy, dog, house, will, more*) whereas there are only a few in Italian (for example *ieri* 'yesterday,' *sotto* 'under,' *mai* 'never').

The words of **polysynthetic** languages, rare in the languages familiar to us but frequent, for example, in the Yup'ik languages spoken in the western region of Alaska and in the eastern point of Siberia, tend to consist of a large number of morphemes, be they lexical or grammatical (they are, thus, morphologically complex words). An example from these languages is that of the word *angya-ghlla-ng-yug-tuq* which contains a single lexical morpheme, *angya* (= 'boat'), followed by several grammatical morphemes, which are able to express concepts commonly expressed in European languages by autonomous words, such as verbs and nouns. The meaning of this word corresponds to that of a whole sentence of English: "he wants to acquire a large boat" (the example is from Comrie 1981: 41):

(6) *angya   -ghlla-          ng-       yug            -tuq*
    boat    AUGMENTATIVE  ACQUIRE   DESIDERATIVE   -3$^{RD}$ SING
    'he wants to acquire a large boat'

From a morphological point of view, on a scale of one to ten, with ten being the most typical and one being the least typical word, the polysynthetic word is the least typical, because it resembles a whole sentence and is composed of many pieces (the morphemes) each of which contributes to the overall meaning of the word. Using the terminology of Seiler we introduced in section 1.2.2, each morpheme "describes" a part of the word's content. At the opposite end of the scale we find isolating words, where there is a one-to-one mapping between morphemes and words, and where the content is not "described" but rather "labeled."

   In **agglutinating** languages words are formed by a lexical morpheme and one or more inflectional and derivational morphemes in a rigid order. These morphemes have the characteristic of carrying one and the same meaning in all contexts and, therefore, they contribute to form words that are highly regular as to their morphological structure and the predictability of their meaning. This is the basic word type of languages such as Turkish, in which the syntactic relations are expressed through suffixes. The following is an example:

(7) *arkadaş* 'friend'
    *arkadaşlar* 'friends'
    *arkadaşlarım* 'my friends'
    *arkadaşlarımla* 'with my friends'

It should be noted that, although agglutinating words are often regarded as typical of languages such as Turkish and Korean, they can be found in Germanic and Romance languages as well. Examples are: the class of English adverbs ending in -*ly*, which are formed according to a very regular mechanism by adding -*ly* to adjectival bases (*curiously, happily*, etc.); the equivalent class of Italian adverbs ending in -*mente* (*curiosamente, felicemente*, etc.); the class of words formed by productive concatenation of suffixes, such as Engl. *home-less-ness, care-less-ness*, and so forth. Unlike Turkish, however, these examples are peripheral in the morphological system of English and particularly of Italian, where a single morpheme may express multiple meanings and the same meaning may be expressed by multiple morphemes. Languages displaying such characteristics are called **fusional**. An example is the It. verbal form *cantavano* 'they sang,' where *cant-* is the lexical morpheme 'sing,' *a* identifies the inflectional class of the verb, *v-* conflates tense, imperfective aspect and indicative mood (subjunctive mood would be *ss-*), and -*ano* lexicalizes both number (plural) and person (3rd).

(8)  *cant-*                *a-*                    *v-*                          *-ano*
     LEXICAL MORPHEME    INFLECTIONAL CLASS    TENSE                       PLUR
                                                IMPERFECTIVE ASPECT    3ʳᵈ
                                                INDICATIVE MOOD

Finally, the words of **introflexive** languages, such as the Semitic languages (for example Arabic and Hebrew), are considered to be a sub-type of the **fusional** type, because these languages too display no one-to-one relations between morphemes and meanings. The words of introflexive languages, however, are built in a different way, namely, by inserting a morpheme made up of vowels into a lexical root consisting of consonants. The root carries a very generic meaning and is incomplete when taken alone; it becomes a word only when it is completed by this insertion. An example is the Arabic root *ktb*, which may denote various objects and activities related to writing:

(9)  *ktb*   *kataba* 'he wrote'
            *takātaba* 'he corresponded'
            *'iktataba* 'he copied'
            *kitāb* 'book'
            *kātib* 'writer'
            *kutubī* 'book seller'
            *'istiktāb* 'dictation'

We have this to some extent in English too, for example with *run-ran, sing-sang, write-wrote;* however, in the Semitic languages this type of patterning is the rule while in English it is an exception.

## Further reading

Pinker (1999) and Singleton (2000) provide good introductions to words and the lexicon.

On the mental lexicon, see Aitchinson (1987). A state-of-the-art survey on the composition of the mental lexicon can be found in Lieber (2010: 177).

General remarks on the distinction between the mental lexicon of an individual and the lexicon of a language can be found in Booij (2007: 18).

A detailed discussion of the interplay between lexical storage and online construction can be found in Jackendoff (2002), chapter 6 and Pinker (1999).

Recent discussions about the notion of word from a morphological perspective can be found in Aronoff and Fudeman (2005), Booij (2007), and Lieber (2010); as a general reference, see Lyons (1968), section 5.4.

An extensive account of grammatical semantics is Frawley (1992).

For a collection of contributions on several aspects of lexicology, see Cruse et al. (2002) and Hanks (2007).

On lexicography, see Zgusta (1971), Landau (2001), Jackson (2002) and Atkins and Rundell (2008). On syntax in lexicography, Osswald (2014). For a quick survey on computers and lexicography, cf. Atkins and Rundell (2008: 112–13). For linguistic notions useful for lexicographic practice, Atkins and Rundell (2008), chapter 5.

On corpus-based lexicography, see Hanks (2013) and references therein.

On lexical semantics, see Cruse (1986), Cruse (1999) [2nd edn. 2004, 3rd edn. 2011], Murphy (2010).

On lexicalization, see Talmy (1985); from a morphological perspective, Booij (2007), chapter 1.4.

Lexical typology is discussed in Koptjevskaja-Tamm (2008).

On morphology, see Aronoff and Fudermann (2005); with focus on semantics, Lieber (2010); in a constructionist perspective Booij (2007).

On multi-word expressions, see Zgusta (1967, 1971); from a computational perspective, Calzolari et al. (2002) and Sag et al. (2002).

Compounds are dealt with extensively in Lieber and Štekauer (2009).

On idioms, Nunberg et al. (1994); Jackendoff (1997), chapter 7.

On lexical resources, including computational lexicons, see the European Language Resources Association (ELRA) catalogue (http://catalog.elra. info/) and the Linguistic Data Consortium (LDC) (http://www.ldc.upenn. edu/).

# 2

# Lexical information

Our focus in this chapter is lexical information, i.e. the information encoded in words. We examine how this information is understood, how it is organized, and how it interacts with the so-called encyclopedic (or world or commonsense) knowledge, i.e. the knowledge that words evoke and that comes into play in their actual use.

## 2.1. Types of lexical information

**Lexical information** is the information encoded in words. This information determines how we use a word and why we choose that word over another when we talk, and accounts for the difference it makes when we substitute that word for another. Lexical information can be seen as the sum of a word's linguistic properties; for example, the meaning of a word is part of its lexical information and it is also one of its linguistic properties (specifically, the semantic property). On the other hand, a word can be seen as a bundle of information because, as we shall see, it encodes information of different kinds (for an introduction to lexical information, with a focus on verbs, see Fillmore 1968).

Intuitively, the most evident information associated with every word is its **meaning**, which is basically the word's informational value. It is possible to distinguish several types of word meanings. A primary distinction is that between **grammatical** (i.e. functional) and **lexical** (i.e. non-functional) meaning, according to which two main types of words may be identified: function words and content words respectively. As we saw in section 1.3, this distinction is inherent in lexical items, but is also inextricably linked to the linguistic means through which a given content is expressed; for example, one and the same notion such as plurality can be expressed by either lexical or morphological means and therefore be interpreted as either lexical or grammatical. The examples in Chapter 1 illustrate this point.

The second distinction to be made is between **denotative meaning** (or **denotation** or **extension**) and **connotative meaning** (or **connotation** or **intension**). The denotation of a word (also called its **descriptive** or **referential** or **logical meaning**) is its ability to refer not only to a single object but, generically, to the entire class of entities that share that object's characteristics (Lyons 1968). For example, when we say "I don't like fish," the word *fish* refers generically to (or denotes) the flesh of the class of entities in the world that belong to the type "fish," among which there are longer fish, shorter fish, the fish I ate yesterday, and so forth. Note that this ability is typical of common nouns and not of proper nouns; in fact, with the sentence "John is tall" we cannot refer to all the people called John but only to a specific John.

According to the traditional view, the denotation of a word may be single, as with Engl. *lamp*, denoting the device for giving light, or multiple, as with Engl. *paper*, which denotes, *inter alia*, the material used for writing ("recycled paper") and an essay published in an academic journal ("a technical paper"). A word with a single denotation is called *monosemous*, while a word with multiple denotations is referred to as *polysemous*.

The task of identifying the denotative meaning of a word, and especially of telling the different meanings apart when the word appears to have multiple denotations, is a notoriously difficult task. As it happens, words tend to systematically take on different denotations depending on the context of use, a fact which has brought many researchers to arguing that words in isolation are better seen as having a meaning potential rather than fully specified meaning(s). We will examine this theoretical stance in Chapter 3; for now we will abstract away from the problem of sensitivity of meaning to context, and characterize the denotation of a word as the most "objective" part of its meaning, that is, the part which is stable across the members of a linguistic community and enables the exchange of information that speakers have in mind when they use that word.

The connotative meaning of a word concerns, instead, those aspects of its meaning that have the character of add-ons. That is to say, they are aspects of meaning that add an extra to the base meaning (the denotative meaning) for example:

- the speaker's attitude toward the word's referent. This is the so-called **emotional, affective**, or **expressive meaning**. An example is *mom*, carrying a specific emotional connotation, as opposed to *mother*, which is neutral in this regard.
- the speaker's attitude towards the situation of utterance and his/her relationship with the hearer. This determines the level of formality/informality the speaker chooses in communication (**stylistic meaning**). For instance: *bike* belongs to a lower register than *bicycle* ("I'll take my bike"); *guy* is informal whereas *man* is neutral ("I know that guy"); *buck* is colloquial as opposed to *dollar* ("This gadget costs 15 bucks"), and so forth.

> Word pairings such as *mom* and *mother*, *guy* and *man*, etc. have the same denotation but a different connotation. That is, the difference between these words does not lie in their referent (the entity to which they refer), which is substantially the same, but in the properties ascribed to the referent by the speaker.

Often, in everyday language, when we talk about the connotation of a word, we simply mean the positive or negative associations that a word evokes. For example the term *bureaucracy* is associated with negative connotations such as excessive regulations causing delays, and so on.

A third type of meaning is *pragmatic meaning*. **Pragmatic meaning** arises only in particular contexts of use: for example, in "Look, I didn't know about that," the meaning of the word *look* is not its basic meaning but corresponds roughly to a demand of attention to what one is going to say. Pragmatic meanings are assumed not to reside in the lexicon and to be generated in the context of use; however, certain pragmatic meanings tend to lexicalize and become systematically associated with a word; this is generally reflected in the fact that they are reported in dictionaries.

Yet another type of meaning is the so-called **collocational meaning** (from the expression *meaning by collocation*, cf. Firth 1957, 194), i.e. the meaning that a word acquires only in combination (in collocation) with a particular word or set of words. Examples are the meaning that *heavy* takes on in combination with *drinker* (= excessive), that *warm* takes on in combination with *welcome* (= affectionate), that *to launch* takes on in combination with *product* (= introduce to the public), that *to pay* takes on with *attention* (= dedicate), that It. *portare* 'bring, carry' takes on with *pazienza* 'patience' (= have), and so on.

The distinction between denotation and collocational meaning is controversial. According to some authors, collocational meaning should be kept distinct from denotative meaning, whereas other authors do not distinguish between the two, claiming that all words do in fact acquire their meanings only in combination with other words. Under this view, there is no need to separate the two; if they are separated, however, the identification of the collocational meaning(s) of a word requires logically that its denotational meaning(s) is/are fixed first.

All of these aspects contribute to defining the meaning of a word along different dimensions. Note that a word, depending on its denotation, can combine with certain words and not with others: a *table* may *creak* but not *smile*; a *drink* may be *pleasant* but not *fascinating*; one can *read a book* but not *a lamp*; *drink an orange juice* but not *an orange*, and so forth. Moreover, based on its denotation a word establishes associations with other words, for example words with a similar meaning (*buy/purchase*), an opposite meaning (*live/die*), a more specific meaning (*eat/devour*), and so forth. Some authors argue that these associations should be included in the information that makes up a word, because to know what a word means involves being able to correctly place it in a network of relations of this type. An extreme version of this position is found in the idea that meaning is definable only on a relational basis.

Added to the fact that a word has a meaning, there exist other properties that a word carries. For example, when pronounced, words have a **sound**, characterized by an orderly set of individual sound segments called phonemes, a syllabic structure, a stress, and, in languages such as Chinese and Thai, a specific tone when used in a particular sense. The sound of a word may be transcribed using the International Phonetic Alphabet (IPA). For example the English word *game* can be transcribed as follows: [geim] (English IPA). A word's sound may have a corresponding **graphic form**, consisting of the set of characters through which the sound is rendered in the writing system of the language. Needless to say, this holds true only for languages that have a written tradition.

There is often no one-to-one correspondence between the sound of a word and its transcription; the relation is rather a one-to-many or many-to-one. For example, the complex sound [ei] in the English word *table* is rendered with a single graphic symbol *a*, while the simple sound [i] of *guitar* is rendered with the complex graphic symbol *ui*. Similarly, in *psychology*, the sound [s] is rendered graphically as *ps*. Finally, a single sound can be written in different ways: the sound [i:] can be written as *e* (as in *be*), *ee* (as in *bee*), *ea* (as in *bean*), *ie* (as in *brief*), *ei* (as in *receive*), *ey* (as in *key*), *i* (as in *ravine*), even *ae* (as in *encyclopaedia*) (Singleton, 2000).

Languages vary in relation to how much sound and spelling diverge. English and French are languages with a loose correspondence between the two, while Italian and Finnish are languages where the level of consistency of correspondence between letters and sounds is very high (although mismatches can be observed in Italian as well; for example Italian has three different graphic symbols (*c*, *ch*, *q*) to transcribe the same sound ([ˈk]) which appears in [ˈkɔrpo] (*corpo* 'body'), [ˈkjuzo] (*chiuso* 'closed'), and [ˈkwadro] (*quadro* 'painting') and two different sounds ([s], [z]) for the same graphic symbol *s* (*scarpa* 'shoe,' *sbaglio* 'mistake'); finally, Italian appears to possess a graphic symbol corresponding to no sound (*h* in *hanno* 'have')). Finally, there are languages in which the basis of the writing system is the syllable rather than the individual sound. This is the case of the Japanese *kana* script, which is used in two forms, *hiragana* and *katakana*, to represent, on the one hand, particles, verb inflections etc. and, on the other, words borrowed from Western languages such as English.

A very different kind of writing system is that which takes meanings rather than sounds as its starting point, as in the case of Chinese *ideograms*. These meaning-based systems often develop historically from systems in which the objects referred to in writing are represented through drawings.

As well as an informational content, a sound and, in some cases, a written form, a word has **morphological properties**. Two basic types of morphological properties can be distinguished: morphological structure and morphological behavior. As regards morphological structure, words which are made up of more than one morpheme (therefore, derived words such as *careful* and compound words such as *bottleneck* or *empty-handed*) can be said to have an inner morphological structure, while words consisting of one single morpheme (such as many English words: *bar, run, with, late, light, just*) do not (section 1.4.2). Morphological structure is important because it provides the basis for structuring the vocabulary of a language into (morphological) word families, i.e. sets of words that share one or more morphemes. Word families can be seen not only as word groupings sharing a common root (*flower, flowery, flowering*; see section 1.1) but also as groups of words that share the same derivational endings; for example, on the basis of the derivational ending, English can be said to have a class of *-able* adjectives (*reasonable, valuable, comfortable*), a class of *-ize* verbs (*apologize, criticize, summarize*), a class of *-ation* nouns (*translation, sensation, civilization*), and so forth.

Turning now to morphological behavior, in languages that have inflection, words may fall into one particular inflectional class, which predicts how they behave in actual use. For example, the color adjectives *rosa* 'rose' and *viola* 'purple' in Italian fall into the class of invariable adjectives, which means that they do not change their form when number or gender changes (compare "un vestito ros*a*" 'a pink dress' with "due vestiti ros*a*" 'two pink dresses' and not "due vestiti ros*i*" 'two pink-plur. dresses'). This behavior contrasts with that of most color adjectives in Italian, which are inflected for gender and number: see for example "un vestito rosso" 'a red dress,' "due vestiti ros*i*" 'two red dresses' (and not "due vestiti ros*o*"), and so forth.

Another property of words is that of belonging to a certain **word class** (or **lexical category**) that is, of being a verb, a noun, an adjective, an adverb, and so forth. This property can be pinned down from the analysis of both the syntactic and the morphological behavior of words. Consider first the syntactic behavior; a word clearly licenses some syntactic contexts and excludes others depending on the category to which it belongs. The English word *meal*, for example, can be preceded by an article (*a meal*) or accompanied by an adjective (*a tasty meal*), but it cannot be modified by an adverb (*\*a well meal*), because the adverb is the word class that modifies verbs, not nouns such as *meal*. We call a context *nominal, verbal*, or *adjectival* precisely to indicate the word's typical environment, consisting of the phrase (i.e. the structured group of words) of which the word is the head.

> Note that under this view, the class associated with a word can be seen as the first point of contact of the lexicon with the syntax.

Turning now to morphology, morphological modifications are also indicative of the class to which a word belongs. For example, in inflectional languages, verbs, and not nouns, are usually marked for tense and modified accordingly (as in "I walk" (present), "I walked" (past), "I will walk" (future) etc.).

With regards to word classes, there is much to say. First, although it is true of all words that they are associated with a class (except, perhaps, of *interjections* such as *oh, wow, ugh,* etc.), it appears that a large number of words may take on different classes in different contexts. This phenomenon is very frequent in languages with poor (inflectional) morphology, such as English, where, for example, the word *back,* originally the name of a body part, may be used as an adjective (*the back door*), as an adverb (*please call me back; don't look back*), and finally also as a verb (*to back a claim*) (examples are taken from Ježek and Ramat 2009).

(1)   a.  She tapped him on the *back.*
      b.  Lock the *back* door.
      c.  Please call me *back.*
      d.  Don't look *back.*
      e.  *Back* a claim.

This phenomenon is the norm in isolating languages, which have little or no morphology, such as Chinese, where, for example, *bing* may mean 'get sick' (verb) but also 'illness' (noun) (the example is taken from Li and Thompson 1981: 42):

(2) *bing*

| ta | de | *bing* | hao | le |
|----|----|--------|-----|-----|
| 3SING | GEN | illness | to improve | PERF |

'his illness improved'

| ta | *bing* | le | san | tian |
|----|--------|-----|-----|------|
| 3SING | to get ill | PERF | three | day |

'he was ill for three days'

The phenomenon is also present, albeit rare, in languages with rich morphology, such as Italian, where for example *dubbio* 'doubt' may appear as a noun or an adjective:

(3) *dubbio*

| Ho un dubbio atroce. | 'I have a terrible doubt' | (*dubbio* = noun) |
| Questo mi sembra un caso dubbio. | 'This seems a doubtful case to me' | (*dubbio* = adjective) |

This raises questions about what, exactly, is the category associated with these words. There are several possible ways to answer this question. In the first place, one might argue that words that exhibit multiple classes contain information about all the categories they are able to take on in context (for example, in the case of Ch. *bing*, both verb and noun). This solution, however, is uneconomical and not satisfactory particularly in the case of isolating languages, where **categorial flexibility** represents the norm rather than the exception. An alternative approach is to assume that the lexicon contains a different lexical entry for each use (for example *dubbio*1 and *dubbio*2 in the Italian example above). Also this second hypothesis is uneconomical, as well as not very plausible from a psychological and cognitive point of view. A third option is to maintain that a word has a "default" category associated with it, and may, by *conversion*, acquire other uses in context, which must be regarded as derived. Derived forms may be more or less lexicalized. Consider for example Engl. *bottle*, which is a noun which has been turned into a verb; both uses are familiar to the speaker and it is plausible to assume that they are both stored in the speaker's lexicon.

(4)   a. I bought a *bottle* of wine. (bottle = noun)
      b. We *bottle* the wine in November every year. (bottle = verb).

On the other hand, converted uses as in (5b) are highly context-dependent and one might think of them as online construction originated in discourse:

(5)   a. We need to tell them *why*. (*why* = adverb)
      b. The *whys* of people's actions. (*why* = noun)

Finally, *green* used as verb (as in (6c)) suggests an intermediate case:

(6)   a. The leaves are bright *green*. (*green* = adjective)
      b. Both rooms overlooked the *green*. (*green* = noun, meaning 'an area planted with grass')
      c. My job is to *green* our company. (*green* = verb, meaning 'to make it more environmentally friendly')

A fourth interpretation is more radical, and applicable only to languages where word classes are not distinguished through morphology. According to this interpretation, words do not contain information about their lexical category, i.e. they are underspecified with respect to this property, and acquire it only in the syntax, i.e. when they are combined with other words. In this view, if a word is inserted into a nominal syntax (thus, for example, preceded by a determiner and/or modified by an adjective), it behaves like a noun, if it is inserted into adjectival syntax (for example, followed by a noun in English), it behaves like an adjective, and so forth. In a lexicon of this kind words are **precategorial**, i.e. they do not belong to a particular lexical category (cf. Sasse 1993 and Bisang 2008).

$$\begin{bmatrix} \text{meaning} \\ \text{sound structure} \\ \text{morphological structure} \\ \text{?word class} \end{bmatrix}$$

**Figure 2.1** Lexical information

Figure 2.1 offers a scheme of what we discussed so far. The term *structure* highlights the fact that the information encoded at each level of the representation constitutes a structured set.

The properties we examined so far are shared, in different ways, by all words. That is to say, all words have a meaning, a sound structure (at least a potential one: as we have noted, the sound structure is not realized in written usage), morphological properties (even words without internal structure—that is, monomorphemic words—have morphological properties that can be defined as the absence of such characteristics), and a minimal syntactic behavior that we can relate to the lexical category/ies to which they belong.

There are, however, words that have some extra properties. They are those words that have the ability to predicate properties of entities or relations between entities, and must include these entities as part of their lexical make-up in order to have a full meaning. For example, the meaning of *shine* contains specification of the entity to which the property of shining applies (the sun, or other sources of light); the meaning of *warm up* specifies what type of entity (a location, a person) gets warm, and so on. Typically, this information is represented in terms of **argument structure** associated with the word in question (called the **predicate**), and the single entities are known as **arguments**.

The meaning of words which includes an array of arguments (verbs in most cases, but also deverbal nouns, prepositions, and adjectives) also includes specification of what is generally known as *Aktionsart* (German for "kind of action") **actionality** or **lexical aspect**. This information concerns the particular way a word presents the relation it expresses from the point of view of its temporal structure, particularly its constituent phases; in other words, how the **event** it reports (understood as a cover term for all situation types) unrolls through time. In this perspective, the verb *sleep*, for example, presents a situation in its progress ("The children sleep"), while *fall asleep*

*Shared by all words*:

$$\begin{bmatrix} \text{meaning} \\ \text{sound structure} \\ \text{morphological structure} \\ \text{?word class} \end{bmatrix}$$

*Specific to words which function as predicates*:

$$\begin{bmatrix} \text{argument structure} \\ \textit{Aktionsart} \end{bmatrix}$$

**Figure 2.2** Lexical information (revised)

presents the same situation focusing on its initial phase (in relation to *sleep*); the verb *build* presents an event that lasts in time and ends with a result (the coming into being of a construction); *explode* describes an instantaneous happening, that ends at the same instant in which it starts (i.e. initial point and end point coincide); finally, *remain* introduces a state that persists in time.

To sum up, from a structural point of view, words denoting properties or relations contain information other words do not possess: the specification of the number and type of entities to which the properties or relations apply, and the way in which the denoted properties and relations unfold in time. We can now revise the provisional structure proposed in Figure 2.1 on this basis, as in Figure 2.2.

It is important to note that the informational structures in Figure 2.2 are interconnected in multiple ways. For example, the argument structure and the *Aktionsart* intertwine inasmuch as the entities specified in the argument structure associated with a word correspond to the entities which play a role in the different phases of the event that the word describes. Consider *run*: it expresses a situation in its progress with one argument (the runner). We shall return to this point in Chapter 4 and turn now to the distinction between lexical information and encyclopedic knowledge.

## 2.2. Lexical information and encyclopedic knowledge

By common consent, words denote classes of entities and are associated with conceptual categories (cf. Chapter 1), for example a *dog* denotes an animal, a *table* denotes an artifact, *bread* denotes a kind of food, a *park* denotes a location, *run* denotes a process, *love* denotes a state, and so forth. A *conceptual category* may be analyzed as a set of salient attributes or properties, for example the concept dog has properties: *breathes, barks, wags its tail, has fur*, and so forth. But which properties of a concept are genuinely distinctive and enter into the lexical make-up of a word and which ones do not? In this section we elaborate on these points.

First, it is important to remember that there are deep controversies regarding what piece of information associated with a word should enter into its definition and constitute what is called its *lexical information*. Generally, it is assumed that encyclopedic knowledge should be excluded (Marconi 1997: 43–7). **Encyclopedic knowledge** is the large body of knowledge that people possess about the entities and events denoted by words as a result of their experience of the world. Because encyclopedic knowledge has to do with the speaker's perception of the world, and the analogies speakers establish between objects and events, rather than with their linguistic knowledge, it is also called **world knowledge** or **commonsense knowledge**.

As an example of how the distinction between lexical information and commonsense knowledge may be applied, consider the case of *bread*. One might argue that the lexical information associated with the word *bread* includes its form (*bread* is a mass noun), the materials it is made of (*bread* is made of flour, water, yeast, and salt), and its purpose (*bread* is a kind of food, therefore it is intended to be eaten). On the other end, the encyclopedic knowledge we have about *bread* concerns: the range of actions we can do with it (slice it, butter it, toast it, but not, for example, *build it, *cross it, *turn it on, etc.); the temporary characteristics that it may have (crusty, stale, but not *fast, *broad, etc.); the fact that it is often stuffed with cheese or spread with butter; how we can store it in order to keep it fresh; how long it stays fresh; its smell; its price, and so on. Commonsense knowledge is thought of including, but not being limited to, information about the typical behavior of objects, their localization and sensory properties, emotions they may evoke (desirable, undesirable, good, bad), typical participants, goals behind human actions, and so on.

The distinction between lexical information and encyclopedic knowledge is very difficult to draw. According to some authors, it is not even necessary (for example, Haiman 1980). Others believe it should be conceived as a continuum rather than a dichotomy. Opinions differ because there is no consensus about what criteria must be satisfied for a piece of information to qualify as encyclopedic knowledge instead of linguistic meaning, or vice versa.

Those who make a distinction take different positions on the subject. According to the **minimalist position**, nothing of what we know about, say, the entity called *dog* is part of the lexical information associated with the word *dog*, except for those features that are necessary to define it as a domestic animal (as opposed to a wild one) and allow us to distinguish it from other entities falling into the same category. According to the **maximalist position**, the opposite is instead true, that is, the lexical information associated with the word *dog* incorporates our knowledge that dogs can be aggressive (and therefore bite and attack), that they have an acute sense of smell, that they like to chase cats, and so on. Likewise, the lexical information associated with the word *peach* includes, in a minimalist perspective, specification that it is a kind of fruit, and, in a maximalist perspective, that it can be more or less ripe, more or less velvety, more or less juicy, and so forth. This additional knowledge about dogs or peaches is what we know from our individual experience.

A third position is intermediate, and **linguistically motivated**. According to this position, the information encoded in a word amounts to those aspects that influence how the word behaves grammatically and how it may be interpreted in different contexts. One way of identifying these aspects is to examine the distribution of words in context. For example, the expression *quick coffee* means 'coffee which is drunk quickly'; this comes across as a sign that the meaning of *coffee* contributes information regarding the activity of *drinking*, while this appears not to be the case with *water*, which, in the context of *quick* means 'that moves quickly' rather than "which is drunk quickly." According to this methodology, if a piece of knowledge is exploited in our understanding of linguistic expressions, it is likely to be part of lexical information.

A radically different position is that taken by those who hold that the distinction between lexical information and encyclopedic knowledge is artificial or useless, and should be eliminated. This position is dominant in cognitive semantics and pragmatics (cf. section 3.3). According to this position, words give access to concepts, and all the properties that enter into the constitution of a concept can in principle be exploited in language through the use of words. The contexts is which words are used determine which property/ies of the concept is/are activated in the specific case. In this view, there is no distinction between the meaning of a word and the information associated with the conceptual category the word gives access to. The lexicon is interpreted as the access node into the vast repository of information associated with conceptual categories.

From the above discussion, we can conclude the following: wherever the border between lexical information and encyclopedic knowledge may be (if it exists), the amount and type of information that different users of the same language associate with a given word must roughly coincide for the word to be used successfully in communication, otherwise one user would mean one thing, another user something else. Since, however, it is clearly not true that all speakers share the same knowledge that they associate with a lexical item, the best way to define lexical knowledge is to see it as the set of overlapping knowledge associated with lexical items language users converge on.

## Further reading

On the scope of linguistic semantics, as distinct from non-linguistic knowledge, see Jackendoff (2002: 281–7).

On lexical knowledge from a computational perspective, Pustejovsky and Boguraev (1993).

On lexical competence, see Marconi (1997).

Pragmatic meaning is discussed in Carston (2002).

For an overview of the relations between pragmatics and semantics, Recanati (2004), chapters 6 and 9.

# 3

# The meaning of words

In this chapter, we address several issues related to the meaning of words: the main problem that we face when describing the meaning of words; lexical ambiguity and polysemy; the nature of word meaning; how word meaning is built up syntagmatically; and how it may be represented using formal tools.

## 3.1. What, exactly, do words mean?

One of the crucial problems in lexical analysis is that of determining precisely what words mean. The study of this aspect of the lexicon is called **lexical semantics**. The task of defining the meaning of words, as easy as it might appear, is instead difficult, for two related reasons.

First, many words take on a different meaning depending on the context in which they are used. For example, the word *next* means 'spatial proximity' in "the couple at the *next* table" and 'temporal sequence' in "the *next* train is delayed." The coexistence of many possible meanings for a word is traditionally referred to as *polysemy*, and it is conceived as a list of established senses stored in the lexical entry. We will see in a moment how this view is challenged today by approaches that see polysemy in relation to contextual sensitivity of meaning (Pustejovsky 1995, Cruse 2004, Recanati 2012).

Second, although word meaning is the basic unit for building the meaning of expressions made up of multiple words, the meaning of complex expressions is rarely the mere sum of the meanings of the individual words. As an example, consider the English expression *plastic bag* and compare it with *grocery bag*. The meaning of both combinations consists of the meaning of the two constituent nouns, plus an unexpressed semantic relation between the members (cf. Levi 1978); precisely, *plastic bag* means 'bag-MADE_OF-plastic' while *grocery bag* means 'bag-MEANT_TO_CONTAIN-grocery'.

The analysis of the meaning of complex linguistic expressions does not properly belong to lexical semantics but rather to **phrasal** (or **sentence**) **semantics,** that is, the branch of semantics dedicated to the analysis of how the meaning of complex expressions is obtained starting from the meaning of the constituent words. Nevertheless, lexical and **compositional semantics** clearly overlap; if, on the one hand, words contribute to building the meaning of sentences, on the other, context appears to influence the way words are interpreted. The two aspects must therefore be regarded as complementary, and lexical semantics cannot but take both into account in the task of defining the meaning of single words.

Before we go on to a detailed look at various aspects of word polysemy in section 3.2, it is important to define clearly the notion of context in light of the role that context is supposed to play in the interpretation of words. The **context** of a word can be generically defined as the set of words that immediately precede or follow it, that is, its immediate linguistic environment. A more precise definition, however, distinguishes between syntactic and semantic context, and then situational (or pragmatic) context.

The **syntactic context** of a word is the set of words it co-occurs with, understood from the point of view of their syntactic properties. On the basis of the analysis of these properties, it is possible to establish whether the syntactic context of a word is nominal, verbal, adjectival, and so forth. For example, in English, the context [Det Adj __ ] (where the underscore stands for the word we are examining, and the rest for its context) is a nominal context; that is, it is an expression headed by a noun, such as "a great man."

The **semantic context** of a word is the set of words it occurs with as seen from the point of view of their semantic properties. It is this notion of context that is particularly important when we address the problem of assigning meaning to words. To understand why, consider the following expressions:

**(1)**    I broke a *glass*. (*glass* = object)

I drank a *glass*. (*glass* = liquid: wine, beer, water ... )

In (1) the word *glass* changes its meaning despite the fact that the syntactic context remains unchanged. In fact, nothing changes in the two sentences except for the verb. It follows that there is only one possible factor causing the difference in meaning of *glass*: the meaning of the verb. We can draw the conclusion that when words combine, the meaning of one influences the meaning of the other. It is precisely by analyzing the ways in which words influence each other when they co-occur that we can gain insight about what their actual meaning(s) is/are and how they acquire one particular interpretation instead of another in a given context.

Finally, **situational** (or **pragmatic** or **extra-linguistic**) context is the context needed to assign a meaning to a word, when this is not assigned by its linguistic context. For example, in the sentence "Your friend is cool," the word *cool* can mean either 'fashionable, attractive' or 'unemotional, aloof'; we are not able to determine which of the two meanings should be ascribed to this word unless we consider the situational context in which it is used. Situational context can therefore be defined as those aspects of the communicative situation that come into play in the interpretation of a sentence, which remains ambiguous otherwise (a thorough discussion of the distinction between linguistic and situational context can be found in Recanati 2004, chapter 1).

Some scholars include in context also the background knowledge that we have about objects or situations denoted by the words, thanks to our individual personal experience; for example, the knowledge that the sun can dry our laundry or brown our skin. In this book, we will not use the word context in this sense and use encyclopedic or world or commonsense knowledge instead (see section 2.2). This kind of knowledge does, however, interact with situational context (i.e. the actual context of a communicative act) in providing the framework against which words get interpreted in their actual use.

## 3.2. Ambiguity and polysemy of words

**Lexical ambiguity** is the property of a lexical form of having more than one meaning. It has been suggested that there are two main types of lexical ambiguity (Weinreich 1964). The first is **contrastive ambiguity** or homonymy.

As we already saw in section 1.4.1, this is the case of a lexical form that in a language accidentally carries two or more distinct and unrelated meanings, as in *pole* ('location' as in "magnetic pole") and *pole* ('round object' as in "fibreglass pole"). This type of ambiguity is called contrastive because the two meanings are by nature contradictory, that is, in a given context one automatically excludes the other. As D.A. Cruse suggests, these meanings are *antagonistic* or in competition (Cruse 2004: 106). Antagonistic meanings cannot be activated simultaneously and give rise to what Cruse calls **zeugma** (Cruse 2004: 44, 106). For example, the expression *it is a magnetic and fibreglass pole, in which *magnetic* modifies the 'location' and *fibreglass* the 'round object' meaning of the word form *pole*, is not a meaningful expression in English.

The second type of ambiguity is **complementary ambiguity** or polysemy. This is the case of a lexical form that has multiple meanings that are somehow related to each other and can be seen as corresponding to different manifestations of the same basic meaning in different contexts. Recall the example of *neck* in Chapter 1, which denotes a human or animal body part ("a stiff neck"), by extension the part of a shirt around the neck ("a V-neck sweater"), by similitude the part of a bottle near the mouth ("hold the bottle by the neck"), etc. In this case, there is a (conceptual) contiguity between the various meanings. At times, however, conceptual contiguity is not immediately apparent as with *neck*. For example, as we saw in section 1.2.1, Engl. *chair* means, *inter alia*, a seat (in such contexts as "He pushed his chair back from the table") or a person occupying a specific position in an organization ("He had been appointed chair of the chemistry department"); the two meanings are conceptually and historically related but this relation is not obvious for the speaker. As with contrastive ambiguity, in complementary ambiguity the two meanings cannot be activated simultaneously, with the notable exception of words associated with *complex type nouns* like *book*, to which we shall return in a moment.

For our purposes, let us leave aside contrastive ambiguity and focus on complementary ambiguity in the following, with the goal of examining word polysemy more closely. As we have already noted, many words in language are polysemous, that is, they have more than one meaning; moreover, polysemous words are those in most common use, so that the phenomenon appears even more widespread than it actually is. The phenomenon is consistent with the fact that language speakers prefer to economize on effort whenever possible; one way of achieving this is to exploit the same material (in this case, words) for multiple purposes (in this case, to express multiple meanings). If this were not the case, that is, if every word were to express only one meaning, a lexicon would consist of an extremely large number of words and the task of learning it and retrieving it in actual use would be extremely arduous.

The most polysemous words appear to be verbs; we can say that verbs tend to have a high rate of polysemy. This is shown by several studies; for example, statistical data about English (processed within the WordNet 3.0 project) indicate that the average polysemy of verbs is 2.17 meanings, as opposed to 1.24 meanings for nouns, 1.40 for adjectives, and 1.25 for adverbs. The high rate of polysemy with verbs is probably due to the fact that verb meanings are by definition incomplete and must be saturated by the meaning of nouns that express the participants in the event the verbs describe (section 2.1).

At first, polysemy may appear to be an accidental phenomenon, especially when evaluated in relation to single words and in different languages. However, when we shift our attention from single words to the entire lexicon, it is possible to identify clear polysemy patterns, that is, systematic alternations of meaning that apply to classes of words instead of single words (**regular polysemy** in the terminology introduced by Apresjan 1973). For example, as far as nouns are concerned, we can identify the following regular alternations: *material/countable object, container/content, product/producer, animal/meat, process/result, institution/place/people, property/person with the property, event/food, author/work*, etc. The following are examples of each of these alternations.

Sense alternations in the nominal domain

- *material/countable object*  
  *Bronze* is harder than silver. (= material)  
  One of the finest *bronzes* in the collection. (= countable object)

- *container/content*  
  I broke two *glasses*. (= container)  
  I drank two *glasses*. (= content)

- *product/producer*  
  Their *Honda* spun out of control. (= product)  
  *Honda* immediately withdrew the two affected models. (= producer)

- *animal/meat*  
  The *rabbit* is under the car. (= animal)  
  She served the *rabbit* with beans. (= meat)

- *process/result*  
  The *building* was beginning to take place. (= process)  
  The *building* was burned down. (= result)

- *institution/place/people*    The *university* hired a new professor.
    (= institution)
    The *university* is close to the station. (= place)
    This is a friendly *university*. (= people)
- *property/person with*    He exercises his *authority* over us. (= property)
  *the property*    We have to talk to the *authorities*. (= person)
- *event/food*    It was a long *lunch*. (= event)
    It was a heavy *lunch*. (= food)
- *author/his work*    *Freud* was born in 1856. (= author)
    *Freud* is on the top shelf. (= his work)

Most alternations in the list above are the result of well-known strategies which have been the subject of rhetorical studies since ancient times. For example, the alternation, *container/content* is a typical case of metonymy. **Metonymy** extends the meaning of a word by conceptual contiguity (or *association* in Cruse's terms; see Cruse 2004: 209), starting from the object being referred to, to other things that enter into contact with objects of that type. For example, from *glass* as a 'container' to *glass* as its 'content' (*water, wine*, and so on). In metonymy, we use one referent to actually denote another referent associated with it. The *intended referent* (the referent the speaker intends to talk about) is not expressed. Fauconnier describes the metonymic process as follows: " [...] we establish links between objects of a different nature and the links thus established allow reference to one object in terms of another appropriately linked to it" (Fauconnier 1985). A similar case is that of the *synecdoche*, represented by the alternation *material/countable object*. In this case, the meaning extends by contiguity from indicating the material (*bronze*) to indicating the objects made of that material (a collection of *bronzes*); see also *gold* (the material), which can be used to denote the medal (as in "She won the gold").

Some of the sense alternations in the list above appear to be instances of a special kind of regular polysemy called **inherent polysemy** (Pustejovsky 2008). Inherent polysemy is a kind of polysemy that allows the senses to be activated simultaneously, as in the context below, where *city* means both the 'place' (we live in) and the 'institution' (which hired private contractors):

**(2)**    The *city* we live in hired private contractors to drill ground source wells.

Inherent polysemy can be seen as the linguistic correlate of ontological complexity. In this view, each sense of an *inherently polysemous noun* (*dual aspect noun* in Asher's 2011 terminology) denotes a single aspect of an entity which is inherently complex in its constitution; the basic idea is that no sense extension by way of metonymy applies in this case because we are still referring to the same object, while with metonymy, this is not the case. Cruse uses the term *facet* (Cruse 2004, 114; Croft and Cruse 2004: 116) to refer to the senses of inherent polysemous words. Among the sense alternations that appear to license the activation of more than one sense (referred to as **copredication** in the literature), and are therefore candidates for inherent polysemy, we find: *object/aperture, object/information*, and *event/food*. Below we give an example of copredication for each of these categories, thereby providing linguistic evidence for the claim that they belong to inherent polysemous nouns. Between square brackets, we highlight the words that activate each sense and specify which sense is activated; for example, in the first example, *through* activates the APERTURE sense of *window* and *open* activates its OBJECT sense (particularly, the FRAME sense as opposed to the PANEL sense).

*Inherent polysemy in the nominal domain*
- *object* and    The cat was climbing [through]~aperture~ the [open]~object~
  *aperture*       window.
- *object* and    The book [on the shelf]~object~ is [boring]~information~.
  *information*
- *event* and *food*    We had a [quick]~event~ and [tasty]~food~ lunch on the
                  terrace.

Inherent polysemy patterns such as *object/information* and *object/aperture* are not perceived as polysemy by ordinary speakers. For example, when asked about the senses of *book* or *door*, speakers do not distinguish the informational or the aperture sense from the object sense. Once these differences are pointed out to them, however, they recognize them with no effort (Cruse 2004: 116). This empirical evidence supports the claim that inherent polysemy is a matter of *aspects* (in Asher's terms) or *facets* (in Cruse's terms), rather than of *senses* proper.

   Another basic way of extending the meaning of words is metaphor. **Metaphor** is the process underlying figurative uses in language. When we apply a metaphor, the meaning of a word is reinterpreted due to a similitude that is instituted, tacitly, between two situations (so-called *source* and *target* domain in Lakoff et al. 1991). As a result of this similitude, the word is used in a novel context, in which it acquires a new meaning. Consider the expression "devour a book"; here, the verb *devour* is reinterpreted meta-phorically as "read," due to the similitude instituted between the FOOD (source) domain and the INFORMATION (target) domain. The existence of such a link allows us to talk about books using FOOD terminology. Meta-phorical interpretations for verbs (as opposed to literal ones) can therefore be said to occur when there is a shift in the domain of the referent of one or more of its complements from a source to a target domain (as in the "books as FOOD" example above). Further examples are: "swallow a pill" (lit.) vs. "swallow a story" (fig.) (story as FOOD); "grasp an object" (lit.) vs. "grasp an idea" (fig.) (idea as PHYSICAL OBJECT); "cultivate a plant" (lit.) vs. "cultivate a habit" (fig.) (habit as PLANT); "The animal died" (lit.) vs. "The battery died" (fig.) (battery as LIVING BEING); "arrive at the airport" (lit.) "arrive at a conclusion" (fig.) (conclusion as LOCATION).

While metonymy mainly applies to the nominal domain, metaphor is very productive in the verbal domain. That is, verbal polysemy is often the outcome of metaphorical reinterpretation rather than metonymic extension. Corpus study has also shown that verbs account for around 50% of meta-phors found in texts, the rest shared by nouns, adjectives, adverbs, and specific constructions.

Verbal polysemy may, however, be induced by processes other than metaphor. Consider the case of verbs that exhibit both a *causative* and a non-causative (so-called *inchoative*) use, such as Engl. *heal*: "The therapy healed the wound" 'caused to become healed' / "The wound healed quickly" 'became healed.' In this case, the variation in meaning targets one specific aspect of the verb semantics, particularly the component CAUSE. This type of polysemy may be represented in several ways; for example, one can either assume that the causative meaning is the basic meaning of the verb *heal*, and that the non-causative one is derived by suppression of the cause, or claim that the verb in underspecified as far as the cause goes, and can be used to report an event from both perspectives.

The sense alternations for verbs introduced above are summarized in the following.

Sense alternations in the verbal domain

- *literal/figurative*      John *arrived* at the airport.

    John *arrived* at a conclusion.
- *causative/inchoative*   The therapy *healed* the wound.

    The wound *healed* quickly.

It is worthy of note that in theory, metonymy, synecdoche, and metaphor are procedures that can apply to all the elements of a lexicon, provided that the appropriate conditions are satisfied (for example, the condition that there is conceptual contiguity or similarity between two objects or situations). In practice, however, only some of the meanings that are created through these procedures become lexicalized.

Finally, several studies suggest that a distinction should be drawn between ambiguity and polysemy of words, on the one hand, and **vagueness**, on the other. The latter should be understood as the property of words whose meaning is not exactly determined. Examples of words with a vague meaning are adjectives lexicalizing gradual properties (*tall, low, short, narrow, wide, large, big, hot, cold*, etc.) The expression "it is a big book" is vague in the sense that it does not specify the exact dimension, although *book* restricts the interpretation of *big* to a size that is compatible with the object (compare "a big book" with "a big house"). The following is instead a precise description: "it is a 400-page book." Another class of words with a vague meaning is that of nouns that indicate age ranges, such as *child, adolescent, boy/girl, youth, adult, middle-aged, elderly*, and *old*. For example, the expression "he is still a boy" is not precise, because it does not assert unequivocally the age of the person in question.

## 3.3. Theories on the nature of meaning

Over time, several theories have been proposed as to the nature of meaning. Some proposals come from philosophy (particularly the philosophy of language), others from linguistics, and yet others from psychology and cognitive science. It must be said immediately that when speaking of meaning, a distinction must be made between meaning in a general sense as "value assigned to something" (for example, the meaning of a behavior, of a gesture, and perhaps of an object, if we attach special importance to it) and **linguistic meaning** (which, instead, belongs only to words, sentences, and texts). To achieve an adequate understanding of the notion of linguistic meaning, in this section we provide a brief survey of the main explanatory hypotheses that have been formulated about its nature. In order, they are the **referential** hypothesis, the **mentalist** or **conceptual** hypothesis, the **structural** hypothesis, and the hypothesis based on the notion of **prototypicality**. The last, as we will see later, may be interpreted as one of the developments of the mentalist theory and is currently widely adopted in cognitive approaches to language. Finally, we will allude to the hypothesis about word meaning, which lies behind **distributional semantics** methods, as they are implemented in computational approaches to lexical analysis today.

To inquire into the nature of linguistic meaning is to inquire into how the individual and his thought, external reality, and language are related. As we will see, these three ingredients are present in all the theories of meaning we are going to review, and each one proposes a different interpretation of this relationship.

According to the referential theory of meaning, we use words to refer to things that exist and events that occur in the world. For example, when we say "The chair I bought is uncomfortable," we use the word *chair* to refer to a certain object that exists in reality and satisfies certain characteristics. With the verb *to buy* we refer instead to an event characterized by the presence of a number of participants: the seller, the buyer, the object whose ownership is transferred (the chair in this specific case), the money required for the transaction, etc. According to this theory, the meaning of a word consists primarily in its ability to establish a relation (a **reference**) with the real world.

> As regards reference, it should be clear that reference is not equivalent to meaning; the two expressions "the man I live with" and "my husband" may have the same reference (that is, refer to the same person in reality) but they have a different meaning. This latter distinction was introduced by the German logician G. Frege (1892), who used the term *Bedeutung* to refer to what we here call reference, and the term *Sinn* to refer to what we here call meaning. In the literature, there is serious terminological confusion in this regard, but it need not concern us here; what really matters is to be aware of this distinction.

The referential approach to meaning gained support following the work of a few logicians, mathematicians, and philosophers, such as G. Frege and B. Russell, and particularly the analytical philosophers active in Cambridge, England, between the 1940s and the 1960s. It is difficult to ascertain who among the philosophers active in Cambridge saw themselves as representatives of the analytic approach; at any event, we recall here R. Carnap, L. Wittgenstein, and J.L. Austin. Furthermore, it is worth recalling the American experience, with W.O. Quine among the chief exponents.

Referential theory is the theory of meaning assumed as the basis of the approach known as formal semantics. Under the heading of **formal semantics** we encounter a number of approaches which use models and tools from logic to analyze and represent semantic phenomena in language (for this reason it is also called *logical semantics*). Formal semantics is referential in its core, that is, it is based on the idea that meaning comes into existence through an act of reference. A formal approach to semantics is taken, for example, in Chierchia and McConnell Ginet (1990), de Swart (1998), Heim and Kratzer (1998), Cann et al. (2009). For a concise introduction to formal semantics approaches, see Saeed (2003), chapter 10.

The notion of reference has received different interpretations in the literature. A broad interpretation is the one introduced above, according to which each expression in the language, when it is used, establishes a reference with extra-linguistic reality (objects, situations, actions, events in the world). A narrower interpretation is the one proposed, for example, by the philosopher J. Searle, whose approach to reference rests on the notion of *speech act*. According to Searle (1969), it is necessary to distinguish between two fundamental kinds of speech acts, that is, of acts that we may perform by uttering words: the act of **referring** and the act of **predicating**. By means of the former, we identify objects in the world [ibid., 28], whereas through the latter we ascribe properties to them [ibid., 102]. According to this interpretation, the expression "Sam is drunk" can be analyzed as follows: "Sam" is the reference (or the referring expression), "is drunk" is the predication. Searle argues that establishing a reference is not the undistinguished property of all linguistic acts but only of those that pick out or identify a particular object. These acts commonly consist of nominal expressions, that is, nouns and nominal phrases. Searle calls predications the linguistic acts (in italics in the following examples) by means of which we describe a situation ("Mary *is thinking*"), ascribe a property to an object ("the umbrella *is red*"), or indicate relations between two or more entities, as in "Mary *owns* two houses." Contrary to G. Frege, his position is that predicate expressions do not have a referent.

Other approaches to the study of meaning, such as the **mentalist** or **conceptual** approach (adopted, for example, in Jackendoff 1988), stress the fact that the reference that we may establish with entities in the real world by

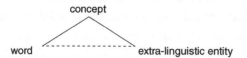

**Figure 3.1** The semiotic triangle

means of words is not direct but mediated by our mental image of these entities. A mental image is what we call a **concept**. According to this assumption, words gain their significance by being associated with a concept. In a simplified way, we can say that according to the conceptual approach, when we speak of *chair* we do not refer directly to the object 'chair' but rather to our mental representation of the class of objects that fall within the category CHAIR (where by "category" we mean the conceptual set of objects that share certain characteristics). This position has often been represented as in Figure 3.1 (where the dashed line suggests that there is no direct relation between words and an extra-linguistic entity, and that this relation is mediated by concepts).

> The most direct reference of the representation in Figure 3.1, called the semiotic triangle, is the study by Ogden and Richards (1923). However, as Eco (1997: 352) observes, already since Plato, but more explicitly since Aristotle, it has been evident that by uttering a word we simultaneously express a thought and refer to a thing.

The mentalist hypothesis does not reject the idea of reference. R. Jackendoff, for example, argues that it is possible to maintain this idea as long as we assume that words do not refer directly to extra-linguistic reality but rather to the way in which this reality is conceptualized and categorized, in other words, to how it is "construed" in the speaker's mind. The same theories of reference do not deny the role of thought as mediator between language and the world. In fact, they fully share the Aristotelian standpoint according to which in language three orders of entities are at play, namely, (a) things, (b) mental images of things (what Aristotle calls "that which is in the mind"), and (c) phonological words (what Aristotle calls "that which is in the voice") (Simone 1990: 462). What mentalist theories argue, however, is more than this, namely that thought plays a role in "construing" reality instead of simply "reproducing" it.

According to the mentalist view, the mediation of conceptual knowledge is necessary to account for such facts as the possibility of using words not only to talk about entities that exist or events that occur in the world but also about abstract or fictional ones. Examples include qualities or emotions (such as *beauty* or *anger*), imaginary objects (mythical creatures such as *unicorns*), hypothetical but possible events, and so forth. What would the reference be in these cases? Furthermore, it is well known that one and the same event can be expressed in language in multiple ways, that is, from different perspectives. For example, the act of John breaking a window with a ball can be reported in several ways: "John broke the glass," "the glass broke," "the glass was broken by John," or even "the ball broke the glass"; if we are not interested in the dynamic aspect of the occurrence and prefer instead to focus on the resulting state, we can also simply say "the glass is broken," "there is broken glass on the floor," and so forth. Based on the observation that words can be used to talk about non-tangible entities and to construct the same aspects of reality in different ways, scholars working within the mentalist framework believe that it is plausible to assume that concepts are mental representations of entities and events, and that words gain their significance by being connected to concepts.

The mentalist approach is widely adopted by cognitive semanticists, who study semantic phenomena emphasizing their relation with general abilities of the human mind, such as categorizing data from experience and organizing them into concepts. Although the assumption that meaning is conceptual in nature is not exclusive to cognitive semanticists and has long been shared by researchers working within different frameworks, the key aspects of the cognitive approach to semantics can be listed as follows: (i) it stresses the psychological aspects of meaning (concepts are psychological entities and not real or sensory data); (ii) it highlights the link between the individual's conceptualizing activity and his physical-perceptive experience; (iii) it establishes a sort of identity between the meaning of a word and the concept it is associated with (Croft and Cruse 2004).

Regarding (i), we have already observed that according to the mentalist approach, a concept is not an accurate picture of reality but an interpretation or a reconstruction of a corner of reality construed by the mind. In this view, the role of the individual and his conceptualizing activity is placed in the foreground with respect to other theories of meaning. As for (ii), the basic idea is that the way in which an individual conceptualizes external data is tied to his sensorial experience. According to this view, abstract categorizations, for example, develop from metaphorization of concrete data. The study of metaphor in language is central in the cognitive approach of G. Lakoff; R. Jackendoff (1996) instead questions the role of perception in the conceptualization activity, still in a cognitive framework. Finally, the position in (iii) poses a series of problems. In the extreme case, those who argue that the conceptual and the semantic dimension are equivalent maintain that everything that we potentially associate with words is part of their meaning. In Chapter 2 we have already observed that such an interpretation does not provide a consistent picture of the nature of word meaning and a satisfactory account of how lexical knowledge is exploited in language use.

---

Several scholars consider it important to maintain a distinction between concepts and meanings. This distinction, they argue, is needed to account for the differences that exist between languages with regard to the ways in which the same concept is encoded in the lexicon, and for the fact that not all concepts are systematically lexicalized.

Schwarze (1997) for example proposes an interesting distinction between **cognitive concepts** on the one hand and **lexicalized concepts** on the other. Only the latter, according to the author, enter into the definition of a word's meaning. The former are unstable entities, have weak borders, can differ individually (according to the criteria that are relevant for the individual) and culturally (according to the criteria that are relevant for the society). Lexicalized concepts, instead, because they are linked to lexical forms (that is, to words), are relatively more stable and are socially shared. If this were not the case, their use would not guarantee success of communication. Cognitive concepts belong to the mental structure (that is, to information as it is categorized in our mind), while lexicalized concepts belong to the realm of linguistic structure (that is, to the semantic information as it is associated with the lexical items of the language). The former can be considered, at an abstract level, universals; the latter are not universal by definition, because they are always lexicalized in a specific language, and may vary from language to language.

---

A third interpretation of the nature of meaning, referred to as the **structural** hypothesis, maintains that meaning is first of all relational in nature. According to this theory, the meaning of a word is not limited to its ability to refer to an object (referential hypothesis) or to point to the mental image we have of this object (mentalist hypothesis); rather, it corresponds to the specific "value" that the word acquires in relation to the other words in the language that belong to the same semantic field and denote analogous objects. For Engl. *chair* these words would be: *stool, seat, stall, throne, bench, recliner, armchair*, etc. According to this interpretation, the key factor in determining the meaning of a word is therefore neither the inherent nature of the denoted object, nor the way in which the object is conceptualized, as much as the number and the type of words that are available in the language to refer to that kind of object; in other words, the way in which the language partitions and hierarchically organizes a given conceptual space by means of words.

The key notion in this approach is not so much that of meaning but that of value. The semantic **value** of a word corresponds to its information content, which, according to the structural hypothesis, is not inherent in the word itself but rather determined by exclusion (Cruse 2004: 246); a word means that which is not meant by the other words that occupy the same semantic field (for a scientific formulation of the concept of *semantic field*, see Trier 1931). By way of illustration, consider the sequence of terms we introduced above (*stool, seat*, etc.); as we proceed in the sequence, the meaning of *chair* becomes narrower and is defined more accurately. In this framework, the relation with the real world is important but secondary in defining the meaning of words, in that meaning is relatively autonomous from reality, and highly dependent on language structure. To conclude, the structural theory of meaning is a theory that stresses the role that language plays in modeling concepts and gives great importance to the relations that hold between words in a language, particularly among words pertaining to the same domain.

A fourth theory of meaning is based on the notion of prototype. As we have already noted, this theory may be seen as one of the developments of the mentalist theory. To date, it is the theory of meaning shared by the majority of scholars working within the cognitive semantics framework. For our purposes, it is useful to first introduce the notion of prototype, and then examine its application to the study of linguistic meaning, particularly word meaning. The primary source for the illustration that follows is Löbner (2013), chapter 11.

The notion of **prototype** intended as best exemplar of a category (for example, the apple and not the olive as best example of the fruit category) has been researched in the first place in the context of anthropology, psychology, and cognitive sciences. The standard references are the studies on colors by psychologist E. Rosch and her colleagues in the early 1970s, although this work clearly built on earlier insights, notably the notion of **family resemblance** by the philosopher L. Wittgenstein (1953). The overall goal of these studies was to understand how we organize our experience of the world from a cognitive perspective, that is, how we build conceptual categories out of external data, especially concrete data. We perform a categorization when, for example, we ascribe an object for drinking to the class of *cups* instead of *glasses*, an object for reading to the class of *novels* instead of *essays*, an object for writing to the class of *pens* instead of *pencils*, a voluntary action to *jumping* instead of *dancing*, to *running* instead of *walking*, to *slicing* instead of *crumbling*, and so forth. We perform this operation on the basis of the properties of objects or events, or, according to the cognitivist perspective, on the basis of the properties of objects and events as we perceive them. In each category, we group objects or events that share similarities; these similarities stem from the fact that these objects share properties that we deem salient for the category. Salient properties answer the question: "What makes this *y* an *x*?." For example: "What makes this *object for drinking*, a *cup*?"; "What makes this *action* a *running action* (instead of a *walking action*)?," and so forth. We also group in the same category objects and events that, despite their differences, turn out to be more like each other than other objects or events on the basis of the properties that we assume as salient. When we categorize data, we proceed by association, contrast, analogy, etc.—in other words, we apply a series of cognitive strategies.

In general, research based on the notion of prototype suggests an interpretation of the notions of *category* and of *categorization process* which is alternative to the traditional view. In the classical model, referred to as the Aristotelian model, a category is conceived as a set of members exhibiting the following three properties. First, the members have equal status—that is, they all have full claim to belong to the category and no member is better than others. Second, the category is defined by a set of features called necessary and sufficient conditions. Third, categories have sharp boundaries—therefore, an entity either does or does not belong to the category; there are no intermediate cases. For example, according to the classical view, the category WOMAN is defined by the necessary and sufficient conditions (adult), (human), and (female). These conditions are **necessary** (if one of them does not apply, the alleged member does not belong to the category) and **sufficient**, because the addition of other features (such as single or married, blonde or brown hair, ugly or beautiful, friendly or unfriendly, clever or unintelligent, and so forth) does not change its status. There are no members that are more woman than other ones, nor, at least in the traditional conception, members that are partly woman and partly something else.

Within prototype theory, a category is interpreted in a different way, namely as a set of members with the best member at its center (the prototype or best exemplar) and the other members coming more or less close to the prototype according to different degrees of similarity. In other words, category membership is graded. Recalling the category CHAIR we introduced above, according to the prototype theory, it may be defined as follows. There is a prototypical member consisting of an object with four legs, a back, and a horizontal surface for a person to sit on, and a series of other members that are more or less similar to the prototype (for example, they don't have a back, they don't have four legs, they have armrests, and so forth).

Category membership is defined by a set of features or conditions that, unlike in the traditional theory of categories, are not required to be necessary; features are often optional and do not have to be globally met by all the members of the category. For example, as we noted above, there are objects we classify as *chairs* even if they lack a back, or objects that we assign to the category of *cups* even if they lack a handle, etc. Note, however, that although features are not all necessary in an Aristotelian sense, they are crucial in that they allow us to establish similarities. The key concept in the theory of prototypes is, precisely, that of **similarity**. According to this theory, categorization is a matter of similarity to a prototype, rather than of adherence to criteria of **necessity** and **sufficiency**. Furthermore, the boundaries of categories with a prototype structure are fuzzy or blurred instead of sharp, at least in the traditional version of the theory. Table 3.1 summarizes what we have said up to now.

Table 3.1. Traditional category and category with a prototype structure

| Traditional category | Category with a prototype structure |
| --- | --- |
| Category has no internal structure. | Category has internal structure (with prototype at its core). |
| Members have the same status. | Members' status with respect to the prototype may vary. |
| Necessity and sufficiency conditions. | Optional conditions of similitude. |
| Category boundaries are sharp. | Category boundaries are fuzzy. |

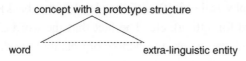

**Figure 3.2** The semiotic triangle (revised)

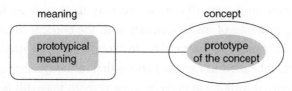

**Figure 3.3** Meaning and concept

The two models of category structure introduced above embody two radically different views of how our mind works in classifying data. If applied to linguistics, and in particular to lexical semantics, the choice of the prototype model over the traditional one has clear consequences on the way word meaning is interpreted and represented. This is particularly true for theories that hold that the meaning of a word coincides with the concept it is associated with (as in many cognitive approaches to meaning). For these theories, adopting the notion of prototype in semantic analysis means in fact shifting from the "meaning = concept" idea to the "meaning = concept with a prototype structure" idea. This position can be illustrated using the semiotic triangle introduced earlier, as shown in Figure 3.2.

From a cognitive semantics perspective, the shift from "concept" to "concept with a prototype structure" requires that not only the concept but also the meaning is conceived as consisting of a prototypical core (roughly corresponding to the prototype of the concept) and a surrounding or peripheral area, the composition of which is graded. This is represented in Figure 3.3.

The best way to illustrate this point is to provide an analysis of the lexical meaning of two words, for example a noun and a verb, based on the notion of prototype.

Let us start with the noun *chair*. We can say that the prototypical meaning of the word *chair* coincides with the prototype of the concept associated with the word *chair* and, therefore, ultimately, with the best member of the category of CHAIRS. To define the prototypical meaning of *chair* we can, then, employ the set of features that identify the prototypical chair, namely (physical object)(with four legs)(with a back)(with a horizontal surface)(used for sitting), etc. The fact that the word *chair*, as we have already observed, can be used to denote objects that are different from the prototype is not surprising and can be seen as the consequence of the fact that in this case the word *chair* is used to refer to a non-prototypical member of the category instead of to the prototypical one.

Turning now to a verb like *walk*, we may analyze it as follows. The prototypical meaning of *walk* coincides with the concept 'move by lifting and setting down each foot in turn' (as in "John walked all afternoon"). The word *walk* may be used to express actions that, although they are different from prototypical walking actions in some respect, may still be reduced to them by virtue of their similarity to the prototype, as in "I saw an old cat/dog/horse/elephant walking past the fence" where *walk* means 'move by lifting and setting down each paw/hoof/etc. in turn'. At some point, however, the **prototype effect** ends. For example, the expression "I saw a spider walking across the floor" is less felicitous, probably because spiders' legs are less amenable to humans' feet than cats' paws are, and the kind of movement that spiders do differs considerably from that of humans. *Crawling* would be the appropriate term in this case.

The notion of prototype is attractive to lexical semantics because it provides a viable explanation for the variability of meaning which characterizes the use of words. Specifically, the ability of words to take on different meanings in different contexts can be related to the fact that word meaning is organized in terms of a prototypical core, consisting of the set of features that define the prototype, and a surrounding area with a scalar structure.

The notion of prototype, however, is not entirely devoid of problems. For example, the idea suggested by many scholars that the actual prototype should not be interpreted as a concrete entity but as an abstract one, i.e. a mental construct consisting of the full set of salient features that characterize the category (for example, for the category BIRD (have a beak)(have wings) and so on), is problematic, as E. Rosch herself acknowledges in her studies. This idea deprives the notion of prototype of perhaps its most fundamental property, namely that of being readily available by means of the best example of the category. Furthermore, this idea appears to clash with experimental data from psychology, which show that prototypicality judgments rest on reference to specific entities instead of abstract concepts. Finally, it has been noted that there appear to be prototypical members even for categories that, by definition, have sharp boundaries. For example, number 3 is perceived as a more significant example of the clear-cut category of odd numbers than 23 or 91 (for an overview of the problems associated with the prototype model of categories, see Riemer 2010: chapter 7.1.4).

In light of these difficulties, many scholars believe nowadays that it is more productive to assume that there exist multiple models of categorization of data from experience, and that these models may co-exist. In point of fact, the prototype-based model of categorization and the traditional one are not mutually exclusive. A prototype can be present even when the conceptual category has clear boundaries that determine what does or does not belong to it. In this perspective, there are categories that have an internal structure that is centered on a prototype and are gradual as to its remaining parts, yet also maintain sharp boundaries with respect to other categories.

New models of categorization are also being developed that challenge the traditional assumption according to which mental representations are fixed and stable. According to the dynamic model of categorization, concepts are not pre-fabricated entities stored in our long-term memory that are accessed by means of words; they are bodies of knowledge assembled on the spur of the moment for the task at hand. Evidence in support of this approach is provided by categories such as the following: 'things to take on a picnic'; 'things on a desk that could be used to drive in a nail'; 'things that can fall on your head'; 'good things to stand on to change a light bulb' (examples are taken from Barsalou 1983). The principle on which these categories are formed is called *construal* in Croft and Cruse (2004).

Let us now turn to the last hypothesis of the nature of meaning included in our review, namely the **distributional hypothesis.** This hypothesis is motivated by referring to the methodology of linguistic analysis developed in the 1950s by the American linguist Z. Harris (Harris 1956) and in parallel work carried out in British lexicology by J.R. Firth (Firth 1957). The basic tenet of this hypothesis is that the meaning of a word correlates with its distribution, i.e. the set of contexts in which it occurs, particularly its local context, that is, the words it stands in a grammatical relation with (for example, the relationship of modification of adjective with nouns, the object relation of nouns with verbs, and so forth). Starting from this assumption, the hypothesis predicts that it is possible to pin down the meaning of words in a relational fashion (that is, the meaning of one word with respect to the meaning of one or more other words) by comparing the set of contexts in which these words occur; the more similar the contexts the more similar the meanings. As a tentative definition, the hypothesis can thus be formulated as follows:

**The distributional hypothesis**: words with similar distributional properties have similar meanings.

The identification procedures of word meaning adopted within the distributional approach are rooted in the structuralist approach. Central to both is the idea that word meaning is inherently differential and that it can be established by comparing words. In distributional analysis, the term of comparison is the set of contexts.

As an example, consider the contextual distribution of Engl. nouns *car* and *train*, and compare it with that of *table*; one can easily observe that the adjectives and verbs with which *car* and *train* co-occur are significantly more similar compared to those of *table*; *cars* and *trains* can be *fast* or *air-conditioned*, while this cannot be said of *tables*; *cars* and *trains* *arrive* and *stop*, while *tables* do not. According to the distributional hypothesis this is empirical evidence (or rather, distributional evidence) that the meanings of *car* and *train* are more similar between them than the meaning of *table*.

The distributional method is of great benefit in identifying not only similarities but also differences between the meanings of words. To illustrate this point, consider again the distribution *car* and *train*, and compare it with that of *taxi* and *ambulance* as objects of verbs. It is easy to see that although all these nouns may all occur as objects of *drive*, their distributional profiles are remarkably different; a car is said to be *parked* or *stolen*, a train is *caught*, *boarded*, or *missed*, and an ambulance is *called*; also, we talk about *taking* a taxi or a train to a destination, but we don't say that we *take* an ambulance to hospital (cf. Ježek and Hanks 2010). According to the distributional hypothesis, differences of contextual distribution of this kind can be interpreted straightforwardly as differences in meaning between the words in question (Harris 1956: 156).

Recent developments in the field of computational semantics have led to a renewed interest in the distributional hypothesis. In particular, the availability of large digitalized corpora and the development of new statistical methods which quickly extract distributional profiles for words from texts have pushed semanticists towards translating the distributional hypothesis into a full-fledged computational model of meaning representation, called the **word-space model** (cf. Sahlgren 2006). We will introduce this model in section 3.5, where we will discuss systems of word meaning representation.

In conclusion, the hypotheses about the nature of meaning surveyed in this section represent different attempts to capture distinct facets of the same, many-sided phenomenon. Meaning can been seen as comprising all these facets. In this view, the notions of *reference, conceptual category, prototype, value within a structure* and *similarity or difference in distribution* can be seen as steps in an effort towards understanding what meaning is and of grasping the most salient characteristics of its linguistic manifestation.

## 3.4. Building meaning syntagmatically

As we mentioned in section 3.1, a theory of linguistic meaning pursues two related goals: to establish what words mean (this is the goal of lexical semantics) and to explain how complex expressions acquire their meaning based on the meaning of their constituent parts (this is the goal of phrasal or sentence semantics). Both these goals face the problem that word meaning is both ambiguous, i.e words can take on different senses, and flexible, i.e. word meaning tends to vary as a function of the other meanings it combines with.

In this section we try to elucidate how the meaning of complex linguistic expressions is built, starting from the meaning of the individual units that compose them. For this purpose, we first introduce the principle of compositionality, which is conventionally assumed to be the most basic principle whereby complex expressions acquire their meaning. We then point to linguistic evidence that calls this principle into question, at least in its traditional formulation. Finally, we examine a model of compositionality which challenges the traditional model and provides an example of how flexibility of meaning in context can be addressed in a formal representational framework.

As noted above, the **principle of compositionality** is the basic principle used in semantics to explain how word meanings combine to make larger meanings and to account for the infinite productivity of messages. This principle is traditionally attributed to the mathematician G. Frege, even though it appears that he never explicitly formulated it in his writings. In any case, according to this principle, the meaning of a complex expression is systematically determined by the composition of the meanings of its component parts and the way they are put together, provided, obviously, that the conditions imposed by the constituents themselves are satisfied. An example is the restriction due to which the noun *chair* in its literal meaning cannot be the subject of the verb *talk* (as in \*that chair is still talking) in that *talk* requires (selects) a human subject (we will discuss these rules in detail in Chapter 6). Therefore:

(3)   "given a expression E formed by the words X, Y, Z, the meaning $M_E$ is the composition of $M_X + M_Y + M_Z$"

The principle in (3) is generally assumed to be a fundamental property of natural languages, and perhaps a reflection of how we build thoughts in our mind out of simpler concepts.

There is, however, good linguistic evidence that suggests that taking the meaning of the expression as the mere "sum" of the meaning of the parts is not sufficient to account for what complex expressions are actually able to denote. On the one hand, there are several complex expressions, which either carry more meaning than what is expressed (as in *black tie dinner* meaning 'a dinner where the participants are assumed to wear a black tie') or mean something different from what is actually said (as in *show someone the door*, where no door is involved). Furthermore, there is the problem of polysemy; given a word with multiple acknowledged meanings, how would the appropriate meaning be selected in context? How is the disambiguation of the senses of a polysemous word achieved in a strict compositional language? How does the adjective *next*, examined in section 3.1, acquire the spatial meaning in combination with *table* and the temporal meaning in combination with *train*? Strictly speaking, the principle of compositionality as formulated above holds only for monosemous words, and does not address the problem of how polysemous words are disambiguated.

From a theoretical perspective, the problems raised above may be addressed in two basic ways. These two ways reflect two opposing views about how lexical meaning is organized. They can be defined as follows:

- sense enumeration models;
- dynamic lexical models.

By a strict interpretation, **sense enumeration** models approach the problem of polysemy claiming that all the meanings that words display in actual use are stored in the lexicon as part of the information encoded by the word. On such a view, polysemous words encode a list of pre-defined meanings and a list of lexical restrictions, which specify the contexts in which the different meanings may be activated. According to this model, the selection of the relevant meaning occurs at the syntagmatic level (i.e. in the context of use), in agreement with these restrictions. We may call this view the traditional view of the lexicon. This is also the standard way dictionaries are put together.

**Dynamic approaches** to lexical meaning argue instead that sense-enumerative lexicons are uneconomic (they require long lists of meanings for each word), incomplete (words in context can potentially take on an infinite number of meanings), and inadequate (the boundaries between meanings are not rigid and tend to overlap). They contend, instead, that words are better conceived as flexible and permeable entities. According to this view, the meaning of each word is expected to vary from occurrence to occurrence as a function of the interaction with the other words it combines with, and of the situation of utterance; the outcome of this interaction (referred to as *modulation, adjustment,* or *fitting* in the literature) generates the meaning of the sentence. These theories, therefore, claim that the syntagmatic dimension prevails in the definition of the lexical meaning, not as the level at which meanings are selected (as in the case of sense enumeration theories) but as the level at which meanings are generated.

Dynamic theories come in two main versions. According to the **core meaning** approach, words have a core meaning from which a predictable set of senses can be obtained by using them in different contexts. The core meaning can then be seen as a range of representative aspects of lexical meaning that determines the space of possible interpretations that the word may have. The **meaning potential** approach assumes instead that words in isolation may be better characterized as having an abstract meaning potential rather than a meaning as such, and that this potential may be exploited in different ways in actual usage. According to this view, (unambiguous) meaning is attached to linguistic units larger than words. A key notion in this approach is the notion of **pattern**, consisting in the minimal syntagmatic structure in which all words are unambiguous or sense-stable. We shall return to the notion of pattern in Chapter 4.

Taking the dynamic approach to lexical meaning does not mean solving the problem of polysemy, as it is still unclear how the contextual variation of word meaning assumed in this approach can be explained, based on the compositionality principle. In fact, the dynamic view requires a revision of how the process of meaning composition works.

An example of how this problem may be approached formally is provided by the composition theory proposed by the American computational linguist J. Pustejovsky (Pustejovsky 1995: 59), who argues that in order to represent the semantic processes that appear to occur when word meanings combine, the following principles are needed, in addition to the compositionality principle:

Principles for strong compositionality (Pustejovsky 1995)
1. co-composition;
2. coercion of the semantic type;
3. selective binding.

These principles extend the notion of compositionality and can be seen as rules that apply to words when they combine with each other; they determine the specific meaning that words take on in the context of other words. They are thought of as operating at a sub-lexical level, that is, to target specific aspects of the meaning of words rather than their meaning in its entirety. This presupposes a multi-layered conception of word meaning, which we will gradually introduce below.

Let us look at some examples of these principles in operation. For current purposes, our illustration is highly simplified with respect to the original model, and the entire formal apparatus is omitted; for an in-depth discussion, see Pustejovsky (1995), chapter 7, 105–40 and (2002).

The principle of **co-composition** can be illustrated by examples of verb–noun combinations. Consider for instance the contexts in (4), where the Engl. verb *take* appears to mean something different depending on what is said to be taken:

**(4)** *take*   Take a tablet. ('ingest')
        Take a train. ('travel with')

When co-composition applies, the meaning of the verb is refined contextually by the information provided by the complement. Specifically, in the case of *take*, *tablet* and *train* provide the information that when they are "taken," a different type of action is performed; a *tablet* is *ingested* and a *train* is *traveled with*. In Pustejovsky's terms, the intended goal associated with the complement (which the author proposes to see as part of the noun's semantic structure) unifies with the verbal meaning, resulting in a novel interpretation of the verb in context. Under this view, the verbal meaning is built up incrementally by combining words, and there is no need to assume a distinct sense of the verb for each use. This procedure is different from the classic composition, because the underlying operation is not a mere arithmetical sum; in co-composition both the predicate and the complement are active in building the resulting interpretation.

Also the principle of **type coercion** (short for *semantic type coercion*) can be illustrated by considering examples of verb–noun combinations such as the following, where the Engl. noun *book* exhibits a different interpretation depending on the verb it combines with.

(5)   Yesterday afternoon I bought a new book.
      Yesterday afternoon I started a new book.

Consider the first example. In the context of *buy*, the meaning of *book* can be described as 'physical object' (books may also be digital files, but we shall assume that a physical support for the information is nevertheless present). In fact, one possible way of rephrasing the expression is the following: "Yesterday afternoon I bought the physical object called book." Consider now the second example. In this case, the paraphrase "Yesterday I started the physical object called book" is not acceptable. According to Pustejovsky, this is because in the context of *start*, *book* does not mean 'physical object.' The author's reasoning goes something like this: *start* requires to be completed by an activity; if the noun filling the complement position does not denote an activity, the verb forces the complement to do so by coercing its semantic type (i.e. the semantic category it is associated with), in this case from physical object to activity. This operation, according to Pustejovsky, is successful with *book* because the meaning of *book* includes information about the activities in which the object book is typically involved, particularly, the goal activity (*read*) and the originating activity (*write*); in this view, coercion can be seen as an exploitation of the noun sub-lexical structure.

Type coercion may occur also with verbs that do not denote a phase of an event but still require an event as object. For example, in the context of *cancel*, *taxi* is interpreted as 'the booking of the taxi,' whereas in the context of *hear*, *bell* is interpreted as 'the ringing of the bell':

(6)   We canceled the *taxi*.            (*taxi* = event of booking the taxi)
      From the house I heard the *bell*.   (*bell* = event of the bell ringing)

Following Pustejovsky, the phenomenon of type coercion is induced not only by verbs but also by prepositions with temporal meaning, such as *before* and *after*, which require to be completed by a complement that denotes an event (for example, "before the departure" = 'before the event of departing, "after the discussion" = 'after the event of discussing'). If they are followed by a noun that denotes a physical object, these prepositions, therefore, coerce the noun's semantic type by exploiting one aspect of the noun's lexical sub-structure, which remains latent in the noun otherwise. For example, in the context of *dessert* in (7), the preposition *before* triggers the activation of the activity of *eating*, which is assumed to be encoded and available in the meaning of the noun:

(7)    We can eat our *dessert* in the sitting room.    (*dessert* = food)
       We took a break before *dessert*.               (*dessert* = event of eating
                                                        the food)

   From the previous discussion, we can conclude that in situations where type coercion and co-composition apply, the meanings of words are not simply added but built in context. Particularly, in the theoretical proposal we have reviewed, co-composition is the mechanism used to account for the contextual interpretation of verbs, while coercion is evoked to account for the contextual flexibility of noun meanings.

   The third principle operating in Pustejovsky's theory of composition is **selective binding**. This principle can be illustrated by resorting to examples of adjective–noun combinations, such as the following:

(8)    This is a *good* knife.
       He is a *good* doctor, but has a difficult character.
       Can you suggest a *good* book for the holidays?

The adjective *good* is polysemous; a good knife cuts well, a good doctor is capable of healing people; a good book is entertaining to read. The interpretation of *good* is clearly determined by the meaning of the noun it occurs with. In selective binding, a link is created between the adjective and the noun, such that the adjective semantically operates on one single aspect of the noun's meaning. In the case of *good*, the adjective operates on the action that satisfies the typical purpose of the referent of the noun in question (*cutting*, *healing*, or *reading*, which, as we have seen, are assumed to be part of the noun's meaning in Pustejovsky's framework). In accordance with this selection, the nouns *knife*, *doctor*, and *book* saturate the core meaning of the adjective, which can be defined as follows: "able to satisfy the typical purpose for which x (that is, the entity denoted by the noun) exists."

Note that the same adjective can operate on different aspects of a noun. Consider the following contexts:

(9)   The film is too long.
      This dress is too long.

In the context of *film*, *long* specifies the duration of the projection; in this case, the adjective modifies the action that renders the film visible, rather than the film itself. By contrast, in the context of *dress*, *long* modifies the dimension of the dress, that is, one of its physical properties. At first, this difference in behavior might be taken as evidence that there is no conventionalized activity associated with the meaning of *dress*; this, however, appears to be contradicted by nominal expressions such as *dinner dress*, whose meaning can be paraphrased as 'dress *to wear* at dinner.' The reason *long* behaves differently with *film* and *dress* remains unclear in the theory.

Finally, not only does an adjective acquire different senses when it is combined with different nouns, as in the case of *good* and *long* above, but the same noun combined with different adjectives contributes to complete the meaning of these adjectives in different ways, depending on what aspect of the meaning of the noun the adjective selects. For example, in the context of *chair*, the adjective *heavy* operates on the chair's material constitution, while the adjective *comfortable* selects the purpose of the object:

(10)   A heavy chair.
       A comfortable chair. (to sit on)

In conclusion, in this section we have examined an alternative interpretation of the process of meaning composition, referred to as strong compositionality. This proposal assumes that when words combine, a number of principles apply in addition to the classic principle of compositionality. These principles rest on the general idea that words are permeable entities with internally structured meanings, and that when they combine, they behave not like monads that add up but as elements that interact functionally. This approach aims at obviating the need to postulate long lists of pre-defined meanings for words and suggests instead that the meaning of complex linguistic expressions is built through processes of mutual adjustment in context.

## Box 3.1. Coercion by construction

For the last 25 years, (type) coercion and related notions such as *type shifting* (a term introduced by B. Partee and M. Root in 1983) and *enriched composition* (Jackendoff 1997) have been a much-debated topic in linguistic literature. According to Lauwers and Willems (2011), the first appearance of the term coercion is in the field of logical semantics with Moens and Steedman (1988), who used the term to refer to the shifts in the *Aktionsart* of a verb due to contextual factors such as the use of the progressive tense, as in (a):

(a)   The light flashed. (point)
      The light was flashing. (iterated activity)

  Since then, coercion has received multiple interpretations, and has been applied to various domains of linguistic analysis. For example in construction grammar (Goldberg 1995, Michaelis 2004), the mechanism of coercion is used to account, *inter alia*, for cases in which a construction (intended as an abstract form-meaning pairing) is successfully filled by words whose meaning clashes with the meaning of the construction. To illustrate this point, consider the expression in (b).

(b)   Sam helped Sally into the car.

The expression in (b) contains a verb (*help*) whose inherent meaning is not compatible with the meaning of motion conveyed by the sentence; in spite of that, the expression is semantically well formed. According to the constructional view, this phenomenon can be accounted for as follows: (i) the sentence instantiates a specific construction (called *caused-motion construction* and meaning roughly 'ENTITY1 causes ENTITY2 to move and be at ENTITY3'); the construction includes the motion component as part of its semantic structure; (ii) the construction is able to contextually "coerce" the verb that fills the predicate position in the structure into a motion reading.

  It is easy to see how in this view coercion becomes a major argument in favor of the existence of constructions, and a general heuristic to identify constructions in the data.

## 3.5. Systems of word meaning representation

Over time several formalisms have been proposed to represent the meaning of words. Some formalisms have a broad scope in the sense that they can be used to represent the meaning of different types of words. These include, for example, the formalism based on **lexical decomposition** (performed through semantic features, semantic primitives or a combination of both), the system based on **meaning postulates**, and more recently, the system based on vectors in **word spaces**. Other representational systems are more specific, in the sense that they are useful for representing meanings that are proper to or prevailing in certain word classes and not in others. These are for example: **event structure**, used to represent the internal temporal structure of events as they are encoded in verbs; **argument structure**, representing those participants in the event expressed by verbs and nouns that have linguistic prominence; **qualia relations**, which are particularly suitable for representing the various facets of the meaning of nouns. The latter three are all specific instances of the decompositional method. In the rest of this section we review the first three systems mentioned above (lexical decomposition, meaning postulates, and word spaces), keeping in mind that the different formalisms imply different views as to how lexical meaning is organized (an overview is in Saeed 2003, chapter 9; see Geeraerts 2010 for a detailed discussion).

Traditionally, word meanings have been described in terms of lists of semantic features. Central to this approach is the idea is that the meaning of a word is made up of smaller units, called **features** or **components**, each of which corresponds to a portion of this meaning. The general strategy to define the meaning of a word in this framework is called lexical decomposition. For example, the features list (human)(adult)(male) defines the meaning of the English word *man*.

But how are features identified? The basic idea is that features can be successfully established by analyzing the oppositions between word pairs in the lexicon. For example, by comparing *man* with *dog* we establish the feature (human); by comparing *man* with *woman* we establish the feature (male) (or (female)); finally, the feature (adult) is established by comparing *man* with *child*. Because they are based on oppositions, features work as binary categories: that is, they are either present or absent. Therefore, it is more accurate to say that the meanings of *man, woman, boy* and *girl* are described by the following sets of features (where "–" means "not"): *man* (+human)(+adult)(+male); *woman* (+human)(+adult)(–male); *boy* (+human)(–adult)(+male); *girl* (+human)(–adult)(–male). In this system, meanings are distinguished from one another by at least one feature. An implication of this strategy is that the inventory of features necessary to define the meaning of all the words of a particular lexicon can be said to be complete only when all words have been analyzed this way.

Features have the property of being stepwise inclusive. That is to say, assuming the verb *walk* has the feature list (+motion)(+instrument) (see Chapter 1), *limp* can be defined by (+motion)(+instrument) plus something else, such as (+manner); in other words, *limp* includes the features of *walk*, i.e. its meaning. Moreover, certain feature lists do not have a corresponding word; for example, as we already noted in Chapter 1, German lacks a generic verb of motion corresponding to the features (+motion)(+direction), such as English *go*; in fact, Germ. *gehen* encodes not only (+motion)(+direction) but also (+instrument).

The analysis based on distinctive features was first applied to phonology and morphology. Only later was it applied to semantics and the lexicon. The first linguistic work in which distinctive features are systematically used to describe the meaning of words is credited to L. Hjelmslev (see Hjelmslev 1961). Afterwards, the feature-based approach (also called **componential analysis** because it pinpoints the components of meanings) was used among others by Z. Harris and subsequently by J. Katz, J. A. Fodor, and then N. Chomsky, who applied it to transformational syntactic theory.

Feature-based analyses allow the elaboration of **taxonomies** (Figure 3.4), that is, classifications of features organized in pyramidal structures. For example, the classification of the concept expressed by *dog* involves several levels; a general or basic level (animal) and other levels with increasing degree of specificity: (vertebrate), (mammal), (carnivore), etc. These levels are defined on the basis of the **entailment** relation holding between the levels, e.g. animal entails animate, and so on.

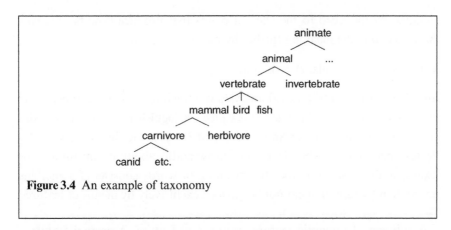

**Figure 3.4** An example of taxonomy

Feature-based analysis has been applied to sub-domains of the lexicon such as the system of words denoting dog sounds (*bark, bay, whimper, growl, howl,* etc.); these may be analyzed by means of features such as (emit a sound), (characteristic of dogs), (complaining), (gnashing the teeth), (rabid), (grumbling), (high-pitched and loud), (low-pitched and dark), (acute and repeated), (loud and prolonged), (hushed), (cubs), (close-mouthed), and more.

An isolated attempt to apply this kind of analysis to an entire lexicon is Alinei (1974). Central to Alinei's work is the idea that words used in dictionary definitions can be employed as semantic features. This is no trivial idea considering that when we define the meaning of a word we tend to break down its meaning into its constituent features. In particular, in defining words, we tend to use the features located at the next higher level in the hierarchy. For example, we define *a terrier* as a dog (i.e. a canid) and not as (animal)(vertebrate)(carnivore); an action of *dragging* as (pulling) instead of (moving), and so forth.

The feature-based formalism works fairly well to describe small groups of words, while it becomes muddled when used to represent an entire lexicon. The reason is twofold; a high number of features are needed and identifying these features, as we already observed, involves comparing all the words belonging to that particular lexicon. Furthermore, some aspects of the meaning of words cannot easily be reduced to features. Consider the word *geranium*. Once the features have been identified that ascribe the entity denoted by the word to the class of plants that produce flowers, it is very hard to define the meaning further by means of features:

**(11)**   *geranium* = (plant) + (blooms) + (???)

In other words, feature-based analyses often witness the appearance of an unanalyzed residue. This residue is called **distinguisher** in Katz and Fodor 1963. According to Katz and Fodor (1963: 187), the distinguishers of a lexical item reflect what is really idiosyncratic about its meaning. The example above suggests that the meaning of words consists of something more than features and cannot be grasped exclusively by means of features.

> A subtype of semantic feature is aspectual feature. **Aspectual features** express single aspects of the inherent temporal structure of an eventuality, as it is encoded in verbs and nouns expressing events (cf. section 2.1). Examples are: (dynamicity), (punctuality), (iterativity), (telicity), (homogeneity), etc. We shall look at these features in Chapter 4.

Another system of word meaning representation based on decomposition is that resting on the notion of semantic primitive. In this case, lexical meaning is conceived as a structure built around one or more **primitives**—that is, elements that cannot be decomposed further. These primitives look like words (for example: CAUSE, BECOME, ACT, DO), but should be conceived as concepts; they are the core components of a word's meaning. For example, the meaning of the English verb *break* contains *inter alia* the primitive CAUSE, because the act of *breaking* causes something (a break); on the other hand, the meaning of *blush* contains the primitive BECOME, because *blush* expresses an event that induces a change of state in someone (become red in the face). Finally, the meaning of *run* does not contain either CAUSE or BECOME, but contains DO, because *running* is an act where the runner DOES something (compare *run* with *fall* and notice how the latter does not contain the primitive DO: in fact, a person that falls does not do anything but rather undergoes something—a fall).

The method of semantic analysis based on primitives follows a decomposition strategy. According to this methodology, the meaning of a word is taken as a whole and broken down into pieces until its core elements are identified (the primitives), beyond which no further decomposition is possible.

Obviously, decomposition techniques cannot be based only on intuitions regarding what a word means and on the comparison with other words.

Rather, they must go hand in hand with the analysis of the syntactic behavior of the word, which must somehow support and not contradict the decompositional analysis into primitives that is being proposed. For example, the verb *blush* can be said not to contain the primitive CAUSE because the expression "Shame blushed Paul" is not a well-formed expression in English. To say that the verb *blush* does not encode the primitive CAUSE does not mean that the event of *blushing* does not have a cause, which, in fact, it certainly does in the real world. It means, instead, that the cause is not part of the meaning of the verb. If the cause needs to be expressed, *blush* must be accompanied by a causative verb such as *make* ("The compliments made Anna blush") or by dependent clauses ("Anna blushed because . . . "). Another example of a verb with no lexical cause is *fall* (*"I fell the book from the table").

It is no coincidence that all the examples we have proposed to illustrate the principles of decompositional analysis based on primitives are taken from the verbal lexicon. In fact, this analysis turned out to be particularly helpful in the analysis of the verbs, whose meanings appear to be organized around primitive notions such as DO, CAUSE, and so forth.

The many decompositional studies of verbs that have been conducted on various languages have shown that there exist certain recurring structures in the meaning of verbs. Scholars working on the topic of verb classification have represented these structures in different ways. Most proposals rely on causal (DO, CAUSE) or temporal/aspectual primitives (BECOME, RESULT); others focus on spatial primitives, such as GO, PATH, and PLACE. Examples of such structures are the *logical structures* of Dowty (1979) and Van Valin and LaPolla (1997); the *lexical conceptual structures* (LCS) of Jackendoff (1990); the *event structures* of T. Parsons (1990) and J. Pustejovsky (1991), and the *event templates* of M. Rappaport Hovav and B. Levin (1998).

As an example, in (12) and (13), we introduce the templates that can be said to be associated with the verbs *blush* and *break*. The notation used is that of Rappaport Hovav and Levin (1998: 108) (for the sake of simplicity, we omit the verbal tense and decompose *break* only partially):

**(12)** *blush*   [BECOME [ x <*red*>]]                     x = Anna
            Anna blushed.

**(13)** *break*   [x CAUSE [BECOME [ y <*broken*>]]]       x = Anna, y = the key
            Anna broke the key.

In the representations in (12)–(13), the verbal meanings are decomposed into their constituent elements. These appear to be of several kinds: the primitives (CAUSE, BECOME), the participants in the event (x (Anna) and y (the key)) and the state resulting from the event, respectively <red> and <broken>. Note that a verb can contain more than one primitive; this is the case of *break*, which, in the context above, contains both CAUSE and BECOME.

Naturally, a verb with multiple contextual interpretations will not have a single representation, but one for each of them. For example, in the context of "Anna broke the key" the default reading of *break* is 'accidentally cause the breakage,' while in the presence of a volitional adverbial, as in "Out of anger, Anna broke all the dishes" it is likely to be 'voluntarily cause the breakage.' In the latter case, the proposed decompositional analysis must then reflect the fact that the subject plays the role of an agent, i.e. that he/she DOES something intentionally, while in the former case, the subject initiates but does not control the action, and it is merely an effector (in the sense of Van Valin and Wilkins 1996):

**(14)**  *break*  [[x DO] CAUSE [BECOME [ y <*broken*>]]]   x = Anna, y = all the
        Anna broke all the dishes.                                    dishes

One interesting property of decompositional representations such as (12)–(14) is that they are predictive of the syntactic behavior of the word being represented. For example, the absence of the primitive CAUSE in the lexical representation for *blush* predicts that it cannot occur in transitive constructions. This property derives from the fact that these representations are grounded on those components of meaning that determine the syntactic behavior.

The decompositional method, however, faces some problems. First, there is disagreement among scholars concerning the list of primitives. Besides DO, CAUSE and BECOME, and a few others, the proposed lists by no means agree in their details. It follows that it is somewhat unclear what these primitives are and how many there might be. To obviate this problem, A. Wierzbicka (1996) proposed a list of about 60 primitives, called **semantic primes**, defined as "a finite set of indefinable universal expressions." Her inventory includes words that are attested in all known languages and that for this reason can be considered universal. Examples are: I, YOU, SOMEONE, PEOPLE; ONE, SOME, ALL; DO, HAPPEN, MOVE, THINK, SEE, HEAR, WANT; THERE IS; HERE, UNDER, ABOVE, FAR, NEAR; NOW, WHEN, BEFORE; GOOD, BAD; BIG, SMALL; IF,

BECAUSE, MAYBE, NOT; PART (OF), KIND (OF); VERY; LIKE. Note that these primitives express universal concepts such as quantity (ONE, SOME, ALL), space (HERE, UNDER, etc.), time (NOW, WHEN, BEFORE), intensity (VERY), etc.

An example of a definition of a word ("explication" in Wierzbicka's terms) based on semantic primes is the following (the example is taken from Wierzbicka 1996: 218):

**(15)**  *top*
      a part of something
      this part is above all the other parts of this something

The strength of Wierzbicka's method to identify universal primitives over other alternatives is that it is based on empirical evidence. At the same time, however, it is labor-intensive, and by definition doomed to remain incomplete. Furthermore, definitions built exclusively on semantic primes have been shown to leave relevant aspects of meaning unrepresented. For example, the definition of *top* in (15) would also work for *tip, crest, summit, roof*, and any upper part that is unconnected to the lower part of an entity, etc.; moreover, (15) includes an improper use of *above*, which in English at least denotes a non-connected part ("the picture hung above the fireplace" as opposed to "the picture sat on top of the table").

A second drawback of primitive-based decomposition methods is that when it is applied, the decomposition strategy requires that lexical meaning is broken down all the way to its root, that is, to its primitives, while meaning might be organized in a different way, as a number of studies on language acquisition seem to suggest. For example, Chierchia and McConnel-Ginet (1990: 452) note that "children acquire words like *kill* and *die* long before they learn words like *cause* and *become*." Along the same lines, Fodor (1987: 161) maintains that "children know about fathers long before they know about males and parents." According to Fodor, this is psychological evidence that the concepts underlying lexical meanings are not organized in a compositional way around a semantic primitive. Particularly, he maintains that concepts are available to the speakers as conceptual atoms (Fodor 1998).

Finally, decompositional analyses performed by means of either features, primitives, or a combination of both do not provide a straightforward explanation of the key ability of words to take on an indefinite variety of possible senses depending on the other words they combine with. For example, does *like* have two different meanings in "I like your sister" and "I like coffee"; and if so, how is this difference to be represented in decompositional terms? And how are metaphorical uses such as "break the silence / a promise / a rule / an engagement" dealt with in traditional decompositional frameworks? No traditional decompositional system, no matter how elaborate or refined, is able to answer this simple question in a straightforward fashion.

A decompositional formalism expressly conceived to address the problem of the semantic flexibility of words is the one based on the notion of **Quale** (Pustejovsky 1995). A Quale (singular of Qualia), from the Latin meaning "of what kind of thing," is a term Pustejovsky borrows from philosophy to indicate a single essential aspect of a word's meaning, defined on the basis of the relation between the concept expressed by the word (for example *dog*) and another concept that the word evokes (for example having fur, barking, tail wagging, licking; cf. section 2.2).

In Pustejovsky's model, it is assumed that the meaning of a word may be represented through four main Qualia relations or roles, which taken together constitute the **Qualia Structure** of the word in question. These are: the Formal, the Constitutive, the Telic, and the Agentive Quale. The **Formal** Quale encodes the information that distinguishes the entity denoted by the word (for example, bread) from other entities within the same conceptual domain (food). The information specified in the Formal answers the following questions: What kind of thing does $x$ denote? For example, *house* denotes a building, *park* denotes a location, *concert* denotes an event, and so forth. The **Constitutive** Quale encodes the relation between the entity denoted by the word and its constitution. The information specified in the Constitutive Quale answers the following questions: What is the entity denoted by $x$ made of, what are its constituents? For example, bread is made of flour, a house is made of bricks, a knife has handle and blade as parts, etc. The **Telic** Quale encodes the purpose of the entity denoted by the word, or its function, if there is one. It is characteristic of words denoting artifacts, i.e. objects that are created by humans with a specific goal in mind: pens, books, chairs, and so on. It answers the question: What is the purpose of the entity denoted by $x$, how does it function? For example, bread is for eating, a house is for living in, a pen is for writing, and so on. Finally, the **Agentive** Quale encodes the factors that cause the origin of the object denoted by the word. This information includes the action that brings this entity into existence and the person that initiates this action. As in the case

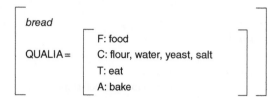

**Figure 3.5** Qualia structure of *bread*

of the Telic, the Agentive is typical of man-made entities. It answers the questions: how did the entity denoted by $x$ come into being, what brought it about? For example, bread is baked, a house is built, and so on.

An example of the Qualia structure of the word *bread* is provided in feature structure notation in Figure 3.5 (where F = Formal, C = Constitutive, T = Telic, and A = Agentive):

The Qualia-based system of lexical representation appears to be effective in capturing contextual variations in the interpretation of words, as any value encoded in the structure can be exploited in context and become the primary denotation. It has been the subject of criticism, particularly based on the observation that it is often difficult to understand exactly what the values of the qualia are supposed to be (a critical examination can be found in Asher 2011: 74 ff.). This problem can be addressed by assuming that the values of the qualia relations can be identified by analyzing the distributional behavior of words and the contextual interpretations that they allow and disallow in different contexts (Pustejovsky and Ježek forthcoming). For example, a house may have several parts, but only those to which we may refer by using the word that denotes the whole (i.e. *house*) may be considered as values of the Constitutive Quale. According to this criterion, *door* may be analyzed as a value of the Constitutive Quale of the noun *house* because in the expression in (16), *house* is actually used to refer to the specific part that is locked, i.e. the door.

**(16)**   Did you lock the house? (C, door)

Further linguistic evidence for the values associated with the Qualia of *house* is provided in (17). In particular, the expression in (17a) may be analyzed as licensed by the Agentive Quale, while (17b) appears to be licensed by the Telic.

**(17)**   a. The house is nearly finished. (A, the building of the house)
           b. A comfortable house. (T, to live in the house)

Based on this empirical evidence, the Qualia structure of *house* may be said to contain the information shown in Figure 3.6.

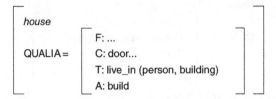

**Figure 3.6** Qualia structure of *house*

To conclude, note that Qualia have some analogies with the procedures by means of which we identify objects: "What does one typically do with a house? One builds it, lives in it, etc."

A different formalism used to represent the meaning of words is the formalism based on **meaning postulates**. This formalism is usually regarded as an alternative to lexical decomposition; nevertheless, there have been attempts to combine the two approaches, as we will see in a moment.

It was R. Carnap who first introduced the term meaning postulate in 1947 (as a general reference, see Carnap 1952). Simplifying, we can define a meaning postulate as a correspondence that is stipulated between lexical items in a language on the basis of their meaning. The basic idea of the meaning postulate approach is that it is possible to elucidate the meaning of a word by postulating a connection with another word, rather than by decomposing its meaning. On the basis of this procedure, the meaning of the English verb *shatter*, for example, rather than being represented by means of lexical decomposition, as in the following example:

**(18)**  *shatter* [x CAUSE [BECOME [y <*broken*><in small pieces>]]] x = the blow,
          The blow shattered the vase.                          y = the vase

can be represented by postulating a connection between *shatter* and *break*, as in (19), where the arrows stands for the relation holding between the two terms:

**(19)**  *shatter* → *break*

Naturally, a connection like that in (19) (called *unilateral entailment* because *shatter* "means" (entails) *break*, but *break* does not mean *shatter*) can be stipulated provided that one of the two words expresses at least one aspect of the meaning of the other.

Clearly, the meaning postulate in (19) does not provide a full definition of the meaning of *shatter*; it only specifies an aspect of that meaning (i.e. the fact that it includes the meaning of *break*). A full definition of *shatter* would require that the meaning postulate forms a two-way implication (that is, an equivalence). This can be attained by adding <in small pieces> to the representation above. This gives the representation in (20), where the bilateral arrow indicates the bidirectionality of the relationship (called *bilateral entailment*):

**(20)**   *shatter* ↔ *break* <in small pieces>

Lexical analysis based on meaning postulates adopts a relational approach to meaning. That is, within this framework, the meaning of a word is defined by establishing links between words, rather than by identifying the semantic primitives that the word encodes. According to some scholars, this way of representing meaning reflects more closely what native speakers do when they attempt to define a word, or assign a meaning to it. For example, if asked about the meaning of *shatter*, a native speaker of English is more likely to provide a definition such as "break (into small pieces)" rather than "cause the fact that something becomes (or is) broken into small pieces."

> The formalism based on meaning postulates is nowadays much exploited to build semantic networks, that is, relational systems that aim at representing the various kinds of semantic links existing among words, such as, for example, the relation between *feather* and *wing* (a *feather* IS PART OF a *wing*), between *horse* and *stable* (a *horse* LIVES IN a *stable*), between *person* and *head* (a *person* HAS a *head* AS PART OF HIS BODY), between *plant* and *green* (*plant* HAS THE COLOUR *green*) and so on (on semantic relationships between words, see Chapter 5).

It should be noted that if the meaning of a word is defined by means of a meaning postulate, that does not exclude the notion that the postulate can be built in a partially decompositional way and, in fact, this is normally the case. For example, in the case of the postulate of equivalence established for *shatter* in (20), the meaning of *shatter* is decomposed into two blocks: *break*, on the one hand, and <in small pieces> on the other. The representation can be said to be a hybrid representation, in that it contains a meaning postulate (indicated by the arrow) and an instance of decomposition (*break* <in small pieces>).

Hybrid representation can be qualified as a method on its own, called *stepwise lexical decomposition* (Dik 1978). A **stepwise decomposition** of the meaning of a word is one that stops when another word is found, the meaning of which is included in the target word, and establishes a meaning postulate on this basis. This latter point can be illustrated by comparing the analysis of *murder*, *kill*, and *die* based exclusively on semantic primitives with the stepwise lexical decomposition of the same verbs based on meaning postulates, and highlighting similarities and differences (the example is taken from Dik 1978 but simplified for our present purposes):

**(21)**   Lexical decomposition based on semantic primitives:

*murder*   DO CAUSE someone BECOME dead in an illegal way

*kill*       CAUSE someone BECOME dead

*die*       BECOME dead

**(22)**   Stepwise lexical decomposition based on meaning postulates:

*murder*   *kill* someone illegally

*kill*       cause somebody to *die*

*die*       become dead

As we can see from the examples, in (21) meaning decomposition for each word takes place until it reaches the semantic primitives that the target word is supposed to include in its meaning. In (22), instead, decomposition is constrained by establishing meaning postulates between words (in this particular case, between *die* and *kill* and between *kill* and *murder*).

The third and last system of word meaning representation we will review is the so-called **word-space model**. The term has come to be used to refer to the techniques used by researchers adopting distributional methods of analysis (see section 3.3) to translate the contextual behavior of words into representations of their meaning. As the name suggests, the model is based on a spatial metaphor, according to which semantic similarity between two words (understood as similarity in their contextual distribution) can be interpreted as spatial proximity. As Sahlgren suggests (Sahlgren 2006), this metaphor actually presupposes another metaphor: the meanings-are-locations metaphor. That is, in order for two meanings to be conceptualized as being close to each other, as the similarity-is-proximity metaphor suggest, they need to possess spatiality. According to Sahlgren, together these two basic metaphors constitute the geometric metaphor of meaning, which can be said to ground the word-space model and can be informally described as follows:

**The geometric metaphor of meaning**: Meanings are locations in a semantic space, and semantic similarity is proximity between the locations (Sahlgren 2006, 19).

At the heart of the word-space model there is the idea that words that tend to combine with the same words occupy locations in the semantic space that are closer to each other than those of words with a different distribution.

But how do we go from distributional information to a geometric representation of meaning? The key notion is the notion of **vector**. In the model, the sum of a word's contexts is tabulated in a matrix of co-occurrence and thereby transformed into a vector with $n$ dimensions; each dimension records the number of times a word occurs in a given context (where context stands for another word, but can also be a region of text or a whole document). In Figure 3.7 we report an example of a co-occurrence matrix (the example is taken from Baroni 2009), in which *dog*, *cat*, and *car* are target words and *runs* and *legs* the context. Context (or distributional) vectors are defined as the rows of the matrix. For example, the co-occurrence-count list for the target word *dog* is (1; 4); that for cat is (1; 5) etc. Such ordered lists of numbers are vectors.

An example of a 2-dimensional vector space representation with three vectors v1 = (1; 5); v2 = (1; 4), and v3 = (4; 0) is given in Figure 3.8.

|      | runs | legs |
|------|------|------|
| dog  | 1    | 4    |
| cat  | 1    | 5    |
| car  | 4    | 0    |

**Figure 3.7** Contexts as vectors

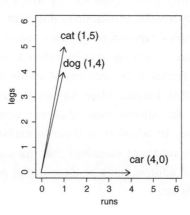

**Figure 3.8** Semantic space

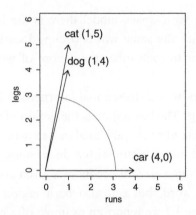

**Figure 3.9** Semantic similarity as angle between vectors

The similarity between words is measured in terms of proximity between the vectors that represent their distribution, as indicated by the arches in Figure 3.9.

It is important to note that word-space semantic representations are inherently relational. That is, a word's distributional vector does not have an inherent value (corresponding for example to traditional semantic components such as (animate), (concrete), etc.), but serves to determine the location of the word in the semantic space and to assess its proximity with other words.

To date, word space models represent a promising and attractive system of lexical representation, complementary to traditional ones. In short, the model faces two main challenges: unveiling the semantic correlates of distributional proximity (that is, elucidating which specific semantic relations are entailed by spatial proximities) and representing the meaning composition for complex expressions (phrases, sentences, etc.).

To conclude, in this section we have introduced three major formalisms that may be used to represent the meaning of words: lexical decomposition (feature-based, primitive-based, and qualia-based), meaning postulates, and word spaces. These formalisms entail different views as to how lexical meaning is organized. In addition to these formalisms, there are others, which are suitable to represent meanings that are associated with specific word types. We shall address some of these in the next chapter, which is dedicated to word classes.

# Further reading

On polysemy, see Ravin and Leacock (2000) and articles therein; see also Nerlich (2003).

On Cruse's facets, see the account in Croft and Cruse (2004), chapter 5.3.

On contextual variation of meaning, see Cruse (1986), chapter 3.2, Pustejovsky (1995), chapter 2, Cruse (2004), chapter 6, Croft and Cruse (2004), chapter 4.5, Cann (2009), chapter 8.3, Asher (2011); from a pragmatic perspective, Recanati (2004).

On semantic flexibility, Recanati (2012).

On enriched composition, Jackendoff (1997), chapter 3.

On *definiciones mínimas* ('minimal definitions'), see Bosque and Mairal (2012).

On the relation between concepts and word meanings, see Murphy (2002), chapter 11.

On dynamic approaches to conceptual categories from a psychological and cognitive perspective, see Croft and Cruse (2004), chapters 4.4 and 4.5.

On metonymy and sense transfer, see Fauconnier (1985), Nunberg (1995), Kleiber (1999b).

On metaphor, see Black (1954). A comprehensive list of source and target domains and mappings between domains can be found in Lakoff et al. (1991).

On compositionality, see the collection of papers in Werning et al. (2012).

On linguistic phenomena challenging simple compositionality, see Jackendoff (1997), chapter 3.

On coercion, see the collection of papers in Lauwers and Willem (2011); for coercions in corpus, see Pustejovsky and Ježek (2008).

On meaning potential, see the discussion in Hanks (2000) and Kilgarriff (1997).

On qualia structure, see Pustejovsky (1995), see Jackendoff (1997, 2002), Van Valin and LaPolla (1997), Van Valin (2005); see Asher (2011), chapter 3.4 for a critical survey. Cruse (2004) and Croft and Cruse (2004: 137 ff.) discuss Qualia as *ways-of-seeing*.

On meaning postulates and meaning definitions, Dik (1997), chapter 4.3.

On compositional distributional semantics, Baroni (2013).

# 4

# The global structure of the lexicon

There are several ways in which the lexicon is highly organized and can be considered a structure—that is, an organized set of related words. In the following, we consider two structuring principles, both delivering groupings of words in the lexicon: word classes and semantic (or sense) relations. Specifically, we look at word classes in this chapter, then turn to semantic relations in Chapter 5; finally, in Chapter 6 we focus on those semantic relations that hold between words that follow one another in text.

## 4.1. Word classes

By the term **word class** we mean a set of words whose members share one or more aspects of their morphological or syntactic behavior. For example, the English words *eat* and *laugh* can be said to belong to the class of verbs, because they can both be conjugated to indicate the time of the action (I laugh, I was laughing); this is a morphological property. Similarly, the words *beautiful* and *new* can be said to be adjectives because they can both modify a noun (as in the *beautiful scenery* and a *new book*), but not a verb (\*answer beautiful, \*dress new). This is a syntactic property. Note that sometimes adjectives appear to modify verbs, as with "It seems/looks/appears beautiful": these, however, are particular types of verbs, to which we will return in due course. Classes of words viewed as groupings of lexical items that share morphological and/or syntactic properties constitute one of the most evident extra-lexical structures (that is, structures that are external to words, concerning multiple words) in a language's lexicon. On the basis of morphological and/or syntactic criteria, it is possible to assign each word of a lexicon to (at least) one class.

> Word classes are referred to as **lexical categories**, **syntactic categories**, or **parts of speech** in the literature. All these terms are appropriate; what they do is focus on different aspects of one and the same phenomenon, according to which words can be clustered together in coherent sets on the basis of properties and functions they exhibit at different levels of linguistic organization, including discourse. Sometimes, **grammatical categories** is also used to indicate categories such as *noun* and *verb*, because word classes, as already stated, may exhibit morphological properties; this terminology is misleading and a distinction should be maintained between grammatical categories such as *tense* and *number* (see section 1.3.2) and lexical categories such as *nouns* and *verbs*.

Languages vary with respect to the kind and number of word classes they have. For example, there are languages that have no articles, such as Latin. Also, word classes may be **variable** in form, that is, prone to morphological modifications (for example, nouns, verbs, adjectives, articles, pronouns in Italian, French, or German) or **invariable**, that is, resistant to morphological modifications (usually, adverbs, prepositions, conjunctions). Finally, from a lexical point of view, there are **open classes** (nouns, verbs, adjectives, adverbs) and **closed classes** (articles, pronouns, prepositions, conjunctions). Open classes gain and lose members relatively rapidly, while closed classes tend to remain constant through time (section 1.3.1).

Some classes are regarded as basic: these are nouns, verbs, adjectives, and adverbs (with some hesitations about the latter, which is sometimes replaced by prepositions). Opinions about what constitutes a lexical class change over time; for example, early grammarians did not consider the class of adjectives to be an autonomous class, and included it in the class of nouns.

The notion of part of speech goes back at least to the classification proposed for classical Greek by Dionysius Thrax (*c.*100 BC). This classification was later resumed and revised by Apollonius Dyscolus in the second century AD and adopted as a model for Latin by Priscian three centuries later. Today, the debate around parts of speech is lively in different branches of linguistics: theoretical linguistics, where research focuses on the identification of the appropriate level for defining word classes— namely lexicon, syntax, or discourse; linguistic typology, devoted to the comparison of word class systems in the world's languages, and neurolinguistics, centered on verifying whether distinctions between word classes, for example between nouns and verbs, are represented in the activity of the brain.

Our discussion of word classes centers around four main issues. These are introduced below and will be developed gradually throughout the chapter.

1. A word class is a cluster of properties. Even though it is possible to assign a word to a class on the basis of a single property (for example, on morphological grounds), class membership involves properties at different levels of linguistic analysis (including, as we shall see, the semantic level, which can be regarded as central). For example, nouns can be inflected for number (morphological property) and modified by adjectives (syntactic property). These properties are assumed to be related; an important issue for current and future research is to pin down the systematic connections between different levels of linguistic organization.

2. The world's languages may lack a particular part of speech (for example, adjectives) but they never lack nouns and verbs (except for controversial cases such as Mundary, an Austroasiatic language of India—discussed at length in Evans and Osada 2005). This suggests that nouns and verbs are basic categories or, at least, that they are more basic than others. The basic character of nouns and verbs is also reflected in the quantity of nouns and verbs present in languages, which, together with adjectives, is much larger than other lexical categories (adverbs, prepositions and so forth). In English, for example, it appears that over half of the vocabulary consists of nouns, about a quarter adjectives, and about a seventh verbs; the rest is made up of exclamations, conjunctions, prepositions, suffixes, etc. In light of the

universal character of nouns and verbs, in our survey we will focus on these two word classes, with the aim of investigating the reasons of their universality.

3. Words may belong to multiple classes. This is infrequent in languages with rich morphology, such as French, Italian, or German, where words have a distinct form for each class (except for nominalized forms, to which we return below); consider for example German *rufen* 'call' (verb) / *der Ruf* 'the act of calling' (noun). On the other hand, in languages with little morphology or languages that have morphology but do not distinguish word classes by means of modification of the word form, this is the norm. This type of language includes English, where a large number of words can take on different part-of-speech values in the context of use; compare "The *mail* arrived before lunch" (*mail* = noun) with "Paul is going to *mail* him a letter" (*mail* = verb).

4. A class can be divided into subclasses. As with classes, subclasses may be identified on the basis of features pertaining to a single level of linguistic analysis. For example, it is possible to identify subclasses of verbs on the basis of the presence or absence of a direct object (syntactic feature). As we saw above, the most interesting research challenge, however, is the study of how features pertaining to different levels interact. An example is the following: Italian verbs expressing natural events such as *piovere* 'rain' or *nevicare* 'snow' (semantic property) lack an overt subject (syntactic property): see "piove da due ore" lit. 'has been raining for two hours.'

## 4.2. Morphological, syntactic, and semantic classes

According to what has just been said, each word class can be independently defined on a morphological, syntactic, or semantic basis. Traditionally, morphology was the first domain to be analyzed systematically, at least in the Western tradition, which is grounded on the study of classical languages with rich morphology such as Latin. Latin showed very well how words lend themselves to different types of morphological modification and may be classified accordingly. For example, given a system of cases, as is the case in Latin, only certain words such as *lupus* ('wolf') and not others such as *vidēre* ('see') are inflected for case (nominative, accusative, etc.). On the other hand, only words like *vidēre*, and not other words like *lupus*, can be conjugated for tense (present, past, etc.).

Syntax-based classifications, on the other hand, have been usually obtained in two ways: (a) by examining the set of words a word may combine with (this is the classification obtained on a distributional basis) and (b) by investigating the kind of modifications a word may undergo (this is the classification obtained on a syntactic basis). The analysis of the distributional profile of a word shows, for example, that only certain words (such as *door*) and not other ones (such as *hastily*) may be preceded by an article (the door, *the hastily). A syntactic analysis highlights instead that only certain words (*eat*) and not other ones (*meal*) may be modified by an adverb (eat well, *meal well).

Turning, finally, to semantics, the question how to classify words on semantic grounds was already a matter of debate in classical antiquity. For example, Aristotle in his *Poetics* distinguished between *ónoma*, a word whose meaning is not endowed with temporality, and *rhēma*, a word whose meaning is endowed with a temporal dimension. In modern times, linguists such as Lyons (1977) have suggested that an adequate basis for semantic classification of words is the ontological correlate. According to this view, words may be grouped into coherent semantic classes by looking at the category of things they refer to (the so-called **ontological category**). Today, the view that distinctions between parts of speech are rooted in our basic ontology of the world has gained considerable recognition in the linguistic community. In the following section, we look at this proposal in more detail.

## 4.3. Relationships between word classes and meaning

There appear to be striking correspondences between the formal properties of words (their morphological and syntactic properties) and the type of meaning they express, though at a rather general level. For example, there is an impressive tendency of words denoting animate and inanimate things such as objects, masses, and substances, to behave linguistically as nouns (*glass, dog, water, traffic*); of words describing actions, states, and processes of things to behave as verbs (*laugh* (for five minutes) and *sit* (for an hour)); of words that denote qualities of things to behave as adjectives, such as *red* in the context of "a red shirt." These correspondences attest the close

**Table 4.1.** Types of entities on the basis of their order

| Order of Entity | Type of Entity |
| --- | --- |
| 1st | persons, animals, places, things |
| 2nd | actions, events, processes, states of affairs |
| 3rd | possible facts |

relationship that exists between conceptual/ontological categorization and linguistic encoding, and several linguists over time, starting from Sapir 1921, have engaged in elaborating systems capable of accounting for these convergences.

Lyons (1977: 439–52) for example proposed a three-output classificatory system of ontological categories (called **entities**) based on their so-called order. These entities consist of different types of "things," as Table 4.1 shows.

According to Lyons' proposal, people, animals, places and things (**first-order entities**) are entities that exist in time, and are relatively constant as to their perceptual properties; actions, events, processes, situations (**second-order entities**) are entities that occur in time, rather than exist in time; possible facts (**third-order entities**) are entities located outside of time and space: we can, therefore, say that they are "true" rather than "real" (beliefs, judgments, expectations, and so on). Following Lyons, first-order entities should be considered to be more basic than either second-order or third-order entities, because an entity is by definition something that exists in time and space, that can be observed, and to which we can refer directly by means of language. Second-order entities, too, are observable in that they occur in the world, but their perception is more conceptual compared to that of first-order entities (while a ball may be touched, the event of kicking it may not). Third order entities, instead, cannot be observed and it cannot be said that they happen in time or are located in space, at least not according to commonsense intuition.

Let us now focus on first- and second-order entities and examine how they relate to the parts of speech. The most obvious observation is the one we made at the beginning of the section; first-order entities tend to be coded as nouns, while second-order entities tend to be coded as verbs. These generalizations are summarized in Table 4.2.

**Table 4.2.** Types of entities and parts of speech

| Order of Entity | Type of Entity | Part of Speech |
|---|---|---|
| 1st | persons, places, things | noun |
| 2nd | actions, events, processes, situations | verb |

Lyons' classification is not uncontroversial, as the author himself recognizes. For example, it does not account for the fact that many languages have nouns that refer to second-order entities. As an example, consider *sunset*, which refers to an event that occurs in time, and not to a physical object. Following Lyons' terminology, we shall call these nouns *second-order nouns* (*action nouns* in traditional grammar). In light of this difficulty, the author proposes to assume the existence, for each word class, of a "focal" subclass, consisting of its most typical members. For nouns, this subclass does not include words such as *sunset* (which is a second-order noun) or *beauty* (which is an abstract noun and therefore denotes an entity which may not be touched), but words such as *sun* and *mountain*, that is, first-order nouns. According to Lyons, semantic/ontological classifications of parts of speech should aim at defining not the whole class, but the distinguished (focal) subclass of the total class.

Echoing Lyons, other linguists have considered the relationship between ontological categories and linguistic categories. In 1979 T. Givón for example proposed an explanatory theory of ontology/word class correlations centered on the notion of temporal stability. In Givón's work, **temporal stability** is defined as the ability of the referent of a category to remain stable over time. According to Givón , this property is scalar, that is, it comes in degrees, and variation in value along the scale correlates with parts-of-speech distinctions.

The following examples illustrate this point. Instances of high time-stable concepts are physical objects; this category is typically associated with nouns in language. On the other hand, concepts with low temporal stability are actions such as *buy* and *kick* and are typically expressed by verbs. Verbs, however, may have relatively higher or lower degrees of low time-stability, depending on whether the event they describe lasts in time; compare *kick* (very low stability, as it is an instantaneous event) with *walk* (higher relative stability, in that it involves duration, but still a low absolute degree of stability) and *own* (the highest stability in the

```
most stable <-------------------------------------------------------> least stable
tree                                    own         walk          kick
noun                                    verb        verb          verb
```

**Figure 4.1** Scale of temporal stability

verbal category, in that a state is durable and no change is implied). Similarly, nouns can be said to be more or less high time-stable; for example, a *flower* can be said to change form and shape faster than a *tree* (at least, according to human perception). Figure 4.1 illustrates Givón 's proposal.

Givón's work recalls the fundamental distinction between what philosophers call *continuants* and *occurrents* (Johnson 1924, section 4) and ontologists *endurants* and *perdurants* (Lewis 1986). Classically, the difference between these two types of entities is related to their behavior in time. **Endurants** are *wholly* present (i.e. all their proper parts are present) at any time they are present. **Perdurants**, on the other hand, extend in time by accumulating different "temporal parts," so that, at any time *t* when they exist, only their temporal parts at *t* are present; other temporal parts (e.g. their previous or future phases) are not present. For example, a piece of paper is wholly present while someone is reading it (it is an *endurant*), while some temporal parts of the reading are not present any more while the reading proceeds (reading is a *perdurant*) (cf. Masolo et al. 2003). Philosophers say that **continuants** are entities that *are in time*, while lacking however temporal parts (so to speak, all their parts flow with them in time). **Occurrents**, on the other hand, are entities that *happen in time*, and can have temporal parts (all their parts are fixed in time).

Both Lyons and Givón incorporate the notions of focal subclass and scale of temporal stability in their semantic classification to account for the internal variation observed within classes. In spite of this, ontology-based classifications still leave some issues unaddressed, such as the fact mentioned above that events are expressed by both verbs and nouns in language. According to some, these issues can be solved by shifting the attention from the ontological level to the level of discourse, particularly, by assuming that the chief factor determining how a given content is categorized in the lexicon in terms of part of speech is not the ontological correlate as to whether the content is *referenced* or *predicated*.

As in Chapter 3, the notions of *reference* and *predication* can be interpreted in several ways. On the one hand, they can be seen as the two fundamental activities of human reasoning, and thus as universal modalities of conceiving things and organizing our thought. In this view, recalling the authors of the grammar of Port-Royal, G. Bossong observes: "The basic features of noun and verb are directly derived from the basic activities of the mind: to conceive entities, i.e. the objects of our thoughts; and to judge about these entities, i.e. to make statements and utterances. The fundamental categories of every conceivable human language are but the reflex of the fundamental categories of our thought" (Bossong 1992: 13). On the other hand, reference and predication can be seen as two basic strategies to introduce the things we want to talk about in our discourse, that is to say, as two distinct modes to organize our utterances—in other words, as discourse strategies. This is the interpretation defended in Hopper and Thompson (1984), which is close in spirit to the one proposed in Searle (1969) and that we review in Chapter 3. According to this interpretation, by performing an act of reference we identify a specific entity and introduce it as a participant into the discourse; that is, we present it as a referent about which we will say something. Instead, when we perform an act of predication, we assert that an event occurs in which the entity referred to is involved or, if the entities are more than one, we establish relationships between them. In this view, reference and predication represent two options we have available for modulating the content of our discourse.

Whatever view one takes of the matter, it is clear that reference and predication are not, strictly speaking, two notions; they are two different ways of imposing form on notions. An an example, consider how one and the same event can be either predicated of an entity, as with *burn* in "the house is burning," or be introduced into the discourse as a participant of another event, as with *fire*: "the *fire* is spreading through the house."

The following conclusions can be drawn from the previous discussion. Verbs are more apt than other words to perform the act of predication, which consists in reporting an event, while nouns are more apt to perform an act of reference, which consists in introducing the entities participating in the event being reported. An act of reference, on the other hand, can target either an entity or an event; this duality grounds Lyons' opposition between first-order and second-order nouns (see Table 4.1), to which we will return in section 4.4.2.

## 4.4. Word subclasses

Starting from the major word classes, increasingly fine-grained groupings can be identified in the lexicon. These are the word subclasses, corresponding to more refined lexical structures. In this section, we focus on verbs and nouns and introduce a number of subclasses for each. Our main criterion for verb classification will be the ability of verbs to denote second-order entities (events), examined from various perspectives; for nouns, we will consider their ability to refer to both first-order and second-order entities.

### 4.4.1. Verb classes

Verbs may be classified according to three main criteria, which correspond to three different perspectives from which the event they express may be looked at. The first is the inherent conceptual content of the event, that is, the core meaning of the verb, also called the (verbal) *root* in the literature (Levin and Rappaport Hovav 2005). On the basis of this property, it is possible to identify classes such as motion verbs (*go, walk, climb*, etc.), manner verbs (*wipe, scrub*), perception verbs (*see, smell, hear, listen*), verbs of cognition (*understand, grasp*), verbs of communication (*talk, tell, whisper*), verbs expressing measures (*cost, weigh*), verbs expressing acts of throwing (*throw, hurl*), and so forth. The second characteristics concern the inherent temporal structure of the event, that is, the verb's *Aktionsart*. On the basis of this criterion, one can identify verbs denoting states (*own*), processes (*work, sleep*), punctual events (*find, arrive*), and so on (cf. section 2.1). The third criterion concerns the number and type of event participants which are required for a successful use of the verb in question, from both a grammatical and a semantic point of view. Required participants are called **actants**, **valences** or **arguments**, and their totality is referred to as the **valency** (or **argument**) **structure** of the verb. On the basis of this criterion one can identify verbs requiring one argument (*run, swim*), two (*know, participate*), or three arguments (*put, give*). Finally, there is transitivity, which intersects the first three properties and will be considered separately in our presentation.

The first two properties (core meaning and *Aktionsart*) are semantic in nature. The other two (valency/argument structure and transitivity) can be interpreted as both semantic and syntactic. There is a dependency among the criteria, as we shall see later. For now, let us just say that valency/

argument structure is superordinate to a large set of criteria, including: **subcategorization**, that is, how arguments of a verb are expressed in the syntax, for example whether they are realized as direct or indirect objects; **semantic selection** that is, what type of entity is expected to fill each argument position (animate, inanimate, etc.); and **thematic role**, that is, the role the entities expressing an argument play in the event reported by the verb, for example, whether they are agents, patients, experiencers, recipients, etc. All of these criteria are individually examined below, in the following order: (a) transitivity, (b) valency structure (and associated properties), (c) *Aktionsart*, and (d) core meaning.

### 4.4.1.1. Transitivity and intransitivity

The most traditional classification of verbs distinguishes between transitive and intransitive verbs. A verb that is **transitive** is one that requires a direct object complement (that is, a complement directly connected to the verb), as in the case of *fix* in "John fixed the roof" (*"John fixed" is not, in fact, a meaningful expression). A verb that is **intransitive** is one that is not able to take such a complement, as in the case of *arrive* in *"the guest arrived the gift". Some transitive verbs are well known for allowing uses with or without an explicit direct object: "Since yesterday, I no longer *smoke* (cigarettes)"; "It would be convenient for you to *park* (your car) in front of your house," etc. These are, however, particular uses, and in such cases the object complement is not expressed because it is taken for granted but is nevertheless implied.

A verb's property of being transitive or intransitive goes together with other properties. For example, transitive verbs may be passivized ("the roof was fixed by John" or simply "the roof was fixed"), while intransitive ones cannot (*the gift was arrived). The passivization test suggests that verbs such as *fix* differ from verbs such as *weigh* in that the latter, despite exhibiting a superficial direct object, may not be passivized and cannot be analyzed as transitive on a par with verbs such as *fix*; compare "The cake weighs two kilos" with *Two kilos are weighed by the cake.

As regards intransitive verbs, besides not permitting direct object complements and passivization, they exhibit variation in the syntactic behavior of their subject and can be divided in two main sub-groups based on this feature. **Unaccusative** verbs are intransitive verbs whose subject behaves syntactically as the object of transitive verbs, while **unergative** verbs are intransitive verbs whose subject does not have this property. This property surfaces in languages in various ways. For example, in Italian (a language where this distinction can be clearly observed in the syntax) the subject of unaccusative verbs may be replaced by the pronoun *ne* (1a), while that of unergative verbs never allows such a replacement (1b). Now, since replacement with *ne* is characteristic of the object of transitive verbs (1c), there is a clear parallelism between the object of transitive verbs and the subject of unaccusative ones, in the sense that they behave similarly from a syntactic point of view.

(1)   a. It. Sono arrivate *molte lettere.* → *Ne* sono arrivate molte.
              lit. Are arrived many letters. → Of them, are arrived many.
      b. It. *Molti bambini* hanno dormito. → *\*Ne* hanno dormito molti.
              lit. Many children have slept. → *Of them have sleep many.
      c. It. Abbiamo visto *molti film.* → *Ne* abbiamo visti molti.
              lit. We have seen many movies. → Of them we have seen many.

> Note that this does not mean that all unaccusatives must have a transitive counterpart: in fact many of them don't (see Levin and Rappaport Hovav 1995 for an overview).The *ne*-test (cf. Bolletti and Rizzi 1981) only shows that the subject of verbs like *arrivare* behaves as any object of transitive verbs.

The examples also show that Italian unaccusative verbs take *essere* 'to be' as auxiliary in compound tenses (1a), while unergative verbs take *avere* 'to have' (1b). Auxiliary selection, together with *ne*-cliticization (the technical term used for the syntactic operation in (1a) and (1b)), are the ultimate tests for unaccusativity in Italian.

For English, the main test for unaccusativity proposed by Levin and Rappaport Hovav (1995) is instead the resultative construction. This test shows that a result state can be asserted of objects of transitive verbs such as the *fence* in "Tom painted the fence *green*" and of subjects of unaccusative verbs such as the *lake* in "The lake froze *solid*" but not of subjects of unergative verbs such as *Sue* in *"Sue laughed *silly*", except when a reflexive is added ("Sue laughed herself *silly*") (an overview of the diagnostics for unaccusativity for different languages, is Zaenen 2006). We repeat the examples below, where the word that lexicalizes the result state is in italics:

(2)   a. Tom painted the fence *green*.
      b. The river froze *solid*.

    c. *Sue laughed *silly*.
    d. Sue laughed herself *silly*.

Turning now to semantic considerations, it is generally assumed that transitivity and intransitivity, as described above, are properties a verb has by virtue of its meaning: for example, typical transitive verbs are thought of as expressing events in which one participant initiates an action that "transits" or "is transferred" to another participant, in the sense that as a result of the action the state of the latter is modified, or affected, whereas intransitives do not do so. Several linguists, however, have long recognized that this definition is inadequate; for example, it does not apply to expressions such as "Paul owns two houses" in which the subject's referent does not initiate any action and the state of the object's referent does not undergo any modification as a result of it. With an expression such as "Mark painted a portrait," the point becomes even clearer. In this case, we cannot properly speak of the painting as being affected, because something that does not exist before the event begins, as the painting in the specific case, cannot properly be said to be affected by the event. For these and similar reasons, to arrive at a consistent definition of transitivity it is better to hold to a formal definition such as the one proposed above, according to which transitive verbs are those which require an object complement (either expressed or implied) (a successful attempt to define transitivity in semantic terms, however, can be found in Hopper and Thompson 1980).

As for intransitive verbs their meanings appear to cover a wide range of event types, and it does not seem possible to make relevant generalizations. Even the intuitive insight that intransitive verbs express events which differ from those expressed by transitive verbs does not appear to be fully supported by empirical evidence. There exist, in fact, several synonym verb pairs one of which is transitive and the other intransitive. Examples are: Engl. *search* / *look for*; *inhabit* / *live in* or *on*; *survive* / *live on*; *compile* / *fill in*; *become* / *grow into*; It. *chiamare* 'call' and *telefonare* 'phone.' The following are examples of this type:

(3)   a. Flightless birds inhabit the island. (transitive)
      b. Flightless birds live *on* the island. (intransitive)

(4)   a. It. Devo chiamare Paolo alle sette. (transitive)
        'I must call Paul at seven.'

   b. It. Devo telefonare a Paolo alle sette. (intransitive)
       lit. I must phone *to* Paul at seven.

On the other hand, there appear to exist instead several correlations between the subclass to which an intransitive verb belongs and its inherent semantic and *Aktionsart* properties. The main cross-linguistic generalizations are as follows. Unaccusative verbs tend to express changes of state of the subject (*disappear, redden, dry*); changes of location of the subject associated with directed motion (*arrive, leave*); states (*remain, own*); instantaneous happenings (*occur, happen, take place*). Unergative verbs, on the other hand, describe voluntary actions (*swim, sing, dance*); bodily processes (*shake, breathe, cry*); manners of motion (*run, walk*), and others.

### 4.4.1.2. Valency structure

The view according to which transitive verbs require both a subject and a direct object and intransitive verbs can only take a subject is not sufficient to fully classify verbs along the transitivity parameter. In fact both transitives and intransitives may require an additional complement to complete their meaning, as in "Lisa put the book *on the shelf*" (*Lisa put the book) or "Peter lives *in London*" (*Peter lives). The problem posed by this evidence can be dealt with by analyzing verbs in terms of valency/argument structure; this allows for refinements of the traditional classification of verb in terms of the transitive/intransitive opposition.

   The scientific metaphor of valency applied to verbs is attributed to L. Tesnière (Tesnière 1959), who used it in the context of a description of the syntax of classical languages. In a nutshell, central to Tesnière's proposal is the idea that the verb is the node of the sentence around which the complements form a set. The verb expresses the event (*procès* in Tesnière's terminology) while the complements express the entities that take part in the event. Some of these complements (called *actants* in Tesnière) are essential to complete the meaning of the verb and must be expressed in the syntax (for example, *"Mark put the book" is not a well-formed expression because it lacks mention of the final location of the book); other ones are optional, that is, they may be left out, as the temporal expression "for ten years" in "Mark lived in Rome for ten years"; these are called *circonstants* (circumstantials) in Tesnière. Verbs typically take one, two, or three actants (one-slot, two-slot, and three-slot

**Table 4.3.** Verb classes on the basis of the number of actants

| Verb Classes | Verbs | Examples |
|---|---|---|
| **One-slot Verbs** | *be born, caught* | *A baby girl*₁ was born; *Paul*₁ coughed loudly |
| **Two-slot Verbs** | *rent, live in* | *Sara*₁ rented *a car*₂; *Mark*₁ lives *in Rome*₂ |
| **Three-slot Verbs** | *put, dedicate* | *Lynda*₁ put *the keys*₂ in *the bag*₃; *Lisa*₁ dedicated *her book*₂ to *her father*₃ |

verbs, cf. Table 4.3). Four-slot verbs (such as *transfer* in "The company transferred the money from one bank account to another") are controversial classes and we will not address them here.

It is a matter of debate whether there are verbs with no actants (no-slot verbs). Some scholars claim that even verbs describing natural events such as *snow* and *rain* include one actant from a logical point of view, corresponding to the precipitation that falls on the ground, despite the fact that this actant cannot be expressed in the syntax (see the note in Jackendoff 2002: 135). On this understanding, "It is raining" includes the actant *rain*, "It is snowing" includes the actant *snow*, and so forth. A test supporting this view is that these expressions can be paraphrased as "The rain is falling," "The snow is falling," etc. Note that unlike Romance languages, where verbs expressing natural events do not take any subject (they are the so-called impersonal verbs: It. "Piove" lit. *rains*), in Germanic languages these verbs are construed with an obligatory so-called expletive subject (Dutch "het regent," Engl. "it rains," Germ. "Es regnet").

Valency grammar relies on a conception of sentence structure which differs radically from that of traditional grammar. In traditional grammar, the basic distinction is between the subject on the one hand, and all other complements on the other; no distinction is made between obligatory or optional complements. By contrast, in valency theory, subject and obligatory complements are grouped together in a single class and contrasted to those which are not required by the verb. Valency grammar also differs from

| Traditional grammar | subject | predicate | complements | |
|---|---|---|---|---|
| Valency grammar | actant | predicate | actant(s) | circumstantial(s) |
| Generative grammar | external argument | predicate | internal argument | adjunct(s) |

**Figure 4.2** Sentence structure

the model of sentence structure developed within the generative tradition, based on the **projection principle** formulated in Chomsky (1965; 1981), according to which sentences are formed by projection of complements from the lexicon, particularly from verbs and other predicative items. Chomsky's principle also assumes the notion of obligatoriness that grounds the valency model, but maintains at the same time that obligatory complements are of two sorts, namely **external** and **internal** to the so-called verb phrase, consisting of the verb and its direct and/or indirect objects. This distinction is absent in Tesnière's model, which contends that the higher node in the sentence structure is occupied by the verb and that all actants are equally dependent on it (Tesnière 1959: 109). In this view, Tesnière's model can be said to rely on a simplified syntax with respect to early generative models. A summary of what has just been said is presented in Figure 4.2, where the terms **argument** and **adjunct** replace the terms actant and circumstantial within the generative tradition.

The set of valency slots governed by a verb corresponds to its **valency structure**, or its **valencies**. Valency structure is referred to as **structure actancielle** in Lazard (1994) and **argument structure** in Grimshaw (1990). The notion of argument is borrowed from logic, particularly from the systematization proposed by G. Frege in 1892. Grimshaw's model subsumes the distinction between external/internal argument mentioned above; in her work, the subject is considered to be the most prominent argument in the structure. We shall return to the notion of structural prominence in section 4.4.2.2.

A helpful method to establish the argument structure of a verb is to add an argument to, or subtract one from, the sentence, and to evaluate whether the result is acceptable:

**(5)**  a. *The cold* coughed Paul.
     b. *Sue* has born a child.
     c. *Sara rented.
     b. *Mark lives.
     e. *Lisa dedicated a book. / *Lisa dedicated to her father.

Deciding on the number of arguments of a verb is notoriously complex for several reasons. In the following, we focus on three. First, depending on the verb and the context, the same complement may play the role of an argument or of an adjunct. To understand how, compare the two lists below, where the notion conveyed by the argument is specified between brackets.

**Arguments (that is, complements that are obligatory):**
    a. Our anniversary is *today*.                     (time)
    b. Clelia lives *in Paris*.                        (location)
    c. The last part of the book deals *with politics*.  (topic)

**Adjuncts (that is, complements that are not obligatory):**
    a. I saw Mark *today*.                         (time)
    b. Mark met Clelia *in Paris*.                (location)
    c. We talked all evening *about politics*.     (topic)

Second, certain verbs allow one of their arguments to be left unstated (*defaulted argument* in Pustejovsky 1995), while others appear to imply arguments that cannot be expressed. Verbs allowing an argument to be left unstated are for example Engl. *smoke* and *park* mentioned in section 4.4.1.1. Verbs implying arguments that cannot be expressed are instead verbs like Engl. *phone* and *bag*, which incorporate one of the entities involved in the action; the instrument in the first case ("She phoned the office"), the container in the second ("She bagged the groceries"). These verbs have been analyzed as verbs with an **incorporated argument** in the literature (*shadow argument* in Pustejovsky 1995). The incorporated argument cannot be expressed, unless it is further specified; "*She phoned the office on the phone" is not a well-formed expression in English, while "She phoned the office on the mobile phone" is acceptable.

Third, to pin down the number of arguments of a predicate is difficult because single verbs tend to be associated with multiple argument structures. For example, *start* is one-slot in "The engine started quickly" and two-slot in "The pain starts from the top of the neck." Note that change in argument structure often goes together with change in meaning: *start* means 'begin operating' in the first case and 'originate' in the second. In other words, valencies are inextricably related to meaning.

The evidence discussed above clearly shows that in analyzing valency structures for verbs, it is not sufficient to talk generically of valency. In order to correctly analyze cases such as those discussed above, one needs to draw a preliminary distinction between participants and arguments on the one hand and between semantic and syntactic valency on the other. A **participant** is one of the entities involved in an event; when an event is encoded in a verb, only some of its participants are selected as arguments; others are either incorporated in the verbal meaning (as in the case of *phone* and *bag*) or defocused and coded as adjuncts. In other words participants are semantic/conceptual notions, while arguments are semantic/syntactic objects. Detecting the difference between participants and arguments enables us to draw a distinction between two valency levels: **semantic valency**, corresponding to the set of *participants* involved in the event denoted by a predicate, and **syntactic valency**, defining the set of *arguments* associated with a verb in one of its meanings (examples of mismatches between the two levels can be found in Van Valin and LaPolla 1997: section 4.2).

It should also be noted that in order for valency grammar to be successfully applied to the analysis of verbs it must first be verified if the verb coincides with the sentence's predicate. Although this is mostly true, there are cases to the contrary. Consider for example the expression "Chris is a good father." In spite of the fact that "a good father" cannot be left out, it is not, in this context at least, an argument of *be*; rather, it is the predicate of the sentence, that is, the part of the sentence that asserts something about the subject argument expressed by Chris.

In traditional grammar, nominal expressions that function as the main predicate of the sentence are called **nominal predicates**; they are linked to their subject either directly or by a **copula** (from the Latin 'connection, linking of words'). In languages that have a copula, the verb *be* serves this function, as in the example above. It follows that the underlying argument structure of the sentence with a copula differs from the one in which the verb coincides with the predicate. The following is a simplified representation of this point.

1. Sentence with a verb that coincides with the predicate:

   SUBJECT$_N$   PREDICATE$_V$   ARGUMENT$_N$
   "Chris       met             his father"

2. Sentence with a verb that does not coincide with the predicate:

   SUBJECT$_N$   COPULA$_V$   NOMINAL PREDICATE$_N$
   "Chris       is           a good father"

Besides the copula, other verbs such as Engl. *seem* and *become* appear to play the role of connecting a subject with his predicate. Some scholars contend that these verbs should, however, be kept distinct from the copula. The copula, they argue, is purely a linking element, while copular verbs contribute to the meaning of the expression; compare "Chris is an engineer" with "Chris became an engineer"; "Chris is happy" with "Chris seems happy," and so forth.

In addition to being classified in terms of the number of arguments they require, verbs may be grouped into classes on the basis of how arguments are expressed in the syntax—for example, whether they are realized as subject, direct object, indirect object, and so on. This property is called **subcategorization** (Chomsky 1965: 63 ff.). For example, as we saw in Table 4.3, both *rent* and *live* (in the sense of 'inhabit') require two arguments, but while the second argument of *rent* is realized as direct object ("We rented a car for three days"), the second argument of *live* must be introduced by the preposition *in* ("Peter lives in London" / *Peter lives London). The **subcategorization frame** of a verb, therefore, can be defined as the syntactical surrounding the verb requires.

Table 4.4 provides some examples of basic subcategorization frames for English verbs. In the table, _ stands for the verb position, NP stands for nominal phrase, *prep* stands for the governing preposition of the NP that follows it, S stand for sentence. The proposed representation reflects only the surface structure, and does not distinguish between internal and external arguments. A more accurate syntactic representation based on the notion of syntactic constituent would do that.

**Table 4.4.** Examples of subcategorization frames

| Subcategorization frame | Examples |
|---|---|
| [NP _ ] | *The girl*$_{NP1}$ is smiling |
| [NP _ NP] | *Jane*$_{NP1}$ attended the meeting$_{NP2}$ |
| [NP _ prepNP] | *The price* $_{NP1}$ depends *on the quantity*$_{NP2}$ |
| [NP _ NP prepNP] | *Lisa*$_{NP1}$ dedicated *the book*$_{NP2}$ *to her father*$_{NP3}$ |
| [NP _ prepNP prepNP] | *Sara*$_{NP1}$ asked *her mother*$_{NP2}$ *for some advice*$_{NP3}$ |

In addition to requiring a certain number of arguments and a specific syntactic form for each of them, verbs also require that the arguments be of a particular type from the semantic point of view; in other words, they pose *restrictions* on the semantic class of words with which they combine. These constraints, called **selectional restrictions** in Chomsky (1965, 95), have been originally conceived in terms of features. For example, the verb *drink*, in its literal use, can be said to constrain its subjects to (+ animate) and its objects to (+ liquid); one cannot, in fact, *drink an orange* but only *an orange juice*. This type of information may be regarded as a lexical property of the verb, and in particular of its argument structure. Assuming that the verb *drink* is associated *inter alia* with the subcategorization frame [NP_ NP], selectional restrictions can be informally added to its arguments as follows:

**(6)**   *drink*.v   [NP$_{<animate>}$_ NP$_{<liquid>}$]

Selectional restrictions have been formulated in terms of semantic preferences in Wilks 1975. An additional piece of information associated with arguments is the role their referents play in the event expressed by the verb, also called **thematic role** (Chomsky 1981). In fact, to speak for example of an animate subject is not enough because an animate subject can play very different roles depending on the event at play. The following are examples of this type: "Peter drank an orange juice" (Peter = agent of the action); "Peter received a letter" (Peter = recipient of the action); "Peter underwent surgery" (Peter = recipient but also entity affected by the action).

Since the pioneering work of J. Gruber (1965) and C. Fillmore (1968), many scholars have attempted to compile a list of thematic roles. Their lists differ in both number and type of roles, as well as in their degree of detail. Table 4.5 offers a list of those roles on which the various scholars agree—though often using different terminologies—as well as an example for each role (for a detailed list of roles, see Van Valin and LaPolla 1997; from a computational perspective, Petukhova and Bunt 2008).

Thematic roles constitute a further piece of information that may be added to the verb's subcategorization frame. For the verb *drink*, they can be informally marked as in (7). In (7), the object's referent is analyzed as Patient in that it is consumed during the event; the Subject's referent is analyzed as Agent, although a *drink* event may actually occur accidentally, as in "The child (accidentally) drank some of my medicine."

(7)    *drink*.v    [NP$_{Ag}$ <animate>_ NP$_{Pt}$ <liquid>]

**Table 4.5.** Selected list of thematic roles

| Roles | Definitions | Examples |
|---|---|---|
| *Agent* (Ag) | initiates and carries out the event intentionally | *The children*$_{Ag}$ are swimming |
| *Cause* (Cause) | initiates the event unintentionally | *The wind*$_{Cause}$ broke the window$_{Pt}$ |
| *Experiencer* (Exp) | experiences a perception, emotion, etc. | *Beth*$_{Exp}$ smelt the coffee$_{Source}$ |
| *Patient* (Pt) | is directly affected by the event | *Jack*$_{Ag}$ fixed *the roof*$_{Pt}$ |
| *Theme* (Th) | is involved in the event, but is not affected | *The speaker*$_{Th}$ is wearing *a tie*$_{Th}$ |
| *Result* (Result) | is created during the event | *Peter*$_{Ag}$ wrote *an essay*$_{Result}$ |
| *Recipient* (Rec) | is the goal of the action | *He*$_{Ag}$ sent an email$_{Th}$*to his sister*$_{Rec}$ |
| *Beneficiary* (Ben) | benefits from the event | *Mark*$_{Ben}$ won an award$_{Th}$ |
| *Locative* (Loc) | place where the event takes place | *John*$_{Th}$ lives *in Rome*$_{Loc}$ |
| *Destination* (Dest) | place where the event ends | *John*$_{Ag}$ jumped *into the car*$_{Dest}$ |
| *Source* (Source) | startpoint of the event | *The water*$_{Th}$ came *from the faucet*$_{Source}$ |
| *Instrument* (Instr) | is required by the agent to perform the action | *He*$_{Ag}$ sent the letter$_{Th}$*by fax*$_{Inst}$ |

*Theme* is distinguished from *Patient* by whether it undergoes a change in one of its inherent properties because of the event or not; if it doesn't, then it is a *Theme*; if it does, then it is a *Patient*. *Patient* and *Theme* both fall within the role that Fillmore calls *Objective* (1968).

Thematic roles have been defined in various ways in the literature. One of the most convincing attempts is Dowty (1991), who proposes to analyze roles as sets of lexical entailments of the verb; for example, the verb *cut* entails an animate, intentional, unaffected subject.

## Box 4.1. Frames and patterns

The notions of valency and argument structure are close in spirit to the notions of *(semantic) frame* and *pattern*. Semantic **frame** is the term used in linguistics to define the cognitive conceptual structure evoked by a lexical item, for example the frame *travel* evoked by verbs like *travel* or *commute* and by nouns like *trip* and *journey*. A frame consists of the lexical item evoking the frame and the set of participants evoked by the frame, called **frame elements** and named by their thematic roles. The notion of semantic frame as cognitive schema was first proposed in Fillmore 1992, and it is currently used in the compilation of FrameNet, a repertory of semantic frames for the English language under construction (a detailed description of the project can be found in Ruppenhofer et al. 2010). Below, we report the Frame *travel* as it is represented in FrameNet. The basic description includes the following components: informal definition of the situation the frame is supposed to represent; the set of frame elements associated with the frame, subdivided into core (argumental, defined as those which are "necessary to the central meaning of the frame") and non-core; the set of lexical units that evoke the frame. An example of an English expression instantiating the frame is "Ellen traveled all Europe by train in three weeks with one suitcase."

(i) *Travel* frame
   Definition:
   In this frame a *Traveler* goes on a journey, an activity, generally planned in advance, in which the *Traveler* moves from a *Source* location to a *Goal* along *a Path* or within an *Area*. The journey can be accompanied by *Co-participants* and *Baggage*. The *Duration* or

(continued)

*Distance* of the journey, both generally long, may also be described as may the *Mode of transportation*. Words in this frame emphasize the whole process of getting from one place to another, rather than profiling merely the beginning or the end of the journey.

Core elements:
*Area, Direction, Goal, Mode of transportation, Path, Source, Traveler.*

Non-Core frame elements (selection):
*Baggage, Co-participant, Distance, Duration, Frequency, Purpose, Speed.*

Lexical units (selection):
*travel* (verb and noun), *commute* (verb), *journey* (verb and noun), *tour* (verb and noun), *trip* (noun).

The notion of **pattern** is related to the notion of *frame* but distinct, inasmuch as it focuses on language recurrent structures rather than on cognitive schemata. In the work of P. Hanks and collaborators, for example, a pattern is a recurrent piece of phraseology, associated with a stable meaning (Hanks 2004). Particularly, patterns for verbs consist of valencies plus the so-called semantic types expected for each valency, such as human, location, activity, food, vehicle, and so forth. In Hanks' work, patterns are acquired from corpora through a lexicographic technique called Corpus Pattern Analysis (CPA). This technique is based on the inspection, for each valency slot, of the corresponding *lexical set*, i.e. the statistically relevant list of collocates that, according to empirical analysis, fill that argument position in text. From the lexical set through an abstraction procedure one arrives at the identification of the semantic types.

An example of a pattern for the English verb *attend* is given in (ii). Semantic types are notated in double square brackets with capital initial letters, whereas lexical sets are in curly brackets. Each argument position includes information about its syntactic realization. Moreover, an informal definition of the meaning associated with the pattern is provided. This is expressed in the form of a primary implicature that includes the typing constraints specified in the pattern.

*(continued)*

(ii) Verb *attend*

Pattern: [[Human]-subj] attend [[Activity]-obj]

Lexical set [[Activity]-obj]: {meeting, conference, funeral, ceremony, course, school, seminar, dinner, reception, workshop, wedding, concert, premiere...}

Primary implicature: [[Human]] is present at [[Activity]]

Currently, the CPA technique is being used to build repositories of patterns of verbs for various languages, including English (Hanks and Pustejovsky 2005), Czech, Spanish and Italian (Ježek et al. 2014).

### 4.4.1.3. *Aktionsart*

Another important criterion for verb classification is a verb's ***Aktionsart*** (also called **lexical aspect** or **actionality**). As introduced in Chapter 2, *Aktionsart* concerns the way in which the event expressed by a verb is encoded in language from the point of view of its inherent temporal structure. Traditionally, verbs have been classified into groups with different actional properties based on the following features: (a) presence of change (**dynamicity**), (b) **duration**, and (c) presence or absence of a goal corresponding to the natural end point of the event (**telicity**, from the Greek *télos*, 'end'). These features are identified through syntactic tests, to which we return below. On the basis of the intersection of these three features, the four main verb classes listed in Table 4.6 have been identified (the main reference for the discussion is the so-called Aristotelian classification elaborated by Vendler 1967 and Dowty 1991; the terms in the table are inspired by Simone 2003).

**State-denoting** verbs (**States** in Vendler) such as *own* in "Peter owns two houses," express a situation which has a duration but does not introduce changes, which is why it is considered not dynamic. Furthermore, its phases are homogeneous (that is, alike) so that we can visualize it as a uniform situation. **Verbs of indefinite process** (**Activity terms** in Vendler) such as *walk* in "Peter walks along the path," express an event which has a duration, but is dynamic, because during its execution it introduces a series of changes. For example while walking, Peter progressively moves and changes location

**Table 4.6.** Main Verb classes based on *Aktionsart* properties

| Verb Classes | Dynamicity | Duration | Telicity | Examples |
|---|---|---|---|---|
| **State-denoting verbs** | − | + | − | *own, remain* |
| **Verbs of indefinite process** | + | + | − | *walk, swim* |
| **Verbs of definite process** | + | + | + | *fix, dine* |
| **Punctual verbs** | + | − | + | *find, arrive* |

with respect to the starting point of the walk. In this case, too, the event's phases are considered homogeneous (Vendler 1967: 101) because the event exhibits the so-called *subinterval property*: "subevents of walking are themselves walking events" (Dowty 1979: 67). **Verbs of definite process (Accomplishment terms** in Vendler) such as *fix* in "Peter fixed the car" express an event which has a duration and is dynamic, but, unlike the event expressed by verbs of indefinite process, is characterized by a progression of the event towards an end point, which corresponds to the point in time at which the event can be said to have occurred. In this case, the event's phases are not all alike. If the event is interrupted, it will not be possible to say that it took place, because the act of fixing tends towards a goal that must be reached for the event to become true; this is why the expression "Peter fixed the car but the car is not fixed" is semantically odd. Because of this, these verbs cannot be said to possess the subinterval property. Finally, **punctual** verbs (**Achievement terms** in Vendler) express an event which has no duration and culminates in an instant ("Peter found the keys"). In this case, the initial point and the end point of the event coincide. Punctual verbs may presuppose a preparatory phase; for example, Peter may have looked for the keys for half an hour, or for ten minutes. This preparatory phase is not considered as part of the lexical meaning of the verb (more on this in section 4.4.2.2).

> Punctual events, which are the smallest dynamic events, have minimally two parts, a beginning and an end, the minimum number of points in time required to tell that a change or action occurred (Dowty 1979: 168–73; Beavers 2008: 248).

Besides dynamicity, duration, and telicity, other features may be considered to classify verbs from the point of view of their *Aktionsart*.

*Iterativity*, for example, characterizes verbs that express repeated (iter-ated) instantaneous events, such as *cough* (for five minutes), *flash* (for ten seconds), *blink*, etc. These verbs are called **semelfactives** (from the Latin *semel* 'once') or **points** (Moens and Steedman 1988; Smith 1991: 55ff.); they encode momentary occurrences that can be coerced to an iterative reading in context, for example by adverbial expressions such as "for five minutes." They differ from punctual verbs because the latter do not allow iteration; *"Peter found the keys for five minutes" is not a well-formed expression. *Ingressive* and *egressive* verbs, on the other hand, denote the entrance in or the exit from a new situation, and are evaluated in relation to what happens before or after the event denoted by the verb; for example, It. *incamminarsi* 'start walking' is ingressive with respect to *camminare* 'walk,' because it describes the entrance in the process denoted by the latter; Engl. *find* is egressive with respect to *look for* because it describes the exit from the process of searching, and so forth. *Ingressive* verbs are sometimes called *inceptive* and *inchoative* in the literature, although the labels do not completely overlap. Finally, *incrementality* is helpful to characterize verbs such as *grow* and *ripen*, which describe an event consisting of a sequence of stages in which one participant exhibits different degrees of the prop-erty expressed by the verb, for example for *ripen*, degrees of ripeness (**degree achievements** following Dowty's 1979 terminology; **gradual completion verbs** in Bertinetto and Squartini 1995; **multi-point scalar verbs** in Rappaport Hovav 2008). These verbs are ambiguous between two possible readings, one in which the meaning can be paraphrased as [BECOME *x*], and one in which the meaning is rather [BECOME more *x*]. For example, an expression such as "The tomatoes ripened" without further specification can mean either that the value of ripeness appro-priate for the tomatoes to be used or eaten has been reached, or simply that the tomatoes have become more ripe than they were. Both these readings can be regarded as telic; the former lexicalizes a conventionalized end state whereas the latter lexicalizes one of the possible intermediate states (so-called *comparative end states* in Kearns 2007).

Several analyses have been proposed to represent the comparative component which appears to be present in the meaning of degree achievements, and to account for the ambiguity just noted. Most scholars converge on the idea that these verbs incorporate a *scale of change* in their meaning (intended as an ordered set of values of the property they denote) and a *function* (called *measure function* in Kennedy and Levin 2008) that associates the entity undergoing the change with the values on the scale, and measures the degree to which this entity changes as a result of its participation in the event.

Other verbs which have been associated with incrementality are the so-called **incremental theme verbs** such as *fill, empty, dry, melt, freeze, build, write, eat* (for this terminology, see Dowty 1991 and Tenny 1992). These can be seen as a subtype of verbs denoting definite processes. Similarly to degree achievements, these verbs express an event that brings about a gradual change in value of one (or more) properties of the entity playing the role of Theme; for example, in "fill the glass" each phase corresponds to a different state of the glass. According to the received view, however, they differ from degree achievement because the scale of change is not supplied by the verb but by the argument playing the role of Theme; for example, when the glass is filled, the event of filling necessarily stops. Moreover, these verbs are not ambiguous between intermediate and end state reading as degree achievements are; their telic interpretation always points at the end state. This is why the expression "Peter filled the glass but the glass was not filled" is semantically odd. Finally, another distinction concerns punctual verbs, which may be classified in two groups, depending on whether the event they express encodes a result which can be referred to by the adjectival form, as with *break* ("The glass broke" → "I noticed a broken glass") or not, as in *go off* ("The alarm went off" → *"I noticed a went off alarm"). In the latter case, it is assumed that the verb expresses only the point in time when the change occurs.

The *Aktionsart* of a verb is often difficult to determine because it rarely comes alone. More often, it merges with aspectual information supplied by the verbal tense, which may construe an event as perfective ("he took me home") or imperfective ("he was taking me home"), by periphrases that focus on specific phases of the event ("it is about to rain"), or by syntactic cues such as direct objects that are capable of coercing ongoing processes ("Mark draws") into telic ones ("Mark draws a landscape"). In any case, to pin down the *Aktionsart* of a verb it is not sufficient to rely on intuitive judgments; it is necessary to base judgments on syntactic tests. For example, in order to determine whether or not a verb denotes a state, one can verify whether it admits the imperative or the progressive form. Verbs of state do not, as a rule, admit these two constructions (*Own two houses!, *You are owning two houses). In order to determine whether or not a dynamic verb is durative, one can verify whether it may be introduced by such verbs as *begin*. Only durative verbs allow this ("I began to walk," "I began to fill the glass," *I began to light the candle). Finally, in order to determine whether or not a verb is telic, one can verify whether it admits the expression "for $x$ time" or the expressions "at $x$ time" / "in $x$ time." Only verbs that allow for the latter type of expressions are telic; on this ground, "Peter walked for an hour / *in an hour" is not a telic expression, while "The bomb exploded *for an hour / at five o'clock" is telic. Some verbs, notably degree achievements, appear to admit both types of expressions: "The tomatoes ripened in five days" / "for five days," thus posing a puzzle as for their actional classification, as mentioned above.

It should be noted that tests cannot be applied automatically, because the material used for testing may act on the actional value of the verb itself, and shift it. For example, as noted above, in construction with point verbs, the adverbial expressions "for $x$ time" is not a diagnostic of atelicity but rather a trigger of iterative reading.

To summarize, the major conclusion to be drawn from the discussion in this and the previous section is the following. Valency structure and Aktionsart are inextricably linked; arguments are those participants in the eventuality that are selected as syntactically relevant by the verb, and *Aktionsarten* define how the event denoted by the verb unfolds in time.

## Box 4.2. Representing events

*Aktionsart* properties associated with verbs have been first represented through either feature sets or decomposed structures based on primitives (see section 3.3). For the verb *break* these two formalisms lead to descriptions such as the following:

(continued)

**(i)** *break*
    a. (+ dynamicity)(− duration)(+ telicity)
    b. [[x ACT] CAUSE [BECOME [y <*broken*>]]]

In the early 1990s, however, several scholars proposed to model the *Aktionsart* encoded in predicates using a formalism that focuses on the internal configuration of the event being denoted, called **event structure** (see for example Parsons 1990 and Pustejovsky 1991). This formalism is based on the idea that an event can be broken down into smaller units called **subevents**, which may overlap or precede each other from a temporal point of view; moreover, each subevent is seen as associated with only the arguments that participate in that specific portion of the overall event. For example, the verb *break* can be said to be associated with an event structure consisting of two main subevents, an initial causing act (e1), in which both the person or event responsible for the breaking and the thing about to be broken participate, followed by the result state (e2) of the broken thing. Figure 4.3 shows how this is represented in Pustejovsky's (1991) event structure model (in the figure < marks temporal precedence).

Single subevents of an event can be focused or defocused depending on the context; the event structure notation is useful to visualize these shiftings. For example, the causative use of *break* (as in "Anna broke the key") can be said to focus on the first subevent e1 while in the so-called inchoative variant ("The key broke"), it is the second subevent e2 which is prominent.

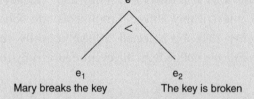

Figure 4.3 Event structure associated with the verb *break*

The subeventual analysis has later been integrated into decomposed structures; in this perspective, the decomposed structure in (ib) is analyzed as a complex event involving a CAUSING subevent followed by a BECOME subevent (Rappaport Hovav and Levin 1998: 108 ff.).

A different formalism to represent *Aktionsart* types is proposed in Croft (2012). Croft uses diagrams that involve two dimensions: the temporal dimension that encodes the progression of the event, and the

*(continued)*

set of states that hold at different points in time during the event. The aspectual diagrams for two putative readings of *see*, namely *see* as indefinite process in "I see Mount Tamalpais" and *see* as punctual occurrence in "I reached the crest of the hill and saw Mount Tamalpais" are given in Figure 4.4 (taken from Croft 2012: 53 ff.). In this figure $t$ represents the time dimension, while $q$ identifies the sequence of (qualitative) states of the event. The solid lines represent the parts of the event under focus in the two readings, i.e. what is denoted by the verb in that context.

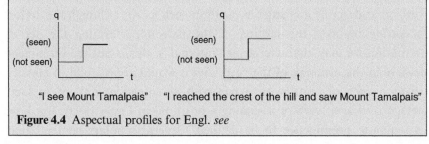

　　　"I see Mount Tamalpais"　　　"I reached the crest of the hill and saw Mount Tamalpais"

**Figure 4.4** Aspectual profiles for Engl. *see*

### 4.4.1.4. The root

To conclude this section devoted to verb classes, we shall look at the most idiosyncratic aspects of a verb's denotation. As we saw above, verbs may be classified according to the inherent characteristics of the event they express, i.e. what type of event it is. The effort to group verbs into categories on the basis of their meaning delivers classes such as, for example: motion verbs (*go, arrive, run, walk*); perception verbs (*see, listen, hear, smell*); verbs of communication (*talk, tell, whisper, twitter*); weather verbs (*rain, drizzle*); psychological verbs (*frighten, fear, bother*); or, at a more abstract level, verbs conveying reciprocity (*collaborate, meet*), reflexivity (*shave, wash oneself*), and so on.

　Most languages lack an extensive semantic classification of verbs; for English, a list of semantic classes derived from the introspective analysis of the set of syntactic structures in which verbs may occur can be found in Levin (1993). The VerbNet project (Kipper Schuler 2005) increases the number of Levin's classes and converts them into a full-fledged online lexical resource with subcategorization frames and event decompositions with primitives such as CAUSE, MOTION, CONTACT, MANNER, for each verb. Finally, the Wordnet project (Fellbaum 1998) proposes a list of 15 general classes for verbs, called **supersenses**, including the following categories: body, change, cognition, communication, competition, consumption, contact, creation, emotion, motion, perception, possession, social, stative, weather.

To identify semantic classes, that is, groupings of verbs with similar meanings, and organize them in a hierarchy that distinguishes for example between types of motion verbs, types of perception verbs, and so on, is intuitively simple but technically complex. In general, the difficulties encountered in classifying verbs in semantic terms can be said to derive primarily from the fact that the meaning of verbs consists of a bundle of features with different semantic prominence. Consider for instance verbs that describe a change in position such as *sit*; although the action of *sitting* involves the motion of the person performing the action (a motion we may characterize as "internal"), this is not the prominent feature in the meaning of the verb, and it would appear odd to classify *sit* as a verb of motion on a par with *enter* and *exit* (it is, in fact, categorized as a 'verb of assuming a position' in Levin 1993). But how is semantic prominence to be defined? Several scholars contend that prominent features are those that are transparent in the syntax, i.e. those that influence a verb syntactic behavior (Levin and Rappaport Hovav 2005: chapter 1); nevertheless, linking an observed syntactic behavior to the appropriate semantic component is a notoriously arduous task.

Another problem is that verbs encode only some aspects of the event they denote while presupposing others. This distinction between denoted and presupposed information is by no means easy to make, although there are clear cases. *Arrive*, for example, presupposes motion but encodes, in fact, the result/effect of such motion, consisting in the fact that the person or thing arrived is located in a place which differs from the one it was located in before the arriving event took place. On this ground, it is reasonable to question whether *arrive* should be considered a verb of change of location rather than a verb of motion, and which criteria are eligible to distinguish between the two.

Related to the previous problem is the problem of polysemy, intended as the property of verbs to exhibit different senses in different syntagmatic environments. A polysemous verb belongs by definition to multiple classes, namely, one for each of its meanings. Engl. *see*, for example, can be classified as a perception verb in "see a star," and as a verb of cognition in "I see your point," and so forth (on perception verbs in a typological perspective, cf. Viberg 1984). *Sit*, on the other hand, is a verb of assuming a position in "He sat in the chair near them" (Levin 1993: 262), while, according to B. Levin at least, it can be regarded as a verb of spatial configuration in stative uses such as "He sits in the corner near the fire" (Levin 1993: 255).

In traditional lexicography, the literal meaning is considered to be the basic meaning and it is therefore assumed as the basis for the classification; Engl. verb *take*, for example, is classified as 'grasp' ("take my hand"), and other uses, such as 'use' ("take the train"), 'ingest' ("take an aspirin") (see Chapter 3) are assumed to be derived.

Finally, assigning verbs to semantic classes is influenced by the degree of granularity of the classes. For example, both *run* and *roll* denote motion events with no inherent end point, but differ inasmuch as the former denotes an intentional action while the latter tends to describe an involuntary movement (see the oddness of "Do you feel like rolling?" as opposed to "Do you feel like running?") (cf. Levin 1993: 264–7).

This all suggests a syntax-informed approach to verb semantic classification. A syntax-informed approach is not driven by syntax but, starting from intuitive groupings identified on a semantic basis, looks for regularities in syntactic behavior of potential members, and divides them into classes based on these regularities. According to this methodology, two verbs with apparently similar meaning fall into different classes if they exhibit significant differences in the way they are used in language.

## 4.4.2. Noun classes

While the main criteria used to classify verbs are all associated with the type of event the verb encodes (from a semantic, aspectual, and syntactic point of view), when it comes to nouns matters are more complicated, because, as we saw in section 4.3, nouns may denote both an event and an entity participating in an event. In what follows, we first focus on nouns that denote *first-order entities*, i.e. *first-order nouns* according to the classification proposed by Lyons (1977). Specifically, we identify several classes of first-order nouns by looking at the correlations between the kind of entity they denote (physical, animate, substance, etc.) and their linguistic properties. We then turn to nouns that denote *second-order entities* (*second order nouns* in Lyons' terminology). Agentive nominals, such as *writer*, which constitute a third major class of nouns, will not be addressed in this context.

When no information to the contrary is given, the term *entity* will be used in the following section as a shorthand term for *first-order entity*. Accordingly, the terms *first-order* or *entity-denoting noun* (or simply *entity noun*) will be used interchangeably. Similarly, *second-order* and *event-denoting noun* (or *event noun*) will be considered synonyms.

### 4.4.2.1. Entity nouns

From the point of view of their information content, entity nouns can be classified on the basis of the type of entity they refer to or, if the entity lends itself to be perceived or conceptualized in different ways, on the basis of the "mode" in which they present this entity. As we shall see, the distinction between "entity" and "way of presenting it" is crucial. For some entities in the world, the nature is inherently defined and univocal. For example, an entity either is or is not animate. In other cases, however, a noun may impose a form on an entity that is inherently not well defined, or can be perceived in different ways, and therefore lends itself to different types of linguistic encoding. Consider the case of physical objects that rarely occur in isolation or that are often referred to as a set. Because of this, these objects are often encoded in the language as a collection whose components cannot be accessed individually. Nouns encoding collections of things are for example Engl. *furniture, jewelry, band*; Dutch *vleeswaar* 'sausages,' *snoepgoed* 'pastries,' 'sweets'; German *Haar* 'hair,' *Obst* 'fruit'; It. *vestiario* 'clothing,' *spazzatura* 'trash,' *traffico* 'traffic,' *folla* 'crowd' and so on. These nouns exhibit a particular grammatical behavior, as we shall see in a moment. Precisely because nouns do not always encode entities as they are found in the world, but may encode the different perspectives through which they are perceived and conceptualized, one speaks, in the case of nouns, of **Seinsart** (or 'mode of being'; Rijkhoff 1991; Dik 1997: 138), in parallel to verbs' *Aktionsart*.

Classifying a noun by establishing what type of entity it refers to requires a language-independent list of the types of entities that exist. A reasoned classification of the types of entities, as we have seen, is called an **ontology**. For our current purposes, we take into consideration only a fragment of an ontology, that is, a restricted number of entity types. The entity types that we consider are identified on the basis of six different dimensions, summarized in Table 4.7. For the sake of simplicity, we present these dimensions as

**Table 4.7.** Types of entity

| Types of entity | Examples |
| --- | --- |
| concrete object / abstract object | building, tennis court, Mark / beauty, belief |
| animate object / inanimate object | Mark, dog / pen, idea |
| natural object / artifact | apple / book |
| shapeless mass / individuated object | blood, gold / chair, Mark, boy |
| member of a class / single individual | boy, idea / Paul, Rome, France, pope |
| independent object / dependent object | woman, house / daughter (of), leg (of), price (of) |

oppositions between two members—for example, for the first dimension, concrete object vs. abstract object—although the dimensions in fact intersect, as we will see shortly.

The first dimension (concrete object vs. abstract object) appears unambiguous from the point of view of the nature of the entity; that which is concrete exists in space, at some point in time, is tangible and can in principle be experienced through the senses (a building, a tennis court, a person called Mark); that which does not, cannot (beauty, love, a belief). Nevertheless, even with respect to this distinction, there are controversial cases. Consider for example imaginary objects such as mythological figures and legendary animals; they are not concrete objects, do not exist at a particular moment in time, and yet are not abstract in the same sense as qualities such as beauty are: they are mental (or fictional) objects. Another problematic case is that of organizations (government, Sony, etc.), which do not have direct spatial qualities like concrete objects but are dependent on a specific location (for example, the place where their head office is located, the legal system of the country in which they are created, and so on). They are **social objects**. Finally, there are entities like the holes in a piece of cheese or the underneath of a table. They cannot be considered concrete in the same way as a chair, but they clearly occupy a region of space.

The second dimension (animate vs. inanimate entity) is more clearly unambiguous: an entity is either animate (Mark, dog) or not (pen), there are no intermediate or questionable cases. Organizations consisting of groups of animates are not strictly speaking animate themselves (e.g. Sony is not an animate entity), even though in ordinary language we say that "Sony is confident that . . . " and "the government thinks that . . . ," and so forth.

A third dimension opposes natural objects (that is, entities that exist in nature, such as an apple, a pine tree, a stone, a lake, a tiger) to artifacts. The latter are entities built by humans for specific purposes (a book, a lamp, a television, and so on). These entities are inherently functional; this is why they are also called **functional objects**. The distinction between natural and artifactuals appears unambiguous, but if we look closer there are controversial cases. For example, what about a bird's nest, or a beavers' dam? These are constructed by non-humans and therefore not artifacts as far as the English language is concerned, but they are not natural objects proper.

A fourth dimension opposes entities consisting of an amount of matter, as substances are (*gold, lead, blood*), to objects that have well-defined and individuated spatial boundaries (*chair, Mark, boy*). A well-known defining characteristic of an amount of matter is that smaller parts of the material are still that material. In other words, a mass can be divided into portions and each portion continues to constitute the initial substance or mass (a piece of gold is gold). Also objects with well-defined spatial boundaries generally have parts, and can be divided into pieces, but, if they are, their parts do not still constitute the initial object (a piece of a chair, for example the armrest, is not a chair).

A fifth distinction is between entities that are inherently unique, i.e. particular individuals such as Paul, and entities that form part of a class (boy, idea etc.).

Finally, a sixth distinction is that between independent entities, i.e. entities that refer directly to something in the world, such as *woman, house, air*, and entities that are dependent on another entity, such as *daughter* (of a mother), *leg* (of a dog), *shape* (of a table), *portrait* (of a man), *price* (of a car).

The distinctions between the types of entities we have introduced in Table 4.7 can be formally represented by means of a taxonomy such as that in Figure 4.5 (taken from Pustejovsky 2001: 100). In Figure 4.5, the focus is on natural kinds, and only a subset of the distinctions discussed above are represented.

The fragment of taxonomy in Figure 4.5 allows us to make an important observation. Entities can be classified in a hierarchy, in which there are

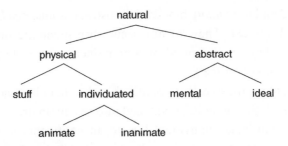

**Figure 4.5** *Taxonomy of natural entities*

superordinate and subordinate elements; for example, a concrete entity is either stuff or individuated. However, this hierarchical classification, as easy as it may seem, poses a number of problems because, as we have already emphasized, entities are characterized by a variety of dimensions that intersect. This is the case with ideas, which may be analyzed as both abstract and individuated, and with beauty, which is instead abstract and mass. Furthermore, there are entities that lend themselves to multiple classifications, as in the case of books, which may be classified as concrete objects but also as abstract ones, because the information they contain is an abstract object. We shall call entities of this type *complex objects* (following Pustejovsky's terminology, cf. Pustejovsky 1995: 149 ff.). The construction of an ontology of entity types must take these facts into account.

To clarify with what kind of entity a noun meaning is associated is important but does not mean saying much about the linguistic properties of the noun itself. What counts from a linguistic point of view is whether there are correlations between the type of entity the noun denotes (i.e. its ontological correlate) and its morphological and/ or syntactic properties.

When comparing different languages (Rijkhoff 1991), the most important distinction that can be drawn from a linguistic perspective within the noun class turns out to be that between **mass nouns** (*gold*, *sand*, *blood*) and nouns that denote bounded (i.e. individuated) objects (*Mark*, *boy*), called **count nouns**. Mass nouns, because they refer to an entity that cannot be counted but only divided into portions and measured, do not take the plural, but rather *classifiers*, such as *grain* of sand, *drop* of blood, *pinch* of salt, *sheet* of paper, *slice* of bread, and other similar terms. Their default use is with singular definite articles (*the* blood) or quantifiers (*much* blood and not \**many* bloods; for abstract nouns, *much* beauty and not \**many* beauties). They do not occur with indefinite ones (\**a* salt) except when they are delimited by a container or by a shape (as in "a coffee" = 'a cup of coffee').

As for **count nouns**, so called because they denote individual things that can be counted, they may be subdivided into two main groups: those that refer to one particular individual (i.e. to an entity that is referentially unique, such as *Mark* or *France*), whose number is therefore 1 (these are the **proper nouns**) and those that refer to a class of individuals, whose number is any number greater than 1. The latter are called **common nouns**. As a rule, proper nouns do not combine with determiners, nor do they take the plural form, because they refer to an individual that does not belong to any class or that, so to speak, belongs to a class consisting of a single member. The only exception is in contexts such as "He doesn't look like a John," in which they take on a specific sense ('the type of person who is named John'). By contrast, common nouns (count nouns denoting classes of individuals), because they refer to entities of which there are multiple instances, naturally require a determiner—either definite (the *boy*; for abstract nouns, the *idea*) or indefinite (a *boy*, an *idea*)—in order to specify, with greater or lesser precision, to which instance of the class they refer to. Furthermore, these nouns naturally occur in the plural form (*boy/boys*, *idea/ideas*) and with plural quantifiers (*many boys*, *many ideas*).

> We may sometimes use a count noun in a mass way (i.e. with mass interpretation). For example, in 'There is tomato in the soup," the tomato is presented as a substance instead of an individuated thing.

Yet another class of nouns is that of nouns denoting a collection of things that functions as a bounded whole, such as Engl. *furniture* or *clothing*. From a linguistic point of view, these nouns behave like mass nouns; they are always singular (\*two furnitures), they are not used with indefinite articles (\*a furniture) and the singular objects that make up the collection can be referred to only by means of a classifier (a piece of furniture) (for an in-depth discussion of the distinction between mass nouns and nouns like *furniture*, see Chierchia 2010).

Finally, **relational nouns**, as the word says, denote entities which are dependent on another entity, such as *mother* (of *x*), *friend* (of *x*), *neighbor* (of

**Table 4.8.** Classes of entity nouns based on formal properties

| Noun classes | Article | Plural | Quantifier | Examples |
|---|---|---|---|---|
| **Mass nouns** | def. | - | sing. | *blood, gold* |
| **Common nouns** | def. and indef. | x | plur. | *boy, idea* |
| **Proper nouns** | - | - | - | *Mark, France* |
| **Relational nouns** | indef. | x | plur. | *friend (of x), neighbor (of x)* |

*x*), and so forth. These nouns behave very much like common nouns as regards determination, with the exception that they appear odd when used with definite articles if there is no explicit mention of the second entity involved in the relation, or if the second entity cannot be retrieved from the immediate context. Consider, for example, "Yesterday I saw the mother" (of whom?).

Table 4.8 summarizes what we have said so far. In the table, "def." stands for definite article "indef." for indefinite article, "x" indicates possibility of co-occurrence, and "-" indicates impossibility.

The noun classes in Table 4.8 exhibit robust correlations between ontological properties and grammatical behavior, particularly types of determination. By contrast, neither the distinction between concrete- and abstract-denoting nouns, nor that between natural- and artifactual-denoting or between animate- and inanimate-denoting nouns appears to be systematically associated with particular morphological or syntactic features in language, at least not with as much regularity and frequency. The grammatical behavior of these nouns appears to be primarily determined by their encoding as mass or count noun.

---

While it is true that certain semantic distinctions do not translate directly into morphological or syntactic properties, they do, however, constrain the ways in which words may combine. For example, all three of the distinctions discussed above play a role in constraining the selection of arguments by a predicate; *build* requires an artifact as object (*I built an apple), *speak* (in its literal sense) requires a human subject (*the chair spoke to me) and so forth.

## 4.4.2.2. Event nouns

Let us now turn to nouns that denote a second-order entity, that is, an event (*second-order nouns* in Lyons' terminology). In traditional grammar, nouns conveying an event meaning are known as **action nouns**. This label is primarily applied to nouns that are morphologically derived from verbs, such as Engl. *training* (from *to train*) or *examination* (from *to examine*) (Comrie 1976). Deverbal nouns, however, do not exhaust the class of nouns that denote an event. This is illustrated in (8):

**(8)**   We took an evening *walk*.
Have you heard the *announcement*?
*Building* began in 2001.
He gave a brief *description* of the project.

The *party* is over.
*Lunch* is ready.
The *meal* lasted an hour and a half.
The *war* lasted three years.
The *crimes* occurred in his property.
How was your *trip* to Istanbul?

The examples in (8) illustrate that from a formal point of view, the class of nouns that denote an event is varied. First, a distinction must be drawn between nouns that are derived from verbs, such as *walk*, *announcement*, *building*, and *description*, and nouns which are not such as *lunch*, *party*, *meal*, *war*, and *crime*. Second, the latter nouns can, in turn, provide the base for deriving a verb (*to lunch*, *to party*) or have no corresponding verb in the lexicon (*meal*, *war*, *crime*, *trip*).

> The distinction between deverbal and non-deverbal action nouns is clearly individuated in the words of Zeno Vendler: "There are certain nouns that are not verb derivatives, yet behave like nominalised verbs [...]. Fires and blizzards, unlike tables, crystals, or cows, can occur, begin, and end, can be sudden or prolonged, can be watched and observed—they are, in a word, events and not objects" (Vendler 1967: 141).

Deverbal nouns are the outcome of a **nominalization** process, that is, a process by which linguistic material which is not a noun, for example a verb, is inserted into nominal syntax and put into noun use (on nominalization, see Box 4.3). Languages have different strategies to turn verbs into nouns. In English, for example, there are two main nominalization strategies: derivation and conversion. In derivation, an affix is added to the base word; this is the case of *announcement*, *building*, and *description* above. In conversion, the same form is used in a nominal syntax; this is the case of *a walk* (in the park). A special type of noun obtained through conversion is the *nominal infinitive* in the Romance languages; it consists in the insertion of the infinitive form of the verb into a nominal syntax. This is illustrated in (9). Recall that in Romance languages, verbal infinitives are marked by a special ending (*-ere* in the case of *insistere* 'insist'); this, however, does not prevent the infinitive being used as a noun, as we can conclude from the example below.

**(9)**   It. Il suo continuo *insistere* mi ha stancato.
'I was tired by his continuously insisting on such and such . . .'

Nominal infinitives are frequent in Romance languages while English tends to use the *-ing* form instead, as shown by the translation above.

---

**Box 4.3. Nominalization**

Nominalization is the general term used in linguistics for the phenomenon according to which linguistic material which is not a noun is used in a nominal context; the outcome of a nominalization is therefore a noun which was originally something else, for example a verb, or a whole sentence. This phenomenon can take different forms and yield different results, on which we focus in the following.

On the one hand, nominalization may consist of an occasional use in a nominal context of linguistic material which is not a noun. An example is the following: It. "Non capisco i suoi *aspettiamo*," lit. I do not understand his "let's wait." In this case, the outcome of the nominalization is a lexical form which is identical to the source verbal form ("aspettiamo") except for its distribution (for example, it occurs with a possessive adjective). Examples of this kind represent occasional uses which are in principle possible with any lexical item or expression but have no impact on the lexicon, in the sense that they do not lead to the creation of new words or new lexicalized word forms.

*(continued)*

On the other hand, nominalization is the process according to which a novel word with nominal function is created, starting from linguistic material which is not a noun. In this case, the outcome of a nominalization can be of several kinds:

(a) a noun with a morphological marker for nominalization, as in the case of Chinese nominalizers *-zi*, *-tou* and *–r* (see *shu* 'pettinare' →*shuzi* 'pettine'; *nian* 'pensare' →*niantou* 'pensiero'), or of Italian suffixes *-ata*, *-aggio*, *-mento* (see *camminare* '(to) walk' →*camminata* '(a) walk"; *lavare* '(to) wash' →*lavaggio* 'an occurrence of washing');
(b) a conversion, as in the case of Engl. (*to*) *run*→ (a) *run*, (*to*) *call*→ (a) *call*;
(c) a compound, as in Japanese *taberu* 'eat' + *mono* 'thing' →*tabe-mono* 'food'; *nomu* 'drink' →*nomi-mono* 'beverage,' *kau* 'buy' →*kai-mono* 'shopping activity.'

In all these cases, nominalization affects the lexical system of the language, because it leads to the coinage of a new word whose form is—with the exception of conversion—distinct from the original one.

The process of nominalization is not systematic from a morphological point of view; for example, some verbs do not have corresponding nominalizations. Moreover, there appear to be no direct correspondences between the meaning of the base word and the nominalization device employed in the derivation process: for example, *agreement* displays a derivational suffix while its synonym *accord* does not.

Whatever form it takes, the noun resulting from a nominalization process is a special kind of noun. To understand how, consider that certain Engl. *-ing* nominal forms take the article but cannot be pluralized ("The dancing was amazing" vs. *"The dancings were amazing") and that It. nominal infinitives are often allowed to be modified by adverbial expressions ("il mangiare in fretta fa male" lit. 'the to eat quickly is bad for you'). In other words, these two noun types may exhibit both verbal and nominal syntax in the same context. This is not the case with other nominalized forms obtained from verbs, such as Engl. *dance* or It. *bevuta*

*(continued)*

'single act of drinking.' The latter have a verbal meaning, but behave syntactically as conventional nouns. If, then, nominalization is viewed as a gradient from verbal to nominal forms, we may then say that Engl. -*ing* forms and Romance nominal infinitives are nouns which are closer to verbs, while action nouns like *dance* and *bevuta* are closer to nouns.

Another interesting property of nominalizations obtained from verbs is that they tend to develop polysemy patterns consisting of meanings with verbal features and meanings with nominal ones. One of the most recurrent patterns is the well-known event / result alternation (cf. Chapter 3). More patterns are listed below. As we can see, the patterns pick out the event and one of the participants in the event, such as the instrument used to accomplish the event, the collective agent performing it, or the place where the event occurs or is carried out (Aprejan 1973, Bierwisch 1990/1991).

Sense alternations for event nouns

- *event / result*      The *drawing* took three hours. (= event)
                        The *drawing* was sold yesterday. (= result)
- *event / means*      A breakdown prevented the *heating*. (= event)
                        They turned off the *heating*. (= instrument)
- *event / agent*      The company will centralize the *administration*. (= event)
                        The *administration* refused to negotiate. (= agent)
- *event / location*   They blocked the *entrance* to the building. (= event)
                        The *entrance* was open. (= location)

It is precisely by virtue of their polysemy patterns that many event nouns are often used as entity nouns in the discourse.

An interesting question is: why would languages with verbs and nouns develop devices to operate shifts between word classes, and enable processes such as nominalizations? In other words, what are the motivations that drive the nominalization process? One possible answer to this question is that languages need devices to shift from predicative to referential mode, and vice versa. From this perspective, nominalization can be seen as a linguistic device that enables the speaker to create referents in the discourse, starting from material which is primarily designed for other uses, that is, predicative use.

Event nouns denote an event, but they do so in fundamentally different ways from verbs; for example, they cannot, as a rule, be inflected for tense. In other words, with a noun such as *run* (as in "go for a run"), there is no way to specify that one is talking about the run which was done yesterday or the one that will be done tomorrow (as when the event is expressed by the verb: *I was running, I ran, I will run*, and so forth). Furthermore, with nouns the event is presented as something to which we can refer and at which we may even point ("Look at that beautiful *sunset*!"), whereas with verbs, it is presented as a change that occurs to something at some point or interval in time ("The sun is setting") or a state in which something participates ("The sun is shining").

As noted above, event nouns are traditionally called **action nouns**, but they are also known as **eventive** or **event-denoting nouns** (Gross and Kiefer 1995) or **unsaturated** nouns (Prandi 2004), as opposed to **entity** (or **entity-denoting**) or **saturated** or **referential** nouns. These labels, however, are not equivalent. For example, the label *unsaturated* highlights the property of these nouns of requiring one or more additional elements to complete their meaning, as with *arrival*, which requires the specification of the thing arrived (a guest, a train, a package, and so on). This property is shared by another class of nouns, i.e. relational nouns such as *sister* (of), *leg* (of) or *price* (of). In this view, the term *unsaturated noun* can be said to apply to all nouns that are relational, while the term *event noun* encompasses only those relational nouns that denote an event. As regards the label *referential*, as we saw in the previous section, it is not interchangeable with the label *entity*. While "entity" points at the ontological correlate of the noun, "referential" defines its discourse function, namely that of picking up something in the world as a referent. In this view, both entity and event noun types can be said to be referential nouns except when they are used predicatively, as *engineer* in "Chris is an engineer" and *walk* in "Chris took a walk" (cf. Chapter 6 section 6.4.4).

Be that as it may, the opposition between entity and event nouns represents the most fundamental distinction within the nominal domain.

A useful test to establish whether a noun refers to an entity or to an event consists in verifying whether it can answer the following question: what happened?

(10)   What happened/took place/occurred?
      There was a *party*, a *concert*, an *arrest*.   (= event noun)
      *A *car*, a *bag*, a *cat*, a *bed* happened.   (= entity noun)

Nouns such as *car, bag, cat, bed* cannot supply an answer to the question posed, because they do not make reference to something that "happens" in time, namely, to an event. Therefore, this test is very useful, although it fails to detect nouns denoting states (such as *tiredness, peace*, etc.), which, as Lyons (1977: 441) appropriately observes, are those second-order nouns that most resemble first-order ones. States do not happen in time, but last in time; therefore a test for durative eventualities such as states is the following: "Peace in the country lasted 500 years."

Another useful test to detect event nouns is their compatibility with adjectives such as *frequent* or *occasional* and preposition such as *during* or *after*, i.e. expressions that select the temporal component which characterizes the meaning of such nouns.

**(11)**  A frequent visit, trip, complaint...     (= event noun)
      *A frequent car, cat, pen, ....     (= entity noun)

**(12)**  During the party, the exhibition .....     (= event noun)
      *During the car, cat, pen, ....     (= entity noun)

> As we saw in Chapter 3, nouns denoting concrete entities may occasionally be coerced to an event reading in context. In this case, these nouns are reinterpreted as one of the conventional activities in which the referent of the noun typically participates. For example, "a frequent train" can be interpreted as a train service which runs frequently.
>
> **(13)**  A frequent train.     (= non-event noun coerced to event noun)

Let us now attempt to identify subclasses for event nouns, as we did for entity nouns. For this purpose, we will use two criteria we already used for classifying verbs: valency structure and *Aktionsart*. We begin with valency structure and then turn to *Aktionsart*.

As regards valency structure, event nouns, like verbs, may take arguments. The main structural difference with verbs is that while verbs "project" their arguments at the sentence level, nouns "project" their arguments at the level of the noun phrase. This is illustrated in (14) for the verb *translate* (14a) and the corresponding action noun *translation* (14b):

**(14)**  a. John translated the book into English.
      b. John's translation of the book into English...

The arguments of an event noun introduce the participants in the event denoted by the noun, and their number and type is defined by how the event is encoded in the noun's meaning. For example, the derived nominal *translation* takes two arguments, the source and the author, and perhaps two additional ones, which can be left implicit, encoding the source and target language:

**(15)**    The translation of the bible (from Hebrew into Latin) by a conservative scholar . . .

---

Entity nouns such as *dog* and *chair* are thought of as not taking arguments. However, if one assumes a rich semantic structure for nouns as that illustrated in section 3.5 under the heading of qualia relations (or roles), one may claim that the complements of entity nouns are arguments to the noun, albeit indirectly, that is, as arguments of the predicates conventionally associated with the noun's primary denotation. To clarify this point, consider the following contrast.

**(16)**    a. Dave's book is interesting.
      b. Dave's dive was spectacular.
      c. Dave's train is late.

In the expression "Dave's book," "Dave's" can denote various types of semantic relations. For example, Dave can be the book's owner, the person who lends it to the speaker or he can be the author, in which case, *Dave* might be said to be the subject argument of the act of writing, which is an action conventionally associated with the noun *book*. Whatever the case, the relation at stake between Dave and the *book* in (a) cannot be clearly identified outside of its context of use. By contrast, in the expression "Dave's dive" (which contains the event noun *dive*), Dave is identified with the agent of the event expressed by the noun *dive* and not, for example, with the person who witnessed the event of diving performed by somebody else (of course he could also be the inventor of the type of dive—as in "the triple back somersault with pike and twist was first performed by Dave at the 1948 Olympics and referred to as Dave's dive ever after"). Finally, with "Dave's train," the train is very likely the train that Dave wants to catch, or the one he is traveling on.

*(continued)*

---

**Table 4.9.** Classes of event nouns on the basis of the number of arguments

| Noun Classes | Nouns | Examples |
|---|---|---|
| No-slot Nouns | *storm* | The storm lasted two hours |
| One-slot Nouns | *birth, dive* | Our son's$_1$ birth occurred in June; Dave's$_1$ dive was spectacular. |
| Two-slot Nouns | *phone call, fear* | The president's$_1$ phone call *to the prime minister*$_2$ lasted ten minutes; Paul's$_1$ fear *of dogs*$_2$ was evident. |
| Three-slot Nouns | *transfer* | The transfer *of funds*$_1$ *from one account*$_2$ *to another*$_3$ took three days. |

> Again, no clear disambiguation is possible outside the context of use; on the other end, as with "Dave's book," the set of possible interpretations appears to be constrained by the activities that are conventionally associated with the denotation of noun, in this case *train* (catching, traveling).

On the basis of the number of arguments, it is possible to identify four main classes of event nouns. These are illustrated in Table 4.9.

No-slot nouns such as *storm* have no arguments. The best candidates for this class are nouns expressing natural events or phenomena. One-slot nouns denote events with one argument. This argument can play an active role, as *Dave* in "Dave's dive," or a passive role. The label "passive" covers all non-active roles, including experiencers, such as Mary in "Mary's astonishment." Two-slot nouns take two arguments; one of these can be considered the "subject" of the noun. The subject should be understood as the argument with higher structural prominence; we return to this in a moment. Again, the subject can play an active role, as in the case of "the president's phone call," where the president is the participant who initiates the event of calling, or a passive role, as in the case of "Paul's fear," in which *Paul* is the experiencer of the state of fear. Finally, three-slot nouns, such as *transfer*, can be said to take three arguments.

It is important to realize that although event nouns take arguments by virtue of their relational meaning, the syntactic expression of their arguments is not obligatory as with verbs. Argument-taking nouns very often appear without their complements, without causing the noun phrases in which they appear to be syntactically incomplete. For example, all the expressions in (17) lack one or more arguments, but are nevertheless well formed:

**(17)**   The dive was spectacular. (agent is lacking)
The phone call lasted ten minutes. (agent and recipient are lacking)
Paul's fear was justified. (cause is lacking)

The fact that event nouns regularly omit their arguments (as opposed to verbs which do that more occasionally) has led many scholars to doubt that for nouns one can actually speak of valency or argument structure as for verbs (see section 4.4.1.2). It has also been noted, however, that even if the arguments of an event noun do not show up in the sentence, they are semantically implied and must be recovered for the sentence to be interpreted. That is, one may choose not to express the agent of a diving event as in (a), but an agent must be present in the semantic interpretation of the expression in (a) for the diving event to be true.

There appear to be different degrees to which a noun's argument may, syntactically, be omitted, determined by the noun's relational strength. That is, when an event noun is highly relational (i.e. largely dependent on its argument(s) for its interpretation), arguments rarely remain unexpressed. This is illustrated in (18):

**(18)**   The city supported the construction.
The city supported the allocation. (of what?)

In (18) *construction* comes without the thing being constructed but the expression is totally acceptable. By contrast, with *allocation* the expression is felt as incomplete. The sentence leaves an open question: *allocation* of what? In this case, we can say that the noun *allocation* is highly relational (i.e. highly dependent on its argument for its interpretation) and its status is similar to that of a verb, which is the relational class of words by definition.

When it is expressed, the argument of a noun cannot be realized as a direct complement; it must always be introduced by a prepositional phrase. To illustrate this point, compare the English verbal expressions "to translate a book" "to analyze the problem," or "to refuse a request" with the corresponding nominal expressions: "the translation *of* the book," "the analysis *of* the problem," "the refusal *of* the request." The same holds for Italian, where the default preposition to introduce a nominal argument is *di*

+ article: "la traduzione *del* libro," "l'analisi *del* problema," etc. Other ways to express a noun's arguments include the so-called Saxon genitive in English ("Jack's phone call"), possessive adjectives ("his phone call)," and relational adjectives, such as *governmental* ("the governmental decision"). Relational adjectives are denominal adjectives, i.e. adjectives obtained by the adjunction of an adjectival suffix to a noun (on the syntax of argument structure for nouns, see Grimshaw 1990 and Alexiadou 2001).

The fact that all arguments of a noun must be introduced by a preposition reduces the structural difference which exists in the verbal domain between the subject and the object argument, and leads to potential ambiguities in the interpretation of the role played by the arguments in the event expressed by the noun. To illustrate this point, consider the nominal expression "fear of the people." Although the argument "of the people" is naturally interpreted as the object of the corresponding verb *fear*, the expression also allows for interpreting it as the subject (that is, as experiencing the fear).

As we argued earlier, for nouns it is difficult to identify the number of arguments because they are not regularly expressed as the arguments of verbs. In the case of deverbal nouns, one could assume in the first instance that the derived noun inherits the argument structure of the corresponding base verb, in terms of both number of arguments and structural relations among them. Up to now, we have followed this assumption. On closer analysis, however, this appears to be dubious. To illustrate this point, consider the English verb *demolish* as in (19a) and compare it with the derived noun *demolition* and with the noun phrases in which *demolition* may appear (19b and 19c):

**(19)**    a. The local authority demolished the building.
        b. Before the building's demolition, its status as a historical monument was revoked.
        c. *Before the local authority's demolition, the building's status as a historical monument was revoked.

The examples in (19) show that with *demolition*, the most natural argument in pre-nominal position is the argument which realizes the object of the corresponding verb. The subject of the verb appears to be expressible only by means of a *by*-phase, and only under the condition that the patient be also expressed and that the order of expression be patient–agent. This is illustrated also in (20b) and (20c).

**(20)**  a. The population tried to delay the demolition of the building by the
city council.
b. *The population tried to delay the demolition by the city council
of the building.
c. ?*The population tried to delay the demolition by the city council.

With English event nouns, the argument expressed in pre-nominal
position usually corresponds to the subject of the corresponding verb. On
this basis, examples like (19) have often been analyzed as **nominal passives**,
that is, constructions where the "alleged" object of the noun has been moved
to subject position (cf. Chomsky 1970; for an overview, Alexiadou 2001: 89
ff.). It might be argued, however, that nouns like *demolition* are inherently
passive, i.e. that their meaning focuses on the participant who undergoes the
effects of the action (*patient-oriented* event nouns). In this view, the argument structure of *demolition* could be said to be construed with the patient
as the argument with highest structural prominence. Given that the argument with highest structural prominence is considered to be the subject,
following this analysis, the argument structure of *demolition* and that of the
corresponding verb *demolish* would not be equivalent.

Not all event nouns derived from two-slot transitive verbs behave like
*demolition*, however. *Classification*, for example, allows for both patients
and agents in pre-nominal position, as shown in (21b) and (21c). In this case,
we can say that the noun is silent with respect to the interpretation of
the entity in the pre-nominal genitive, and that its argument structure is
underspecified as regards the relations of prominence holding among the
arguments.

**(21)**  a. Darwin classified the species.
b. *Darwin's* classification of species introduced a dynamic view to
Linnaeus' classification.
c. The *species'* classification evolved during time from static to
dynamic.

The conclusion we can draw from the previous discussion is that
event nouns, like verbs, may focus on specific aspects of the event they
denote. For example, nouns may pick out only some of the event
participants as arguments, and assign structural prominence to one of
them at the expense of others. If the structural prominence thus
assigned differs from the one assigned by the base verb, the argument

structure of the noun and that of the corresponding verb can be said to diverge.

A second criterion for identifying classes of event nouns is that of *Aktionsart*. On the basis of *Aktionsart* nouns can be divided into the four basic classes listed in Table 4.10 (see section 4.4.1.3 for further discussion).

**State-denoting nouns** denote situations that extend in time but do not entail changes in their participants (therefore they are not dynamic) nor a culminating point (therefore they are not telic). Typical examples are nouns denoting psychological or physical states of people (*fear, anger, courage, richness*, etc.).

**Nouns of indefinite process** denote dynamic events consisting of an indefinite number of phases that follow one another and do not tend towards a goal or end point (therefore they are not telic). In English, these nouns are represented by the *-ing* form of the verb (such as *swimming* in "The water was warm and the swimming was wonderful"), while in Romance languages, as we saw above, it is rather the nominalized form of the verbal infinitive that expresses indefinite processes. This particular type of noun leaves the event open with regard to its duration, more so than other nouns; the event is shown as ongoing.

**Table 4.10.** Classes of event nouns based on *Aktionsart* properties

| Noun classes | Dynamicity | Duration | Telicity | Examples |
|---|---|---|---|---|
| **State-denoting nouns** | − | + | − | *fear, richness* |
| **Nouns of indefinite process** | + | + | − | *swimming* |
| **Nouns of definite process** | + | + | +/− | *walk, construction* |
| **Punctual nouns** | + | − | + | *start* |

**Nouns of definite process** can be grouped in two main categories. Nouns of the first type (*walk, discussion*) denote durative homogeneous events and that can be said to have occurred even if they are interrupted (i.e. "The walk has been interrupted" entails that "The walk took place"). Nouns of the second type, on the other hand, denote durative events whose constitutive phases are not homogeneous. For example, the noun *construction* denotes a process in which the state of the object being built changes progressively as the phases of the event proceed, and we cannot properly say that the building has taken place, until the object has been completed (Parsons 1990). Both these nouns types denote **bounded** events, but only nouns of the second type can be said to denote events that are telic proper, that is, events that encode a goal.

**Punctual nouns** denote an event that ends at the same instant in which it begins, in that it does not take place over a period of time but at a point in time; therefore, we can say that it culminates at the point in time in which it occurs (*start, arrival, refusal, departure*). The event expressed by these nouns may, of course, involve preliminary phases. For example, we can say "His arrival took longer than expected," and refer to the sum of occurrences that took place before he arrived, and delayed his expected arrival time. As with punctual verbs, the standard assumption is, however, that these preliminary circumstances are not part of the semantics of the noun, and that the noun expresses an instantaneous transition between two different states (for *arrival*, the two states would be "not being in a certain location" and "being in a certain location").

Yet another class of nouns is that of **semelfactive** (or **point**) **nouns**. These nouns denote a special kind of punctual event, that is, a momentary happening that usually constitutes a single instance of a larger event. For example, a *flash* or a *hiccup* denotes a single instance of a potential process consisting of repeated instances (as in "multiple flash technique"). In other words, the event denoted by point nouns allows for repetition, while still maintaining the property of uniqueness from a referential point of view. Note that by contrast, the event denoted by punctual nouns such as *arrival* and *departure*, if repeated, cannot form a larger event; they are different events.

> Semelfactive nouns are not included in Table 4.10; their classification involves an additional feature, namely iterativity associated with uniqueness, and their status with respect to telicity is unclear (Smith 1991 for example analyses them as atelic).

Some scholars believe that nouns like *sip* and *step* also belong to semelfactive nouns, because they denote single occurrences of an activity. A *sip*, they claim, is a single instance of a *drink*, a *step* of a *walk*, a *flap* of *a flight*, a *stroke* of a *swim*, etc. (Simone 2003). As noted in Simone (2003: 903), in Arabic a single root is used for both types of nouns (activity vs. point):

**(22)**   *-sh-r-b-*      'to drink'
     *sh-u-r-b*      'the activity of drinking'
     *sh-a-r-b-at*  'each individual act of drinking = sip'

In classic Arabic grammar, the noun indicating the single occurrence is called *ismu al-marrati*, lit. 'noun of once.'

To detect the *Aktionsart* of a noun we can apply the syntactic tests we use for verbs (cf. section 4.4.1.3), with some adjustments. For example, to establish whether a noun refers to an event that extends in time, we can verify whether it is compatible with expressions such as "last for *x* time":

**(23)**   Her happiness lasted for days.
     The dancing lasted till 2am.
     The walk lasted three hours.
     The construction will last six months.
     *The departure lasted 10 minutes.

This test shows that punctual nouns, such as *departure*, don't go well with these expressions (and, in fact, in Table 4.10, they are the only ones that are not durative).

To identify the properties of the different types of durative nouns—for example, whether or not they are dynamic—we can further verify whether they are compatible with expressions such as "it happened / it took place / it occurred." By definition, only that which is dynamic can happen or take place:

**(24)**   *Her happiness took place in the afternoon.
     The dancing will take place in the ballroom.
     The walk took place yesterday.
     The construction will take place in the winter.
     Departures occurred every 30 minutes.

Note that only *happiness*, a state-denoting noun, does not admit these expressions.

Once we know that a noun denotes a dynamic situation, we may perform other tests to verify whether it refers to an indefinite or definite process and, in the latter case, whether it is only temporally bounded, or bounded and telic. For nouns, the tests for **boundedness** rely on the acknowledged parallel between the bounded/unbounded distinction in the verbal domain and the count/mass distinction in the nominal domain (dating back to Bach 1986).

Assuming this parallel, to establish whether a noun denotes a bounded or unbounded event we can check which type of determination it is compatible with. Consider (25):

(25)   a. *We did three swimmings. (unbounded)
       b. We took several walks during the holiday. (bounded)

Nouns denoting unbounded processes such as *swimming* behave as mass nouns and cannot be pluralized, whereas nouns denoting bounded processes such as *walk* can be pluralized.

As for telicity, one can instead verify whether the event can be said to have occurred even though it is interrupted. If it can, the event is not telic; if it cannot, it is telic.

(26)   a. My morning walk was interrupted but I enjoyed it anyway. (atelic)
       b. *The construction [of the bridge] was interrupted but it was visible
          from everywhere. (telic)

We can see that nouns like *walk* yield positive results in the context of *interrupt,* while nouns like *construction* do not.

Let us now focus briefly on the differences and similarities of *Aktionsart* between event nouns and the corresponding base verbs. As with argument structure, one might in the first instance assume a one-to-one correspondence between the *Aktionsart* of a verb and that of its corresponding deverbal noun. For example, one might assume that a verb denoting an indefinite process will yield a noun with the same actional properties. Close scrutiny of this assumption, however, reveals that it is only partially correct. Event nouns may exhibit shifts in the *Aktionsart* value of their base verbs. The type of shift appears to depend on the nominalization strategy at play. For example, as we argued earlier, nominalization attained through the *-ing* strategy in English appears to convey nouns that focus on the progression of the event. This appears to be a general property of *-ing* nominalizations, independently of the actional value of the base verb. That is, although the *-ing* suffix occurs more naturally with nouns denoting indefinite processes, it may also combine with verbs denoting bounded events and act as an unbounding device, defocusing the end state. Because of this characteristic, the *-ing* form is often used in English in place of the "standard" action noun (if it is available), when one wants to focus on the ongoing nature of the event. This is illustrated in (27), where the *-ing* form of the punctual verb *depart* is contrasted with the action noun *departure*:

**(27)**   One day before the *departing* of the ships, . . . (focus on the ongoing
aspect of the event)
One day before the *departure* of the ships, . . .

On the other hand, conversion appears to be a nominalization strategy
which yields the opposite actional value, i.e. boundedness. To illustrate this,
consider the verb *walk*, which denotes an indefinite process, and compare it
with its nominalized form in (25a) which denotes only a bounded portion of
the process.

## 4.5. Word class systems across languages

In this section, we turn to the analysis of systems of word classes in the
languages of the world. All the languages of the world have more than one
word class, but not all languages have the same number of classes, nor the
same classes. As for closed classes (pronouns, conjunctions, prepositions,
articles), we have already mentioned the example of Latin, which lacks the
class of articles (another language with no articles is modern Russian). As
for open classes (nouns, verbs, adjectives, and adverbs), Yurok (a language spoken in Northwest California) and Samoan (an Austronesian
language) are often cited as two examples of languages, which, according
to R. Dixon (1977, 55), have no adjectives (we will return to this observation below; for an in-depth discussion of these aspects, see Schachter
1985).
To be able to compare languages with respect to their word classes it
is first necessary to establish a term of comparison, that is, a universally
valid criterion that allows one to clearly identify the kind and number
of word classes a language has (we will call the set of these properties
its **word class system**) and to compare them with those of other
languages.
The operation of establishing the *tertium comparationis* (i.e. the
neutral background against which a comparison between languages
can be made) is complex because, as we saw in Chapter 2, the distinction between word classes is achieved in different ways in individual
languages, namely by lexical, morphologic, and/or syntactical means.

An ideal language from this point of view is one that has a different lexical root for each single word belonging to a different class (that is, a root for each noun, a root for each verb, and so on). A language that comes close to this ideal is Tunumiisut, an Inuit dialect spoken on the east coast of Greenland. In this language, as P. Mennecier (1995) noted, there is a fairly clear opposition between the two classes of root radicals, which are either exclusively nominal or exclusively verbal.

A language of this type, however, is rare. In most languages, one and the same lexical root is used to form words that belong to different classes. As we saw in section 4.1, this is achieved either by inflection and derivation, as in German and in the Romance languages, or by conversion, as in English. For example, the root *nag-* 'swim' is used in French to form *la nage* (noun) and *nager* (verb), while in English the equivalent word is inserted in different syntactic environments without modifying its form, as in "go for a *swim*" (noun) and "*swim* in the lake" (verb).

The classical approach to word class distinction defines word classes on the basis of morphological analysis (cf. section 4.2). However, there is a widespread consensus nowadays that morphological modification is neither a desirable nor a sufficient criterion to ground the identification of classes of words, especially if the ultimate goal is to compare systems of word classes across languages. Central to this claim is the observation that there exist languages that lack a morphology almost entirely and languages that, despite having morphology, do not distinguish word classes through modification of form but rather on syntactic grounds. Finally, morphological systems of languages vary widely, and the kind of modifications adopted to draw word class distinctions may be very different from language to language.

Not even the semantic (or notional or ontological) criterion appears to be the most appropriate for comparing languages and, in fact, it is probably the weakest from a cross-linguistic perspective. Recall that this criterion relies on the identification of correspondences between the categories of the outside world (as we perceive them) and the word classes, such as between concrete entities and nouns, between actions and verbs, and so on (section 4.3). However, this criterion has long been recognized as not sufficient, not even within a single language; there are nouns that denote events, verbs that denote states, and so forth. As we saw in section 4.3, in spite of this, linguists such as J. Lyons put a lot of effort into developing a hierarchical classification of concepts (concrete, abstract; derived; first-order, second-order, etc.) with the goal of enhancing this criterion, and defused criticisms by appealing to notions such as *focal subclass*. These are extremely interesting generalizations, but from the point of view of the cross-linguistic comparison the notional criterion remains weak.

As it happens, the most appropriate criterion to identify word class systems for individual languages, and to compare them with those of other languages, appears to be the syntactic criterion. Unlike morphology, there is in fact no doubt that all languages have a minimal syntactical organization and that this organization tends to reflect three major universal functions of language: introducing referents in the discourse; asserting something about them; modifying them (see section 4.3 for discussion). For example, in the expression "The car stopped suddenly," *car* introduces the referent, *stop* asserts what happened to it, and *suddenly* modifies the event, while the underlying cause of the stopping is left silent.

A well-known classification of word class systems based primarily on syntactic principles is the one proposed by K. Hengeveld (first illustrated in Hengeveld 1992; for an overview, see Hengeveld et al. 2004). This classification is based on the analysis of a sample of 40 languages representing a high degree of genetic and geographic diversity, and proves to be particularly helpful from a cross-linguistic perspective.

The basic idea of Hengeveld's proposal is that in all languages, independently of their morphological organization, it is possible to identify the class(es) of a word by looking at two distinct but related features:

(a) the function that the word plays in the syntactic unit it may occupy, that is, whether it is the head of that unit or the modifier;
(b) the function of the syntactical unit in which the word may be used, that is, whether it is a unit with predicative function (= a predicate phrase) or with referential function (= a referential phrase).

The intersection of these two criteria enables Hengeveld to identify four syntactic positions: head and modifier or a referential phrase, and head and modifier of a predicate phrase. These correspond to the positions typically occupied by verbs, nouns, adjectives, and adverbs, which may accordingly be defined as follows:

- verb = a word that can be used as the head of a syntactic unit with predicative function (predicate phrase);
- noun = a word that can be used as the head of a syntactical unit with a referential function (referential phrase);
- adjective = a word that can be used as a modifier within a syntactical unit with referential function;
- adverb = a word that can be used as a modifier within modifier of a syntactical unit with predicative function.

Table 4.11 summarizes what we have said thus far.

According to Hengeveld, it is possible to distinguish three major types of word class systems in the world's languages by looking at the different ways in which the words of each language may fill the slots in Table 4.11 (it should be noted that for adverbs, Hengeveld only takes into account the class of manner adverbs). These are (a) differentiated, (b) flexible, and (c) rigid systems.

**Differentiated systems** are systems of languages that have four distinct classes of lexical items to fill each of the syntactical positions in the table. According to the author, English is a case in point, as illustrated in the example below:

(28)    The little$_{\text{ADJECTIVE}}$ girl$_{\text{NOUN}}$ danced$_{\text{VERB}}$ beautifully$_{\text{ADVERB}}$

In English there are of course many cases of conversions between classes, as we discussed above; yet, this does not change the fact that there are well-defined distinct classes of words for each syntactic position. For this reason, these languages may be said to be *specialized languages*.

**Flexible systems** are typical of languages that do not have four separate classes of lexical items, that is, one dedicated to each slot of Table 4.11, but have fewer. Nevertheless, they are languages whose lexical items are able to cover all positions in the grid in the table, because they are polyfunctional, i.e. they have the ability to occupy more than one slot, so that no slot ever remains empty. Dutch, for example, has been claimed to be a language

**Table 4.11.** Words and syntactic slots

|  | Head | Modifier |
|---|---|---|
| **Predicate phrase** | verb | manner adverb |
| **Referential phrase** | noun | adjective |

where the distinction between adjective and manner adverb is absent (in fact, there appear to be some residual morphological distinctions that for purposes of simplification we do not consider here):

**(29)** Dutch   Een *mooi* kind.
'a beautiful child'

Het kind danst *mooi*.
'the child dances in a beautiful way'

As the examples show, the word *mooi* in Dutch may function both as adjective and as adverb; the same lexical item covers two of the functions of the table. This is systematic in the Dutch language.

A group of languages with an extremely flexible system of lexical classes is that of the Austronesian languages. In these languages, the same word may fill up to all four of the syntactic positions in Table 4.11. That is to say, depending on the context the same word can serve as a verb, a noun, an adjective, or an adverb, with no modification of its form. Consider for instance Samoan, a language spoken in the central South Pacific, in a group of islands forming part of Polynesia. In this language, the same lexical item *lā* can be used for example as a verb (that is, head of the predicate phrase) or as a noun (head of the referential phrase) (the example is taken from Hengeveld et al. 2004: 535):

**(30)** Samoan   Ua   mālosi   le   lā              lā = noun
         INGR   strong   ART   sun
         (lit. the sun strongs)
         'the sun is strong'

         Ua   lā   le   aso              lā = verb
         INGR   sun   ART   day
         (lit. the day suns)
         'the day is sunny'

**Rigid systems** are typical of languages that, like languages with flexible systems, do not distinguish between four basic classes (they too are *nonspecialized* languages). Unlike languages with flexible systems, however, words in languages with rigid systems do not have the ability to cover the functions of the missing classes, i.e. they are not flexible or polyfunctional. As a consequence, certain syntactic positions may remain empty and the corresponding categories are simply lacking. Hengeveld notes that to the best of our knowledge there exists no purely rigid language, that is, a language with a single class of words that may cover only one of the functions in Table 4.11. A group of languages often cited as being extremely rigid is, however, the group of the Iroquoian languages. Iroquoian languages, such as Tuscarora, are very much oriented toward a single lexical class, that of the verb. These languages have few nouns, and because verbs cannot perform a nominal function (unlike what happens in Samoan) a predication is often used to express a concept which is typically encoded by a noun in English, such as, for example *boy* = 'he is young'.

(31)  Tuscarora    ra-kwa:tihs
                   M.SUBJ-young
                   (lit. he is young)
                   'boy'

Thus, Tuscarora often uses verbs rather than nouns, whereas Samoan combines the functions of verbs and nouns in a single class of lexical items.
    The situation can be summarized as in Table 4.12.

**Table 4.12.** Flexible, differentiated, and rigid languages

| Extremely flexible class system | verb / noun / adjective / adverb | | | Samoan |
|---|---|---|---|---|
| Fairly flexible class system | verb | noun | adjective / adverb | Dutch |
| Differentiated class system | verb | noun | adjective | adverb | English |
| Extremely rigid class system | verb | — | — | — | (not attested) |

Table 4.12 only captures four types of languages, one of which is not attested. Some languages, however, appear to occupy intermediate positions between these types, that is to say, they show different degrees of flexibility or rigidity. According to Hengeveld, if we include these intermediate systems (Tuscarora falls among these), the total number of types is seven (more examples can be found in Hengeveld et al. 2004).

Words of languages with a flexible system have a high degree of elasticity. Not being tied to a particular function in the construction of predications, they are polyfunctional. Words of languages with a rigid system are, instead, specialized for a single syntactic function.

Interestingly, the combinations of syntactic possibilities for a single lexical class in flexible languages and the lack of lexical classes for certain syntactic functions in rigid languages are not random, but can be described in terms of the following hierarchy.

(32)   Word Class Hierarchy
       Verb > Noun > Adjective > Adverb

This hierarchy represents an implicational scale which, according to Hengeveld, is able to predict the word class system of a language depending on the degree of *flexibility* or *rigidity* exhibited by its lexical items. The hierarchy can be interpreted in many ways. One is the following: if a rigid language lacks adjectives, it will also lack adverbs; if a flexible language has a class of words which can be used both as nouns and as adjectives, it will also be possible to use these words as adverbs. By locating nouns and verbs on the left side of the implicational scale, the hierarchy acknowledges the universal character of these classes compared with the other two. In other words, the scale predicts that when a language lacks one or more word classes, nouns and verbs are the last ones to be lacking.

## Further reading

Lexical categories are discussed in Baker (2003).

On the relation between ontology and the lexicon: from a linguistic perspective, Lyons (1977), Givón (1979), Dik (1997, 136 ff.); from a cognitive perspective, Murphy (2010), chapter 7; in a computational perspective see Hirst (2004) and Huang et al. (2010).

On the correlations between syntactic and semantic properties of unaccusative and unergative verbs, see Van Valin (1990) for Italian and Levin and Rappaport Hovav (1995) for English.

On subcategorization frames for English, see the list compiled within the VerbNet project (Kipper Schuler 2005).

On semelfactives, Smith (1991).

On points, Moens and Steedman (1988).

On scalar analysis of verbs, Hay, Kennedy and Levin (1999), Beavers
(2008), Rappaport Hovav (2008).

A constructive critique to a syntax-informed approach to verb semantic
classification can be found in Boas (2011).

The correlations between modes of determinations and noun classification
are examined in detail in Löbner (2011).

On result nouns, Melloni (2012).

On semantic relations in the English Saxon genitive construction, see Asher
(2011).

# 5

# Paradigmatic structures
# in the lexicon

In this chapter we focus on semantic relations between words. We first examine the relations holding between words that tend to "compete" with each other in the same context and can therefore be said to form a *lexical paradigm* or *lexical set*, as in {*read* / *leaf through* / *skim*} *a book*. In order, the relations we introduce are: hyperonymy/hyponymy (extended to troponymy for verbs); meronymy/holonymy; synonymy; near-synonymy; opposition. Then, we shift our attention to relations between words that do not compete with each other (and are therefore not strictly paradigmatic) but are equally relevant from the point of view of the semantic organization of the lexicon. These are: cause, purpose and temporal entailment. We exclude syntagmatic relations, which will be examined in Chapter 6.

## 5.1. What counts as a paradigmatic relation?

To understand what counts as a paradigmatic relation we must first clarify the meaning of the term *paradigmatic*, as it is used in the study of language.

The first use of this term is often attributed to the Swiss linguist Ferdinand de Saussure, although, as we shall see shortly, Saussure actually used the term *associative*, which has a broader scope than what we today call *paradigmatic*. In fact it was the Danish linguist L. Hjelmslev who coined the term *paradigmatic* as a refinement of Saussure's *rapports associatifs* (Hjelmslev 1961).

Saussure introduced the term *associative* in his effort to classify the relations that exist between two or more elements in a language. These elements may be of different types: words, morphemes, sounds, syntactic structures, and so forth. According to Saussure, the relations between these elements are instead of two types only, namely *associative* or *syntagmatic*. In the rest of this section, we first introduce associative relations, then define syntagmatic ones. Finally, we show how by considering both dimensions together, a specific form of associative relation can be identified, called *paradigmatic*.

An **associative** relation (in the Saussurian sense) is a relation that holds between two or more linguistic elements (in the case we are considering, between two or more words) on the basis of an association. Association is a mental operation; it consists in establishing a link between words that are felt by speakers to be sharing some kind or degree of similarity. According to Saussure, there are two main types of associative relations among words; those based on the words' forms, and those based on the words' meanings. An association of the first type (form-based associations) generates sets of words that either share the lexical morpheme, as in *book, booklet, booking*, or the derivational morpheme, as in *truly, amply, fortunately, happily*. In some cases, however, form-based associations are not grounded on morphological structure but rather on pure sound similarity, such as is the case with the set *big, pig, fig*. Associations based on a word's meaning create instead sets of words such as the following:

**(1)**   *book, volume, dictionary, diary, album, novel, library, bookstore, read, consult, chapter, page, paper, index, publisher, writer.*

In this case, what brings the words together is not a formal feature as in the previous cases but rather one or more aspects of their meaning. Specifically, all of the words in (1) denote objects and actions that have something to do with the object denoted by the word *book*: similar objects (*album, diary, dictionary, novel, volume*), physical parts (*page, sheet*), information parts (*index, chapter, section*), constituent material (*paper*), typical actions (*read, consult*), creators (*publisher, writer*), typical setting (*library, bookstore*), and so forth.

---

We said above that associative relations between words are normally based on similarities either of form or of meaning, but in reality these two dimensions are often available at the same time in a given association. Consider for example the words *book* (*x*) and *bookstore* (*y*). These two words can be said to hold both a formal relation (determined by the presence of the morpheme *book*) and a semantic relation of location, which can be roughly represented as follows:

(2)  $x$ = object which is sold in $y$.
 $y$ = place in which $x$ is sold.

Research on language acquisition has shown that form-based or meaning-based associations seem to play a different role in the learning process. Particularly, it has been claimed that beginners memorize words primarily by associating them on the basis of their formal resemblance, whereas advanced learners tend to memorize words by associating them on the basis of their content (for example, by linking *purse* with *bag, backpack, briefcase,* and so forth). This can be easily explained by the fact that in the early stages of acquisition learners do not know the meaning of words and therefore are capable of activating form-based associations only.

---

The notion of associative relation can be conceived very broadly, including within its scope any association between words that a speaker is able to establish, based on his/her lexical competence; in example (1) above we have taken this view, and included words such as *author, paper, read* in the set of words prompted by the associations with the word *book*. This is not, however, the way Saussure approached the notion. For Saussure, associative relations are defined by contrasting them with another kind of relation that exists between words in a language, namely the syntagmatic relation. In the context of lexical analysis, a **syntagmatic relation** is the relation that holds between terms that can occur together linearly in an expression, to form complex linguistic units such as phrases, sentences, and texts; particularly between terms that stand in an intimate syntactic relationship, such as "subject of," "object of," "modifier of," and so forth. For example, a syntagmatic relation can be said to exist between the adjective *big* and the nouns *book* and *crowd* so that the two may occur together and form expressions such as those in (3):

**(3)**   It is a big book.
It is a big crowd.

Note that in the two expressions, the meaning of the adjective *big* is dependent on the relation at play. That is, in the context of *book*, *big* means 'consisting of many pages,' whereas in the context of *crowd*, it means 'consisting of many people'.

If we now consider both relation types as defined above (associative and syntagmatic), we can narrow the definition of associative relation and finally arrive at the notion of paradigmatic relation. **Paradigmatic** relations are special kinds of associative relations, namely those holding among words that can be substituted for each other in the same context. For example, the empty slot in the sentence "I read the ____ you wrote two years ago" may be filled by the word *book* or such other words as *volume* or *novel*, but not such words as *bookstore*, nor by words such as *table* or *thought*, and so forth. The set of words that can be inserted successfully in the same syntagmatic context constitutes **lexical paradigm** (or **set**). An example of nominal lexical paradigm for the verb *read* in the context above is *book*/*volume*/*novel*. Lexical paradigms involve words that share many semantic properties, but differ in some.

The sum of the paradigmatic relations that exists between the words of a language constitutes its paradigmatic dimension. In a narrow sense, these relations are *in absentia*, in that they concern words that are alternatives to each other in the same context. According to L. Hjelmslev (1961: 36) a paradigmatic relation is such if it responds to an *either/or* function: either we have one element or we have another. The sum of syntagmatic relationships that exists between the words of a language constitutes, instead, its syntagmatic (or horizontal) dimension. In this case, the relation is *in praesentia* or, in Hjelmslev's terminology, it is a *both/and* relation, because the words may co-occur.

The paradigmatic and syntagmatic dimensions of a language are relevant in several ways. They provide us with a framework to analyze lexical phenomena and to make hypotheses of how the lexicon of a language is structured and operates in use. For example, it allows us to claim that when performing a speech act, the speaker selects elements from the paradigmatic system and combines them along the syntagmatic chain.

By examining paradigmatic relations closely, it is possible to represent the lexicon of a given language as an organized set of form-based or meaning-based networks. These networks may be seen as genuine lexical structures. Therefore, paradigmatic relations can be said to generate structures in the lexicon. In the rest of the chapter, we examine some of these relations, focusing on those based on meaning.

## 5.2. Kinds of paradigmatic relations among words

Word associations based on meaning can be of several types and they may recur more or less frequently across the vocabulary. However, the analysis of the possible substitutions of words in specific contexts allows us to identify two basic axes on which further classification can be based. These two axes represent, in a sense, a speculative hypothesis about how the lexicon is structured.

A first axis concerns **vertical relations** (or **hierarchical relations** or **relations of inclusion**), in which one of the terms is superordinate and the other one is subordinate, as in the case of *vehicle* (superordinate) and *car* (subordinate), or *car* (superordinate) and *wheel* (subordinate). As we shall see, the two cases are very different from each other. A second axis concerns **horizontal relations**, such as those of **identity** (*barrier/obstacle*) and **opposition** (*long/short*), in which the terms are not in a subordinate/superordinate relation but rather on the same level.

Before going further in our survey of the main types of semantic relations between words, two points should be made. First, paradigmatic relations between words are primarily associations between meanings, and only secondarily associations between words. Polysemous words, in fact, activate different relations for each meaning; for example the adjective *big* associates with *substantial* or *massive* in its 'large' sense (as in "a big building"), with *bad* in its 'intense' sense (as in "a big headache"), with *important* in its 'significant' sense (as in "a big decision"), and so forth. Second, paradigmatic relations are relations between lexical items that belong to the same word class (for example, noun/noun, adjective/adjective, verb/verb and so forth). On the other hand, associative relations go beyond word classes and may occur between elements that belong to different classes. The following are examples involving verb–noun pairings: *leave / arrival, (to) vote / election, fall asleep / awakening*.

What follows is a description of the most basic semantic relations between words. These are: for vertical relations (a) hyperonymy/hyponymy and (b) meronymy/holonymy; for horizontal relations (a) synonymy (or identity), (b) near synonymy, and (c) opposition (antonymy, complementarity, and converse terms).

## 5.3. Relations of inclusion: hyperonymy/hyponymy; meronymy/holonymy

The hyperonymy/hyponymy relation (for example that existing between *vehicle/car*, *move/walk*, *close/lock*) links two words, one of which (the **hyponym** or *subordinate*) has a more specific meaning than the other (the **hyperonym** or *superordinate*), in the sense that its meaning consists of the meaning of the hyperonym plus some additional features. For example, the meaning of *car* can be paraphrased as (vehicle) + (with engine) + (with four wheels), etc.; the meaning of *walk* can be defined as (move) + (on foot); the meaning of *lock* can be described as (close) + (using a lock) and so forth.

The hyperonymy/hyponymy relation can be examined not only from the point of view of the meanings but also from the point of view of the referents of the words. From this perspective, we can say that the referent of the hyponym is a subtype of (or a kind of) the referent of the hyperonym. This is illustrated in Figure 5.1.

By examining the relations of hyperonymy/hyponymy holding between the words in a lexicon it is possible to build taxonomies, that is, classifications of words based on hierarchical principles, where there are superordinate and subordinate terms. Two fragments of taxonomies are reported in Figure 5.2.

The taxonomies in Figure 5.2 highlight the following properties of the hyperonymy/hyponymy relation:

(a) The hyperonymy/hyponomy relationship is a hierarchical relation, because the hyponym is subordinate to the hyperonym (i.e. it is a subcategory of the hyperonym);

(b) The relations between the referents of an hypernonym and its hyponyms is oriented or asymmetrical: a *car* is a type of a *vehicle*, but a *vehicle* is not a type of *car*; the logical relation of entailment underlying

**Figure 5.1** Hierarchical relations of inclusion

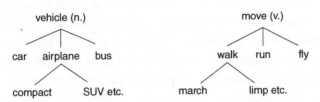

**Figure 5.2** Taxonomies based on relations of hyperonymy/hyponymy

hyponymy (also called a IS_A relation) is unilateral (*car* entails *vehicle* but not the other way round);

(c) The lexicon includes multiple levels of hyperonymy/hyponymy relations; very often, a hyponym is the hyperonym of another word;

(d) The relationship is transitive, because it allows the transfer of semantic information across levels (*property inheritance*): for this reason, we can say that *compact* denotes a type of *car* but we can also say that *compact* denotes a type of *vehicle*. The different levels correspond to a lesser or greater specificity of meaning;

(e) One hyperonym can have multiple hyponyms: these are called **co-hyponyms**. In Figure 5.2, the co-hyponyms are *car, airplane, bus; walk, run, fly; compact, SUV; march, limp*. The semantic relation between co-hyponyms (**co-hyponymy**) is different in nature from the relation between a hyperonym and its hyponym(s): it is horizontal rather than vertical, and involves contrast rather than inclusion (i.e. a car is contrasted with an airplane, a bus, and so forth). Co-hyponyms may be seen as involving roughly the same level of specificity of meaning, although this is clearly an approximation.

The standard test used to identify if two words participate in a hyperonymy/hyponymy relation is based on the criterion of inclusion holding between their referents: "$n_1$ is an $n_2$, but $n_2$ is not an $n_1$." For example, "an *SUV* is a *car* but a *car* is not an *SUV*." Another test for nouns is the following: "an $n_1$ and other types of $n_2$." For example, "an *SUV* and other types of *cars*." For verbs, an important test to identify hyponyms is based on the idea that the structuring principle for verb taxonomies is the notion of manner. The test is as follows: "to $v_1$ is to $v_2$ in a particular/certain manner." For example, "to *walk* is to *move* in a certain manner," "*to murmur* is *to talk* in a certain manner," and so forth. The term "manner" is interpreted here loosely as applicable to several aspects of the event that may be incorporated into the meaning of the hyponymous verb. Manner lexicalization in this sense involves many kinds of semantic elaborations, some of which are illustrated in (4). For verbs, the hyponymy relation is often known as **troponymy**, emphasizing the point that verb inclusion tends to be a matter of "manner" (on troponymy, see Fellbaum 2002).

(4)   Kinds of troponyms
       manner proper (*to move* vs. *to drag, to dance*)
       instrument (*to close* vs. *to button up, to lock, to latch, to hook, to tie, to strap*)
       speed (*to move* vs. *to run, to dart*)
       medium (*to move* vs. *to fly, to sail; to fax* vs. *to phone, to email*)
       intensity (*close* the door vs. *slam* the door, *whisper* vs. *shout; eat* vs. *devour*)

The hyperonymy/hyponymy relationship applies not only to simple words but also to word combinations such as *door / front door, food / junk food, dress / cocktail dress, juice / fruit juice* (see Löbner 2013: 205 on this point). That is, *a cocktail dress* is a type of *dress*, a *front door* is a type of *door*, and so forth. These are pairs of hyperonyms/hyponyms beyond any doubt. On the other hand, a *station wagon* is not a type of *wagon*, but a type of *car*.

If interpreted in a broad sense, the hyperonymy/hyponymy relation can be said to hold also among words that belong to different parts of speech. According to this interpretation, the Engl. noun *exit* (as in "facilitate the exit") may be said to be a hyponym of the verb *to go*; It. verb *colpire* ('to hit') may be interpreted as a hyperonym of noun *martellata* ('a hit with a hammer'). This is a particular interpretation of the hyponymy relation, however, and not the usual one; moreover, it does not meet the conditions of the tests we introduced above.

Although the hyperonymy/hyponymy relation is perhaps the most crucial component of the lexical architecture, it must be acknowledged that this relation is more apt to describe the relations that hold between words belonging to certain word classes than others. In particular, hyponymy is an important structuring principle in the case of nouns and verbs, though

with different modalities, as we saw above. In the case of adjectives, however, the most powerful structuring axis seems to be that of opposition. That
is, an adjective tends to be defined by opposition to something rather than as
a hyperonym or a hyponym of something; for example, *young* is characterized as the opposite of *old, dry* is characterized as the opposite of *wet*, and so
on. Nevertheless, for certain adjectives it is possible to think of a hypero-
nymy/hyponymy structure. The following is an example of hierarchy for the
adjective *colored* as opposed to white, black, or neutral (Figure 5.3).

Finally, the hyponymy relation is useful to represent the inferences that
we can make through the use of words: for example, from the fact that
someone is said to have walked we can infer that he has moved.

The two terms participating in a hyperonymy/hyponymy relation tend not to
co-occur in the same context, since they are in a paradigmatic relation with each
other. We may, however, occasionally find both terms in constructions such as
those shown in (5), where $n_1$ stands for the hyponym and $n_2$ for the hyperonym:

**(5)** Constructions for the Hyperonymy/Hyponymy relation
  $n_2$ such as $n_1$: *events* such as *lectures, walks, tours*, and *meetings*;
  such $n_2$ as $n_1$: such *areas* as *children's playground*;
  $n_1$ and other $n_2$: *rum* and other *spirits*;
  $n_1$ or other $n_2$: *insects* or other *animals*;
  $n_2$, including $n_1$: *recyclable materials* including *glass*;
  $n_2$ especially $n_1$: *cool temperate countries* especially *Europe* and *North
    America*;
  favorite $n_2$ is $n_1$: *Mario's favorite food* is *pasta*.

Constructions as in (5) are frequently exploited for the automatic extraction of
hyponymy relations from texts, for example in Cimiano and Wenderoth (2005).

A meronymy/holonymy relationship (for example, that existing between
*door handle / door, sleeve / shirt, pedal / bicycle, wheel / car, arm / body*)
connects two terms of which one (the **meronym**) denotes the part and the
other (the **holonym**) denotes the whole. It is especially terms that denote

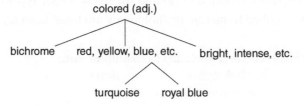

**Figure 5.3** A hyperonymy/hyponymy structure for adjectives

concrete objects (including, as we shall see, places) that often participate in a meronymic relation.

---

Defining what counts as a part of an entity goes beyond the realm of languages and occupies a prominent role in philosophy and ontology. The matter is debated especially within the theory of mereology (the study of the relation between part and whole). In a way, the word "part" may be used to indicate any portion of a given entity, regardless of whether, for example, that portion is attached to the rest of the object, as with "the handle of a door," or undetached, as "the cap of a pen." However, among ontologists it is often assumed that the "legitimate" parts of an object are those that display the following characteristics:

a. they are available in discourse as individual units;
b. they make a functional contribution to the entity they are part of;
c. they are cognitively salient.

Autonomy as individual unit and functionality with respect to the whole depend on the context of application: a *handle* is attached to *spoon* and *knife*, but detachable from *doors* and *windows*; a *handle* is functional with *knife* but not in the same way with *mug*. Cognitive salience, on the other hand, rules out arbitrarily demarcated portions of an object, such as "the lower part of the wall," which is clearly part of the wall, but not to be identified as a legitimate "part" of the wall, since it refers to a part of the wall with no clear boundaries.

   Finally, a well-formed meronymy relation consists of elements of the same general type; a part of some concrete entity will also be a concrete entity, part of some time period will also be a time period, and so forth.

---

   There are different types of relations based on meronymy/holonymy. The most typical cases consist of the relations between a whole and its constituent parts, as discussed above, and between a whole and the material it is made of. These are reported in (a) and (b) below. Other types of relations that can be ascribed to meronymy/holonymy are listed from (c) to (f):

(a)   relationship between a whole and its constituent parts:
   *hand*       is a holonym of          *finger*
   *finger*     is a meronym (part) of   *hand*

(b)  relationship between an object and the material or substance it is made of:
    *river*        is a holonym of                                *water*
    *water*      is a meronym (substance) of          *river*

(c)  relationship between a set and its members:
    *team*       is a holonym of                               *athlete*
    *athlete*    is a meronym (member) of            *team*

(d)  relationship between a whole and its natural constituents:
    *sand*       is a holonym of                               *grain*
    *grain*      is a meronym (element) of            *sand*

(e)  relationship between a whole and one of its portions:
    *bread*      is a holonym of                               *slice*
    *slice*       is a meronym (portion) of          *bread, cake*

(f)  relationship between an area and a smaller area inside it:
    *city*         is a holonym of                             *city center*
    *city center*  is a meronym (element) of           *city*

As we can see from the examples, a meronym can be a constituent part of an object, the material (or substance) from which an object is made, and, in a broader sense, a member of a set, a constituent element of a mass, a portion of something, or an area inside a larger one. In some cases, a meronym can have multiple holonyms (*slice* is a meronym of *bread, cheese, cake*, etc.); conversely, there can be multiple **co-meronyms** of a holonym (*sleeve, collar, cuff, button* are co-meronyms of *shirt*). Only count nouns have parts and possibly material relations, while mass nouns (such as *bread* and *sand* above) have no distinction between material and parts (see section 4.4.2.1).

A special relation that is frequently subsumed under the meronymy relation is the **locative relation** (or relation of localization) that links an object with the typical place where it is found. In this view, one may say that *dogs* are "parts" of a *doghouse*, *books* are "part" of a *library*, *plants* are "part" of a *park*, *flowers* are part of a *garden*, and so on. This is illustrated in (g):

(g)  relationship between an object and the place where it is frequently found:
    *library*   is a holonym of                *book*
    *book*     is a meronym (element) of  *library*

As with hyperonymy, words have different meronyms for each meaning or facet of meaning. For example, *book* has different meronyms for its physical facet and its information facet, as shown below.

**(6)**   *book*   physical facet:
        *book*    is a holonym of          *page*
                                                  *cover*
        *page*    is a meronym (part) of  *book*
                                                  *volume*
        information facet:
        *book*    is a holonym of          *chapter*
                                                  *index*
        *chapter*  is a meronym (part) of  *book*
                                                *volume*

Meronymy relationships can be represented as in Figure 5.4 (this is a partial representation of the meronymy relations in which these words participate). This representation highlights the fact that meronymy, like hyponymy, is a relationship of inclusion (e.g. *bicycle* "includes" *wheel*).

The lexical systems created by hyperonymy/hyponymy relations (see Figure 5.2) and those created by meronymy/holonymy relations (see Figure 5.4) appear identical in these two representations. That is, they both look like well-formed taxonomies, that is sequences of progressively larger categories in which each category includes all the previous ones, with branches and a hierarchy of levels (Murphy 2002: 199). Nevertheless, the two systems are in fact fundamentally different and should not be confused; while an hyponym denotes a *type* of something, a meronym denotes a *part* of something. This fact becomes obvious if we think of the referents. A car is not a part of a vehicle; it is a type of vehicle. Likewise, the wheel is not a bicycle type but a bicycle part. While a car is a vehicle, a wheel is not a bicycle. Furthermore, while the referent of a hyponym inherits the properties of the referent of the hyperonym (for example, a tulip has petals, scent, etc. like a flower), the referent of a meronym does not inherit the properties

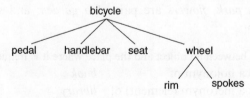

**Figure 5.4** Meronymy relations

of the referent of its holonym (a wheel does not have the properties of a bicycle). Finally, meronymy relations are not all equally transitive, as those of hyperonymy/hyponymy are; while it is normal to say that spokes are bicycle parts, it appears odd to claim that a finger is part of an arm or a handle is part of a room.

A naïve test to identify meronymy is the following: "*x* has (a) *y*" ("a bicycle has a pedal"). This test is misleading, however; in fact, we can say "I have a book" but the book is not a part of me (possession is inalienable in the first case, alienable in the second; see Lyons (1977: 312), on this point). The following tests are more appropriate; for meronymy: "*x* is a part of *y*" (the *pedal* is a part of the *bicycle*); for holonymy: "*x* has *y* as part" (the *bicycle* has *pedal* as part). Another test focusing on the constituting material instead of the parts is: "*x* is made of *y*" ("the ring is made of gold").

As we already observed in Chapter 3, the meronymy relation is linguistically relevant because in many languages the word that denotes the part is often used to denote the whole. This shift in meaning is called *synecdoche*; more broadly, it is an instance of metonymy. Examples are: "I'll take the wheel!" (= I will drive the car), "He no longer has a roof over his head" (= he is homeless), "He painted his room white" (= the walls, the ceiling of the room), "Did you lock the car?" (= the door of the car), "I picked up the telephone" (= the handset, in old-fashioned phones), "Let's pedal home" (= Let's bike home), and so forth. Furthermore, *associative anaphora*, that is, the first mentioning of an entity in a text that can somehow be associated with a previously mentioned entity, is often grounded on meronymy relations, as noted by Kleiber (1999a) among others—for example: "The *house* is close to the beach. The *windows* overlook the ocean." As noted above, however, in general not all parts of an object have equal status. It is the typical parts—that is, those that characterize an object as such and are not optional—that allow meaning shifts along the meronymy relation.

Nouns denoting parts of larger objects are frequently encoded in the language as relational nouns (cf. section 4.4.2.1), especially if the part denoted is highly dependent on the whole. In language, there is sometime a dedicated sense of a word to name a salient part of an object. Some examples follow:

(7)  Engl.  The *foot* of the stairs.
     Engl.  The *hands* of the watch.
     It.    La *radice* del naso.        'the root of the nose'
     It.    Il *collo* del piede.        'the instep (of a foot)'

In a broad sense, as with hyperonymy/hyponymy, the meronymy/holonymy relation may also be said to be valid across word classes. Here is an example: *to pedal / bicycle*.

To conclude, we review some of the constructions in which both terms participating in a meronymy relation may co-occur in context. These are shown in (8), where $n_1$ stands for the meronymic expression and $n_2$ for the holonym:

**(8)**   Constructions for the meronymy/holonymy relation
   $n_2$'s $n_1$: the *room*'s *wall*
   $n_1$ of $n_2$: the *door* of the *car*
   $n_1$ is a part of $n_2$: the *brain* is a very sensitive part of the *body*
   $n_2$ made of $n_1$: *monuments* made of *stone* and *marble*
   $n_1$ of $n_2$: *house* of *wood*
   $n_2$ consists of $n_1$: the *orchestra* consists of 90 *performers*
   $n_2$ containing $n_1$: a *forest* containing dead *trees*.

Assuming a scalar view of the paradigmatic dimension, it can be said that meronymy is less paradigmatic than hyponymy, because with the exception of *synecdoche*, the two terms of a meronymy relation are not substitutable for each other. Their most typical use is either in constructions where both terms of the relation are present (as in (8) above) or in expressions where only the part-denoting term is expressed. An example is: "I found the door open," where the object of which the door is a part (the car, the room) is left unexpressed.

## 5.4. Relations of identity: synonymy, near-synonymy

There are different definitions of synonymy. Two words are **synonyms** when they mean the same (*misery / poverty, to mix / to blend, rocky / stony, enough / sufficient*). This notion applies to simple words, but it can be used for larger expressions as well; compare for example "this is *serious*" vs. "this is *no laughing matter*." In this view, synonymy is the relationship of semantic equivalence between two words that can always be substituted for each other without changing the meaning of the sentence in which they occur.

This definition of synonymy, however, applies very rarely. The reason is obvious. Since most words are polysemous, the case in which two words are substitutable for each other in all of their meanings is rare. Typically, this is the case of monosemous words, such as *umbrella* and *parasol*, where, however, *parasol* is a less common word and denotes in fact a subtype of *umbrella*, and therefore cannot be said to be perfectly synonymous with *umbrella*. Moreover, *umbrella* also has a figurative meaning, as in "under the umbrella of the UN," which *parasol* does not have. More frequently, two words are interchangeable only in one or more specific contexts of use. For example, *package* can be substituted for *box* in a context such as "a box of cookies" but not in a context like "the upper right hand box on the screen" or in the context of "sand box"; *hard* is interchangeable with *difficult* in "hard work" but not in "hard cover"; *persistent* is interchangeable with *continuous* in "persistent rain" but not in "a persistent person," in which case the word *tenacious* is appropriate, and so forth.

A more accurate definition of synonymy is the following: synonymy is the relationship that exists between two words that, in a given context (i.e. in a given meaning) can be substituted for each other without consequences for the interpretation of the sentence, that is, without affecting a sentence's truth value. On the basis of this definition, two words are synonyms not only when they can always be substituted (**absolute synonyms**) but also when they can be in at least one context of use (**contextual synonyms**, as in the cases of *box* and *package* above).

All of the definitions of synonymy introduced above rely on the substitution test (the possibility of replacing one word with another). If we use the substitution test in order to define synonymy, only words of the same word class can be said to be synonyms (verbs with verbs, nouns with nouns, etc.). On this basis, *arrival* and *to arrive*, *departure* and *to depart* are not synonyms.

To identify synonyms, it is necessary to first analyze the contexts in which the terms are used. Furthermore, we can apply a number of tests. These tests bring to light a logical property of synonymy, namely, that of encoding a so-called **mutual** or **bilateral entailment**. A classic test to identify synonyms for nouns and adjectives is the following, consisting of two parts: "it is (an) *x*, therefore it is (a) *y*"; "it is (a) *y*, therefore it is (an) *x*." For example, "it is a *snack*, therefore it is a *light meal*," "it is a *light meal*, therefore it is a *snack*"; "it is *quick*, therefore it is *fast*," "it is *fast*, therefore it is *quick*." This test does not work for hyperonymy/hyponymy relations, which are based on a **unilateral entailment**: "it is a *dog*, therefore it is an *animal*"; *it is an *animal*, therefore it is a *dog*. Furthermore, it rules out meronyms: *it is a *sleeve*, therefore it is a *shirt*; *it is a *shirt*, therefore it is a *sleeve*. A test to identify synonyms for verbs, is, instead, the following (this test, too, consists of two parts): "something/some-one *x*, therefore something/someone *y*"; "something/someone *y*, therefore something/someone *x*." For example, "the event *happened*, therefore the event *took place*"; "the event *took place*, therefore the event *happened*"; "we *participated* in the ceremony, therefore we *took part* in it"; "we *took part* in the ceremony, therefore we *participated* in it," and so forth.

The test must be satisfied in both directions to identify synonymy. If only the first half is satisfied, it could still be hyponymy; see for example "John *walked*, therefore John *moved*."

**Near-synonyms** (*tool* / *utensil*, *jug* / *bottle*, *chaos* / *mess*, *bite* / *morsel*, *full* / *overflowing*, *to whisper* / *to murmur*, *to chat* / *to converse*, *liberty* / *freedom*) are word pairs that give odd results in the synonymy tests. For example: "? if John chats, then he converses," "? if John converses, then he chats." These word pairs have been called different things; for example, they have been said to be **analogous** or **similar terms**. These definitions, however, are vague and generic. In fact, from the point of view of their meaning, co-hyponyms of a general term can also be said to be similar terms: see for example *to fly*, *to run*, *to walk* as co-hyponyms of *to move*.

There are certain parameters that allow us to clarify in what way two near-synonyms diverge. These are illustrated below. These parameters are not mutually exclusive and, in fact, can add up. Cases 3 to 5 are also called *synonymy variants*:

1. degree: the two terms express roughly the same concept, for example a physical property, but they differ inasmuch as one expresses a higher or lower value of that property along a reference scale. For example: *over-flowing* as opposed to *full*, *huge* as opposed to *big*, *soaked* as opposed to *wet*, and so forth.
2. manner: two near-synonymous verbs denote an activity of the same type, but carried out in different manners. For example: *to whisper*, *to murmur*, to *mumble*. Note that these verbs are near-synonymous with each other and co-hyponyms of *to talk*. As noted above, near-synonymy is not a necessary property of co-hyponyms, however.
3. connotation: the two terms have the same denotation but a different connotation, especially in regard to register (formal, colloquial, vulgar). For example: *mother* / *mom*, *work* / *job*, *to do* / *to perform*, *to carry out* / *to execute*, *to pass away* / *to die*, *delicious* / *yummy*, *silent* (as in "a silent night") / *quiet*, etc.

4. domain: the two terms have the same denotation, but are used in different domains (*priority* / *right of way* (traffic)).
5. geographic area: the two terms have the same denotation but are used in different geographic areas (Engl. *pop* / Amer. *soda*; Tuscan *babbo* / Northern It. *papà* 'dad').

Other cases of near-synonyms are less easily classifiable. That is, although it is possible to identify in what meaning dimension two near-synonyms differ, it does not appear possible to make generalizations and build a class of phenomena on that basis. In other words, they are single cases and the relation they bear is more idiosyncratic. Among these we find: *tea* / *infusion*; *remedy* / *treatment*; *profession* / *work* / *occupation*. Good candidates for near-synonymy in English are word pairs that differ from each other with respect to their etymology (e.g. Germanic or Latin): *vivid* / *bright*, *quiet* / *silent*, and so forth.

## 5.5. Relations of opposition: antonymy, complementarity, converse terms

The category of opposites includes pairs of terms that contrast with each other with respect to one key aspect of their meaning, such that together they exhaust this aspect completely. Examples include the following: *easy* / *difficult*, *to open* / *to close*, *to rise* / *to fall*. We will examine their differences in a moment. Paradoxically, the first step in the process of identifying a relationship of opposition often consists in identifying something that the meanings of the words under examination have in common. A second step is to identify the key aspect in which the two meanings oppose each other. For example, given two terms such as Engl. *to rise* and *to fall*, starting from the identification of a shared element ('movement along an axis') we may identify the key point of differentiation ('directionality'), on which base we finally identify a relation of opposition. This is illustrated in Figure 5.5, where the shared features are marked in gray (see Löbner 2013: 208 for further remarks on this point).

There are several ways in which words may oppose each other as regards their meaning. Consider the relationship between *rise* and *fall* and notice how it differs from that between *buy* and *steal*; although it is possible to identify a shared element of meaning between *buy* and *steal* to rise — | motion along an axis | — to fall (opposite direction of motion)

**Figure 5.5** The identification of a shared feature and a distinguishing feature in an opposition

('gain / obtain possession of something') and a key point of differentiation ('compensation with money'), most people would say that the opposite of *buy* is *sell*, not *steal*, and that *buy* and *steal* may be different and indeed mutually exclusive (*incompatibles* in Cruse's 1986 terms), but not opposite.

Opposites cannot be true simultaneously of the same entity, for example a price cannot be said to rise and fall at exactly the same point in time. Similarly, "*The task is both *easy* and *difficult*" is ruled out because *easy* and *difficult* are opposites, while "The task is both *lengthy* and *easy*" is well-formed because *lengthy* and *easy* are not opposites. The "it is both *x* and *y*" test can be seen as a basic test to identify an opposition. This test, however, does not tell us what kind of opposition it is. Among the various types of oppositions that can be said to exist among words, we focus on **antonymy**, **complementarity**, and **converseness**, which appear to recur frequently across the vocabulary and are relatively easy to systematize.

**Antonyms** are word pairs that denote a property (*easy / difficult, wide / narrow*) or a change in property (*to clean / to soil; to lengthen / to shorten*) that has the characteristic of being gradual from a conceptual point of view. Two antonyms, therefore, oppose each other in relation to a scale of values for a given property, of which they specify the two poles (or bounds). For this reason in the case of antonyms one may also speak of **polar** (Pustejovsky 2001) or **scalar** opposition.

From a logical point of view, antonyms are contraries, not contradictories; the negation of one term is not equivalent to the opposite term. For example, *not easy* does not necessarily mean *difficult*. How is this possible? There is a region along the property's scale (roughly corresponding to an interval in its central part) that is neutral, so to speak, with respect to the two terms, which as we noted above tend to locate themselves on two poles. This region is neutral in the sense that one cannot refer to it with either one of the two terms; in fact, something can be said to be neither *easy* nor *difficult* (Figure 5.6). This characteristic is self-evident in such everyday expressions as: "It is not expensive but neither is it cheap."

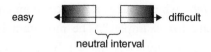

**Figure 5.6** Relation of polar opposition

The zero value on the scale (that is, the absence of the property) is denoted by neither of the two terms. In fact, we cannot say that something is *very tiny* if it has *no spatial extent*, or that it is *extremely slow* if it is *stationary*. One of the two antonyms approaches zero size, but never reaches it.

In the world's languages it is easy to find series of terms that identify very refined gradations of a specific property, for example:

1. Temperature: *freezing, cold, lukewarm, warm, hot, boiling, burning*;
2. Age: *baby* (infant), *child, teenager, boy/girl, youth, adult, elderly, old*;
3. Tempo in music: *fortissimo, forte, mezzo forte, piano, pianissimo*;
4 Quality: *horrible, bad, mediocre, good, very good, excellent*; etc.

Potentially, along a scale of this type we could have very many terms lexicalizing different degrees along the scale. In reality, as a rule, we have just a few and use words called degree modifiers (such as *a bit, more, very*) to refine the concept. For example, we say "These sleeves are *very* long"; "This film is *moderately* funny," etc.

The standard tests to determine whether two words are antonyms are the following: "it is neither *x* nor *y*"; "it is quite / moderately / lightly / a bit / very / really *x, y*." For example: "This task is neither *easy* nor *difficult*"; "This task is very, moderately *difficult*." The "neither *x* nor *y*" test verifies whether it is possible to negate both terms simultaneously, and whether there is a neutral interval with respect to the two terms. The second test verifies whether the terms of the opposition express a scalable dimension.

In general, the maximal and minimal values of the property denoted by an antonym are not absolute but are dependent on the referent to which it is applied; a *tall* mountain will, therefore, have different dimensions from a *tall* person. In many cases, there is an average value that is used as a reference. This, however, appears not to be the case with all antonyms; *flat* for example can be said to encode a maximal value of the property, independently of the object it is applied to. This is captured by the "completely" test, i.e. the test that verifies whether the antonym can be modified by *completely*, which makes reference to an end point as part of its meaning; compare for example "*The mountain is completely tall" with "The wooden top is completely flat": only the latter (*flat*) and not the former (*tall*) can be said to encode a lexical end point (see Hay, Kennedy, and Levin 1999).

Finally, antonyms may be oriented. Consider the following tests applied to *clean / dirty*: "This dress is a bit dirty" vs. "?This dress is a bit clean"; "How dirty is it?" vs. "?How clean is it?." The test suggests that *clean* is the unmarked member in the opposition, that is, the one which is implied by the other, and therefore the most basic.

Two expressions are **complementary** (*to accept / to reject, to pass / to fail, to remember / to forget, true / false, awake / asleep, alive / dead, cause / effect*) when they oppose each other with regard to a distinction that is not polar but binary; in other words, complementaries partition a conceptual domain into mutually exclusive compartments. For this reason, this opposition can also be called **binary opposition** (Pustejovsky 2001).

Complementary terms exclude each other and there is never an intermediate term. Therefore, a binary opposition corresponds to the relationship "*x* is equivalent to non-*y*": *accept* is equivalent to *non-reject*, *true* is equivalent to *non-false*, and so on. There is no underlying scale of values, although in the literature binary opposition is nowadays often referred to as a two-point scale (as opposed to the multi-point scale of antonyms): see for example Beavers 2008 and Rappaport Hovav 2008 as examples of scholars who use this terminology.

The standard test to identify complementary terms is the same as that employed for antonyms, with the difference that in the case of complementarities, the result is negative: "neither *x* nor *y*" (*he was neither *accepted* nor *rejected*; *it is neither *true* nor *false*). Complementary terms fail the test because the opposition they encode is exclusive, in the sense that the assertion of one term entails the negation of the other (and vice versa); there are no intermediate cases. It is not possible to negate both terms simultaneously.

**Converses** (*to buy / to sell, father / son*) are terms whose meaning involves necessarily a relation between at least two elements. That is, a father is such only in relation to someone: if there are no children, there is no father; on the other hand, a person can sell something only if there is a buyer, and so forth. Therefore, converse terms are inherently relational. The underlying relation is asymmetrical—that is, it is seen from the point of view of one of the two participants, which for convenience we call *x* and *y*:

| Point of view of *x* | Point of view of *y* |
|---|---|
| *x sells* something to *y* | *y buys* something from *x* |
| *x* is *y*'s *father* | *y* is *x*'s *son* |

The characteristic of two converse terms is that each expresses the underlying relation in the opposite way from the other. Therefore, not all relational terms are converses, but only those with reversed or converted roles. In the case of verbs, role conversion may be obtained not only by means of word pairs but also by means of the passive construction, as shown in the example below:

| Point of view of *x* | Point of view of *y* |
|---|---|
| x *watches* y | y *is watched by* x |

Finally, opposites expressing a direction relative to a certain axis are called **directional opposites**. It is possible to identify four main reference axes, three of which are defined by the positioning of our body in space and its symmetrical structure:

1. primary horizontal axis (front/back)
2. vertical axis (head/feet)
3. lateral axis (left/right)
4. time axis (past/present/future)

On the basis of these axes, we can characterize pairs of opposites with regard to directions, such as the following: *front / back; in front of / behind; to advance / to recede; top / bottom; high / low; up / down; above / below; to rise / to fall; to the left of / to the right of; yesterday / today; next / last; to precede / to follow; before / after*, etc.

Besides the main types of opposites discussed above (antonyms, complementaries, converses), there are many other categories of opposite which apply to narrow ranges of vocabulary. One case in point refers to terms which denote reversed actions or events (**reversives**), such as *build / destroy, assemble / disperse, wrap / unwrap, arrive / leave, start / finish, appear / disappear*, and many more.

## 5.6. Other relations: cause, purpose, temporal entailment

In the lexicon one can identify a large number of semantic relations between words that cannot be ascribed to the main relation types introduced above or that appear to crisscross them. These relations are not strictly paradigmatic, that is, they do not involve terms that can be substituted for each other in the same context. Nevertheless, they contribute to highlight the structure of the semantic lexicon and may be considered to be present in the lexical competence of a speaker. In this section, we will briefly introduce some of these relation types. In order they are: the causal relation, the relation of purpose, and the relation of temporal entailment.

A **causal** relation (or relation of **causation**) links such verb pairs as *to kill* / *to die*, *to buy* / *to own*, *to aim* / *to hit*, *to teach* / *to learn*, *to search* / *to find*. In fact, as we saw in Chapter 3, one can say: *to kill* CAUSES *to die*. This relation can be paraphrased as follows: "the event expressed by $v_1$ causes the event expressed by $v_2$ to occur." The causal relation is factive (according to Lyons' 1977 terminology) when it applies necessarily, as in the case of *to kill* which necessarily causes *to die*, or non-factive, as in the following cases: *to aim* MAY CAUSE *to hit*; *to search* MAY CAUSE *to find*; *to teach* MAY CAUSE *to learn*; *to order* MAY CAUSE *to obey*; *to play* MAY CAUSE *to win*; *to try* MAY CAUSE *to succeed*; *to iron* MAY CAUSE *to burn*, and so on. The paraphrase is as follows: "the event expressed by $v_1$ is likely to cause the event expressed by $v_1$ to occur." Finally, the causal relation can be said to link words belonging to different lexical classes, for example a verb and a noun, as in the case of *to try* (in a court of law) / *conviction*. In this case, the relation can be paraphrased as follows: *to try* MAY CAUSE *conviction*. Finally, the causal relation may link two nouns. For example, the relation between *writer* and *book* may be analyzed as a relation of causation (i.e. the *writer* CAUSES the *book* to exist). This holds true for all nouns that denote individuals that create something (*sculptor/statue*, *painter/painting*, and so on). Other kinds of relations between nouns that can be interpreted loosely as causal are for example the product relation *cow/milk* (*cow* CAUSES *milk* to exist), and the relation holding between *foot* and *footprint* (*foot* MAY CAUSE *footprint*).

The cause relation may be seen in relation to **purpose**. For example, the purpose of *searching* something is to *find* it, the goal of *trying* is *to succeed*, the goal of *teaching* is that someone *learns*, the goal of *eating* is *to nourish oneself*, the goal of *play* is to *win*, and so on. The purpose relation can be paraphrased as follows: "the event expressed by $v_1$ has the event expressed by $v_2$ as purpose/intended goal." Involuntary actions lack a purpose, i.e. *break* associates by default with no purpose, as it is typically done unintentionally.

While many relations of non-factive causation can be analyzed as purpose relation, this is not always the case. For example, *to iron* MAY CAUSE *to burn* and *to try* MAY CAUSE *to fail*, but *to burn* is certainly not the ultimate purpose of ironing nor is *to fail* the goal of *to try*.

A relation of purpose can be said to exist also between two nouns: for instance the instrument relation existing between *brush* and *color paint*, or between *nail* and the noun *hammer*, may be subsumed under the purpose relation, if it is interpreted loosely as 'to be used in some action with an intended goal.' Finally, the purpose relation links a noun with a verb that specifies the activity that satisfies the noun's typical function: *fork* and *eat*, *sandwich* and *eat*, *pen* and *write*, and so on. In this case, however, the relation is best characterized as syntagmatic. Therefore, we will postpone the discussion of this relation type to the next chapter.

As for the relation of **temporal entailment**, recall, first of all, that, from a general point of view, entailment is at the core of various relations that we have already discussed, such as hyperonymy/hyponymy and cause. The same relation, however, allows us to identify other types of association between words. In particular, in the case of verbs and event nouns, more types of association can be identified by analyzing the internal temporal structure of the event they express, particularly the phases or stages the event is made of, and how these phases relate to each other (if they precede each other, if they are co-extensive, and so on).

For example, if we consider the verb pairs *to sleep / to snore*, *to buy / to pay*, *to eat / to swallow*, *to phone / to dial*, we can say that a relation exists between these verb pairs such that *to snore* ENTAILS *to sleep*, *to buy* ENTAILS *to pay*, *to eat* ENTAILS *to swallow*, *to phone* ENTAILS *to dial*. In the first case, the event of *snoring* is necessarily included, from the temporal point of view, in the event of *sleeping* (one snores only while sleeping, while one can continue to sleep without snoring). The entailment relation is in this case unilateral (or unidirectional) and we may talk of **temporal inclusion**. A possible paraphrase is: "The event expressed by $v_1$ overlaps with the event expressed by $v_2$ and is included in it." Temporal inclusion holds also with *to buy / to pay*, *to eat / to swallow*, *to phone / to dial*. For example, the event of *buying* can be said to include the event of *paying* as one of its constituent aspects.

Temporal inclusion between verbs resembles meronymy between nouns: a single temporal part constitutes for the verb a part of the entire event (see, however, Fellbaum 1998 on this point). Note also that it is possible to define an order between the parts that form an event: for example *to eat* HAS *to swallow* AS LAST PART, *to phone* HAS *to dial* AS FIRST PART, and so on. Note that being a part of an event is not the same thing as being a **prerequisite** or **precondition** for an event to happen. For example, *to eat* precedes *to digest*, but the relation in this case is not one of being a part but rather a relation of *backward presupposition* (Fellbaum 1998) or *precedence* (Ruppenhofer et al. 2010). In other words, *to digest* HAS PREREQUISITE *to eat*, *to get up* HAS PREREQUISITE *to wake up*, and so on. This can be paraphrased as follows: "The event expressed by $v_1$ has the event expressed by $v_2$ as a precondition."

Verbs participating in a troponymy relation are always **temporally co-extensive** with each other; for example, *to walk* is *to move* in a certain manner, and the two actions described by the two verbs take place at the same time, i.e. they begin and end at the same time. The paraphrase is: "The event expressed by $v_1$ is simultaneous with the event expressed by $v_2$." It could be argued that in order to move, first a certain action needs to be done with the legs to cause the movement of the body to begin. This fine-grained analysis, however, need not detain us here.

To conclude, as referred to above, the relations presented in this section are no less important from a qualitative point of view than the ones introduced in the previous sections; they are either more idiosyncratic or they apply to smaller sections of the vocabulary. For these reasons, they have received less attention within the lexicographic tradition over the years. Nevertheless, they play a central role in structuring our lexical knowledge, on a par with the main axes identified by hyponymy, opposition, and so forth.

## 5.7. Lexical configurations

The relationships we have described in this chapter do not exhaust all of the possible semantic relations between words. They do, however, allow us to identify the most typical lexical configurations. By **lexical configuration** we mean a word's relation profile from the point of view of its meaning, that is, the set and type of semantic relations it activates in each contextual interpretation (*synonymy, opposition, hyperonymy, cause*, etc.). Each word of a lexicon can be said to activate a different configuration. A few examples will illustrate this point. The word *pessimism* does not appear to have any synonyms and can be characterized on the basis of its opposite, *optimism* and a group of near-synonyms with a more accentuated meaning (*hopelessness, defeatism, nihilism*). The word *full* has a similar profile: no synonyms, an antonym (*empty*) and a few intensifying near-synonyms (*bursting, overflowing, brimming, packed*). *To rain* does not have synonyms but only hyponyms (*to pour, to drizzle*). *Subject* (in the meaning of 'member of a reign') is a relational term and can be characterized only on the basis of its converts (*monarch, sovereign*). *To subscribe* has no synonyms, a reverse opposite (*to unsubscribe*), and a few near-synonyms (*to sign up, to join*).

As noted above, in the case of polysemous words, the configuration varies depending on the meaning in question. For example, *whale* does not have opposites in its 'animal' sense and can be characterized by a technical hyperonym (*cetaceous*) and a number of hyponyms (*blue whale, humpback whale, killer whale*). By contrast, it has several synonyms and opposites in its figurative sense of 'big person,' such as *giant, hulk*, and so forth.

It is not only individual words but also word classes that have lexical configurations, or profiles. In this regard, numerous studies carried out with the goal of building large lexical-semantic networks of individual languages (such as WordNet, Fellbaum 1998, and EuroWordNet, Vossen 1998) have yielded interesting results. As referred to earlier, nouns tend to organize themselves along the hyperonymy/hyponymy axis and generate deep hyponymic chains (up to 12 levels). Verbs cluster along the hyperonymy/hyponymy axis as well, but form hyponymic chains that are shallower than those formed by nouns (four levels at most) and tend to extend horizontally rather than vertically (recall that for nouns the hyponym is a "type" of the hyperonym, while in the case of verbs it is a "manner" of the hyperonym). Furthermore, verbs organize themselves around different types of oppositions depending on their meaning. For example, motion verbs form pairs of opposites along the direction axis (*to rise* / *to fall*) while verbs of possession are more often converse opposites (*to give* / *to take, to buy* / *to sell*). Finally, adjectives rarely form hyperonymic chains and tend, instead, to organize themselves along the axis of opposition (polar/scalar or binary).

## Further reading

On semantic network theory and analysis, Quillian (1968).

On lexical relations, see Cruse (1986).

On semantic relations among words, see Miller et al. (1990).

On semantic relations among verbs, see Fellbaum (1998), chapter 3.

On relations among frames, see Ruppenhofer et al. (2010), chapter 6.

On mereology from an ontological perspective, see Simons (1987).

On automatic extraction of semantic relation from text, see Poesio and
    Almuhareb (2008).

# 6

# Syntagmatic structures
# in the lexicon

In this chapter, we examine syntagmatic relations between words in more detail. We first illustrate how a syntagmatic relation may be understood, then examine the most significant word combinations, focusing on combinations of verbs with nouns, and nouns with adjectives. Also, we briefly discuss the notion of construction, as it is intended today in linguistic studies. In closing, we revisit the topic of complex words discussed in Chapter 1 in the light of the content covered in this chapter.

## 6.1. What is a syntagmatic relation?

To explain what a syntagmatic relation is we shall start by looking at what is meant by the term syntagmatic. Syntagmatic relates to *syntagm*. According to the standard definition, a syntagm is a linguistic expression consisting of a sequence of linguistic units. These units may be of different kinds: phonemes (which together form syllables), morphemes (which together form words), words (which together form phrases), and so forth. In our discussion, we will look at syntagms as word combinations. In particular, we will focus on those syntagms in which the words are in a particular grammatical relationship, such as the verb–object relationship. These combinations are called *phrases*. Phrases can be defined as the structured union of multiple words that function as their syntactic "head." For example, the sequence "the boy who always wears a hat" is a noun phrase (NP), because its head is a noun and the whole phrase can be substituted in its entirety for a noun, such as *Chris*. In this view, when we talk about the syntagmatic (or horizontal) dimension of a language, we refer generically to the phenomenon of word combination, which results in phrases but also in higher linguistic units, such as sentences and texts.

Word combination can be seen as the necessary consequence of the linear character of language, which, as Saussure noted, rules out the possibility of pronouncing two elements at once (unlike music) and requires that elements be combined in temporal sequence, that is, one after another. This property of language, however, does not entail that linear order plays a role in the syntax; in fact syntax appears to be much more sophisticated and involve long-distance relations and dependencies between words.

Words that combine do so based on syntagmatic relations that they bear *in potens* because of their meanings. Their actual combination activates different kinds of processes. One of these processes concerns the mutual adjustments that the meanings of the individual words undergo in the context of other words. We examined this process in detail in section 3.4. In this chapter, we address this same process from the perspective of combinatory phenomena between words. We first give a review of the most common types of syntagmatic relations that can be observed between words, then turn to the description of the main types of syntagmatic constraints operating in word combinations. Finally, we give an overview of the most common types of word combinations that can be identified on the basis of these constraints.

## 6.2. Syntagmatic relations: role, attribution, and manner

As noted by A. Cruse, syntagmatic relations hold in specific syntactic contexts; for example, *chair* (in its primary meaning) can be the object but not the subject of *see*. Starting from this observation, linguistic studies contribute to isolating three main types of semantic relations between words in syntactic context. These are the relation of role, the relation of attribution, and the relation of manner. The relation of roles has already been introduced in Chapter 4 in relation to verb classes; here we will review it briefly, and then focus on the other two relations.

The relation of **role** links a verb to a noun when the noun denotes one of the participants that plays a role in the event expressed by the verb. For example, the relation between *to paint* and *paintbrush* can be said to be a relation between the action expressed by the verb and the instrument used in the action. As we saw in Chapter 4, the relation may involve other roles: the agent (*to bark / dog*), the patient (*to give birth* (*to*) / *child*), the location (*to sleep / bed*), etc. This is illustrated in Table 6.1.

The relation of role can be looked at not only from the point of view of the word expressing the event, as in Table 6.1, but also from the perspective of the word expressing the participant. In this view, it is possible to identify the roles for objects shown in Table 6.2 (notice the analogies with the Qualia roles introduced in Chapter 3).

**Table 6.1.** The relation of role (for events)

| event | agent of the event | *to bark / dog* |
|---|---|---|
| | patient of the event | *to give birth* (*to*) / *child* |
| | theme of the event | *to drive / car* |
| | resulting object | *to paint / portrait* |
| | instrument used to perform the action | *to paint / paintbrush* |
| | location where the action takes place | *to sleep / bed* |

**Table 6.2.** The relation of role (for objects)

| object | event defining the object | *pedestrian / to walk* |
|---|---|---|
| | | *passenger / to travel* |
| | event for which the object is made | *fork / to eat* |
| | | *printer / to print* |
| | event bringing about the object | *book / to write* |
| | | *path / to walk* |

**Table 6.3.** The relation of attribution

| object | attribute of the object | *hair/blonde* |
|---|---|---|
| | | |

**Table 6.4.** The relation of manner

| event | manner of the event | *damage/severely* |
|---|---|---|
| | | |

Let us now look at the relation of attribution, i.e. the relation that links an adjective with a noun, when the adjective expresses an attribute or property of the referent of the noun, for example color, length, shape, weight, and so forth. For example, *blonde* predicates a specific value (pale yellow) of the color property of *hair* and very few other things (*moustache, beard, eyebrow,* etc.): it may, of course, be extended to a person with that property ("a blonde actress," "a blonde girl," and so on, or even be used metonymically to indicate the person, as in the famous expression "Gentlemen prefer blondes") (Table 6.3).

Finally, the relation of **manner** connects an adverb (for example, *severely*) with a verb (for example, *damage*), when the former expresses the manner in which the event expressed by the verb takes place (Table 6.4). As explained in section 5.3., manner is used here as a general term that subsumes several properties of the event, including, for example, degree of force. Other examples are: *to grasp / firmly, to throw / forcefully.*

## 6.3. Impossible word combinations: why?

The fact that words cannot be combined at will is a truism. For example, words cannot be lined up in random order, but must follow a precise order, determined by the syntax of the language to which they belong. This order concerns the sequence of words inside a phrase and the sequence of phrases in sentences. From this point of view, the sequence "the striped sweater that you are wearing" is correct, while "the sweater that you are striped wearing" is not. At times, given the same words, more than one linear order is allowed, but the interpretation changes, as in the case of "Paul saw Mary" / "Mary saw Paul."

Rules that regulate word order are not the only types of rules that constrain how words may combine. Other rules concern, for example, the way in which the argument(s) of a verb is/are expressed syntactically. For example, in English, the expression "I flew to New York" is syntactically appropriate, while "*I flew New York" is not.

Even if they satisfy a language's syntactic constraints, certain word sequences can still turn out to be odd. For example, the expressions "The chair I spoke with yesterday" or "I bought two pounds of courage" are abnormal. The reason these combinations are odd does not have to do with the order of the words or with other syntactical rules but with the content of the words. A chair in its literal meaning is an inanimate object and it is therefore unthinkable that it would speak, courage is a frame of mind and can be neither bought nor weighed. These expressions are syntactically correct but conceptually *impossible*. The words that compose the expressions are *incompatible* or *ill matched* from the point of view of their meaning.

The existence of semantic constraints on the ways in which words may be combined, that is to say, of rules that constraint the possible combinations, has attracted the attention of many scholars, especially within the structural and generative traditions, which we will briefly review below.

## 6.3.1. Selectional restrictions and lexical solidarities

It is in the structuralist tradition that one finds the first systematic observations regarding the nature of syntagmatic relations in the lexicon. W. Porzig is the first scholar to have systematically noted that among the words that line up in text we can identify semantic relations ( "*Bedeutungsbeziehungen*" in Porzig's terms) that favor their co-occurrence and at the same time constrain their compatibility with other words. Porzig observed (1934: 70): "part of the content or essence of the German verb *gehen* (*to walk*) is that it requires human feet, because a dog does not walk on the street and a cat does not walk along the wall: in these cases the German verb would be *laufen*." Years later, still within the structuralist tradition, E. Coseriu (1967) devoted a lot of attention to the analysis and classification of the semantic relations that exist between word pairs such as *nose / aquiline, dog / to bark, to flower / plant, to cut down / tree*. Coseriu calls these word pairs *lexical solidarities*. **Lexical solidarity** is defined as a linguistically encoded semantic relation such that one of the two terms (for example, *nose*) functions as a distinctive feature of the other (*aquiline*). According to Coseriu, a lexical solidarity is an asymmetrical kind of relation. As Coseriu (1967: 15) points out, "In a solidarity, there is always one term which determines and another which is determined." For example, for Coseriu *nose* is included from the point of view of content in *aquiline*, but *nose* does not include *aquiline*, because one can say other things about a nose, other than asserting that it is aquiline.

About the same time, syntagmatic meaning relations were addressed in generative grammar by Chomsky (1965) under the heading of **selection**. The term selection had already been used in 1943 by Danish linguist L. Hjelmslev to describe the syntagmatic process occurring between two elements when one element (the selector) unilaterally determines another one (the selected). The process of selection is thought of as operating at multiple levels. The one of interest for the current discussion is argument selection, i.e. the operation by which a predicate, by virtue of its meaning, can be said to select a range of possible arguments and to exclude others. For example, Engl. verb *hear* selects an animate subject and excludes inanimate ones, which, by definition, cannot hear anything. For this reason, Chomsky calls this type of restriction *selectional restriction* (see section 4.4.1.2).

Further analysis of syntagmatic meaning relations among words can be found in the works of scholars from various theoretical backgrounds, including Lyons (1968: 440), Apresjan (1992: 15 ff.), and Dik (1997: 91–7).

## 6.3.2. Types of constraints on word combinations

As mentioned earlier, research on incompatibility between words has contributed to identifying different types of syntagmatic relations but has missed an important fact; constraints on word combinations are of different natures even if when violated they produce the same result, namely word combinations which are ruled out as odd or may be interpreted only if the meaning of one of the members is reinterpreted contextually (this is the case of coercion, cf. section 3.4). We claim instead that for purposes of lexical analysis and classification, it is convenient to draw a distinction between three different types of constraints operating on word combinations.

### 1. *Conceptual or ontological restrictions*

These restrictions on word combinations derive from the inherent properties of the word's referents, of which we are aware as a result of our experience of the world—experience that we tend not to contradict when we speak. It is on the basis of this type of restriction that sentences such as "The chair I spoke with yesterday" are unacceptable. A combination of words that violates this type of restriction expresses a *conceptual conflict*, which cannot be resolved in any way, because it is inconsistent from an ontological point of view, that is, from the point of view of how the world is and how we perceive it. Conceptual/ontological restrictions determine which words are compatible with each other and which ones are not, i.e. they are the basic level at which compatibility among words is established.

### 2. *Lexical restrictions based on a semantic solidarity*

Lexical restrictions are similar to ontological restrictions—their violation results in conflicting word combinations—but their nature is different, because they are based on a lexical conflict rather than an ontological one. A *lexical conflict* concerns the way in which a certain concept is lexicalized in a language.

To clarify this point, consider the following examples. French, as is known, has two terms to indicate the concept of "growing" applied to living things: *grandir* for people, and *pousser* (preferably) for plants. The word sequence "Un terrain où il ne grandit que l'herbe" ('a ground where only grass grows') is therefore ruled out as odd. The combination, however, does not violate an ontological constraint but rather the lexical solidarity that exists in French (but not in other languages, such as Italian) between *grandir* and a specific class of objects. German provides us with similar examples. For example, German distinguishes between eating by human beings (*essen*) and eating by animals (*fressen*). If the verb *fressen* is used with a human subject, as in the case of "Er ißt nicht, er frißt!" ('he does not eat, he "frißt"') it activates a metaphor in which the human being takes on the properties of an animal. Dutch has *snuiten*, a specific term dedicated to the act of blowing one's nose ("zijn neus snuiten"), while *blazen* is used for all other blowing situations (for example, for wind, or to indicate the act of blowing something into someone's face, the act of blowing glass, etc.). Therefore, "Jan blies zijn neus" is incorrect, but in this case, too, the reason can be said to be lexical, not ontological. In English the word *tall* applies to people, whereas *high* applies to buildings, mountains, etc. Therefore, a word combination such as "the boy is high for his age" sounds odd. One last example is It. "Luca calzava una cravatta rossa" 'Luca was wearing a red tie.' This sequence violates a semantic solidarity that is typical of Italian, namely, the one that links the verb *calzare* to *scarpe* 'shoes' and *guanti* 'gloves.' In other words, *calzare* can be said of *shoes* and *gloves* (as in "Luca calzava gli scarponi da sci" 'Luca was wearing his ski boots') but not of *ties*. The conflict that arises from the violation of a semantic solidarity can be easily resolved by substituting the "conflicting" verb for a hyperonym/super-ordinate with a looser restriction. For example, in the case of *calzare*, with the hyperonym *indossare* ('to wear,' used for clothing in general). Words on which a lexical constraint holds are not merely compatible; they are connected by a solidarity. The figure below summarizes what we have said so far:

violation of an ontological constraint   →   conceptual conflict   →   irreversible
violation of a lexical solidarity          →   lexical conflict        →   reversible

In many cases it is difficult to distinguish whether a word combination is ruled out due to the violation of a conceptual constraint or to a lexical solidarity and at times only a vast cross-linguistic comparison allows us to resolve the question or, at least, to collect data in support of one or the other hypothesis. For example, the combination "I drank an orange" may at first appear to give rise to a conceptual conflict; however, it has been noted that the fact of having two (or more) verbs to denote the action of ingesting, distinguished on the basis of whether they apply to ingesting solid or liquid food (in English, *to eat* or *to drink*, respectively) is a characteristic of certain languages but not of other ones. As Coseriu points out, there are, in fact, languages, such as Persian, that appear to have a single word to refer to both actions (the word is *khordan*). For this reason, and because the conflict can be resolved by replacing *to drink* with a hyperonym with looser constraints such as *to ingest*, it is appropriate to consider this a case of lexical restriction.

### 3. *Lexical restrictions based on a solidarity institutionalized by use*

These restrictions can neither be directly ascribed to ontological constraints (therefore, they are not conceptual), nor to obvious syntagmatic relations between word meanings. That is to say, word combinations on which these restrictions apply are not predictable only on the basis of the ontological category or of the meaning associated with the words involved, as in 1 and 2 above. Rather, they are restricted by a constraint that seems to be rooted in language use, that is, in the tendency of languages to express a given content by means of preferential word pairs, although other combinations are in principle possible from a semantic perspective. These conventionalized or institutionalized word pairs are often called collocations (see section 6.4.3 for a discussion of the various interpretations of the notion of collocation in lexical studies).

Lexical restrictions institutionalized by use can often be formulated in terms of preferences rather than requirements. For example, although both *high winds* and *heavy winds* are attested in English, the first pair is preferred, together with *strong winds*, and the second one is extremely rare. On the other hand, the standard adjective to express magnitude with *rain* is *heavy* (while *strong rain* is ruled out and *?high rain* is extremely infrequent, according to corpus data).

In some cases, however, the choice of the collocate appears instead to be obligatory, in the sense that no lexical variability is allowed. Consider the following list of examples from different languages: Engl. *shake a fist* but not *give a fist*, *have a conversation* but not *?take a conversation*, *make a choice* but not *?take a choice*, *tell a lie* but not *say a lie*; Dutch *koffie zetten* (lit. 'to put (on) coffee') but not *koffie maken* (lit. 'to do coffee'); *thee maken* (lit. 'to make tea') and not *thee zetten* (lit. 'to put (on) tea'); It. *avere paura* (lit. 'to have fear') but not *avere tristezza* (lit. 'to have sadness'), *essere in ansia* ('to be in apprehension') but not *essere in angoscia* (lit. 'to be in anguish'), and so forth.

Although it remains an open question whether differences in distribution such as those above are due to differences in denotation (for example, whether differences in distribution of *high* and *heavy* to express magnitude with natural events like *wind* or *rain* have to do with differences in the inherent meaning of the two adjectives), these combinations are felt by speakers as a typical way of saying a certain thing, i.e. as combinations characterized by a certain degree of conventionality.

Note that in all of the above, replacing the term that violates the restriction with the conventional one can easily cure the violation of this type of restriction. This, as we saw above, is not possible when the restriction which is violated is conceptual/ontological.

It is interesting to note that restrictions usually add up. The most common situation is as follows: conceptual restrictions (1 above) interact with lexical ones (2) and, in addition, language use fixes some combinations as most conventional with respect to others (3).

To conclude, we can provisionally identify three main situations as regards word (in)compatibility: (i) words that do not go together, such as *tasty* and *film*; (ii) words that are compatible, such as *film* and *long*, and (iii) words that tend to go together, such as *blond* and *hair* and *heavy* and *rain*. More will be said about these distinctions in section 6.4.3.

### 6.3.2.1. *Context fitting*

Even when they violate a restriction, certain word combinations are interpreted. This is possible because, as we saw in Chapter 3, word meanings are flexible and are apt to be adjusted in order to fit their context, and also with the aid of commonsense knowledge. Consider the English verb *answer* in the context in (1):

**(1)**    He answered the door.

The combination in (1) technically qualifies as a conflicting combination from an ontological point of view, as a door cannot be answered in the real world. Nevertheless, the combination is perfectly understandable with the aid of pragmatic knowledge, and is interpreted as making reference to the response of a person to an action of somebody knocking or ringing at the door.

### 6.3.2.2. *Redundancy*

As noted in Bosque (2004a) among others, some word combinations are not possible because they are *redundant* (or *pleonastic*, in Cruse's 2004 terms). That is, a member of the combination somehow repeats a piece of lexical information provided by another member. Verbs with incorporated arguments are a case in point; they entail one or more participants that, being already incorporated in the verb, cannot be expressed, unless they are more specifically described. For example, the expression "He smelled gas with his nose" is redundant because the meaning of *nose* is already contained in the meaning of *smell*.

**(2)**    *He smelled gas with his nose.

In *to smell* and *nose*, as well as in *to walk* and *foot*, *to see* and *eye*, *to bite* and *teeth*, the incorporated role is the instrument role (Lyons 1977: 262); in *to swim* and *water*, as in (3), it is the medium.

**(3)**    *We were swimming in water.

Redundancy may be eliminated by introducing an element that contributes new information, as in (4):

**(4)**    We were swimming in cold water.

Note that redundancy does not always lead to incompatibility between words. In some cases, language exploits redundancy in a pragmatic fashion, as in (5).

**(5)**    I saw it with my own eyes!

Apart from the role relation, redundancy may be present also in the relation of attribution. As noted by both Cruse 2004 and Bosque 2004b, occasionally, an adjective may also reinforce an aspect that is already present in the noun's meaning, as in the case of *rapid explosion*, *invited guest*, *mental thought*, *round circle*, *final end*.

Finally, we may have redundancy in the manner relation that links a verb to an adverb: for example between *devour* and *voraciously* ("He devoured his portion voraciously"), between *whisper* and *softly* ("they were whispering softly"), and between *collaborate* and *together*, where *together* repeats information already present in the verb.

When redundancy leads to ungrammatical expressions, as in (2) and (3) above, it can be used as a test to identify what actually makes part of the lexical information of a word.

## 6.4. Types of word combinations

In this section we focus on classifying word combinations into types. This can be done according to several criteria. We shall concentrate on three:

1. The presence of semantic restrictions on the combination,
2. The possibility of predicting the meaning of the combination,
3. The lexical and syntactic variability of the combination.

As regards 1, we will adopt the threefold distinction between kinds of restrictions introduced in section 6.3.2. Therefore, we will distinguish between (a) conceptual/ontological restriction, (b) lexical restriction based on a semantic solidarity, and (c) lexical restriction institutionalized by usage.

As regards 2, two different but related aspects will be taken into account: predictability of the meaning of the combination and availability of the words' referents in the discourse. Predictability of meaning can be defined as the property of a word combination whose meaning may be built up in a compositional fashion starting from the meaning of its members. This is sometimes referred to as *semantic transparency*, a term we will not use here. On the other hand, a referent can be said to be available in the discourse when it is identified with precision. The standard test used to identify if the referent of a word is available in the discourse is based on the substitutability of the word in question for a pronoun. For example, in the English compound *wine glass*, *wine* can be said not to be available as a referent, because combinations such as *"I drank a wine glass and enjoyed *it* very much" are anomalous. By contrast, in the expression a *glass of wine*, the referent of *wine* can be said to be available in the discourse as it can be accessed through a pronoun, as in "I drank a glass of wine and I enjoyed *it* (= the wine) very much."

Finally, as regards 3, we will consider two other properties of word combinations, namely **lexical variability**, i.e. the possibility of substituting the members of the combination (as in "I saw *the movie / the picture / John*"; "to hang *the laundry / the clothes*"; "*read / write / publish* a book," etc.) and **syntactic variability**, that is, the ability of the members of the combination to undergo syntactic operations such as relativization, passivization, and so forth: for example "I saw the movie," "The movie I saw ...," "The movie was seen by ...," etc. (for this terminology, see Sag et al. 2002). These two aspects together will allow us to assess the **distributional variability** and **degree of cohesiveness** of a word combination, also referred to as *figement* in the French tradition (Gross 1996a).

---

In our analysis of verb–noun combinations, the syntactic modifications that appear to be most relevant to distinguish between different types of combinations are: (a) modification of the determination of the noun, (b) relativization of the noun, (c) displacement of the noun in the structure, (d) passivization of the combination, and (e) insertion of words between the members of the combination. Several examples of these modifications are given below.

Taken together, the three criteria above allow us to identify the types introduced below.

## 6.4.1. Free combinations

In principle, a **free combination** is the combination of two or more words on which no restriction applies. It should be made clear that no combination exists in language that is completely free. In fact, any combination involves at least some conceptual/ontological restriction, owing to the nature of the word referents, which display more or less typical attributes or uses, and simultaneously rule out others. For example, the word *bread*, as we noted in Chapter 2, occurs with adjectives expressing attributes such as *fresh, crunchy, homemade, moldy*, or *stale; white, brown*, or *whole-meal*, and with verbs expressing actions such as *bake, butter, eat, toast, cut, slice*, and *buy*, but rules out other words, because they denote properties or actions that cannot be applied/ascribed to bread. For example, one cannot *drink, melt*, or *praise* bread; *bread* cannot be said to be *angry* or *boring*, and so forth. Note that certain words may in principle occur with *bread* but appear not to. This is because the action or property they express is odd when applied to bread ("odd" in an ontological sense), and people do not talk about bread in this way. This is why *wash bread*, although imaginable, sounds odd and will not be found in a corpus.

Once we have made clear that all word combinations involve at least some conceptual/ontological restrictions, a combination can still be classified as free when it exhibits the following characteristics:

1. It is created *ad hoc* by the speaker on the spur of the moment for the purpose of the speech act he intends to make. Note that this single criterion rules out idioms, fixed or semi-fixed phrases, and word sequences with more or less frozen status, including compounds.
2. The members can be combined with other words, therefore substituted, while keeping the same meaning ("wash/build/sell the *car*") or, in the case of polysemous terms, while keeping one of their conventional meanings.
3. The referents denoted by the words are available in the discourse and for this reason we can also refer to them for example by means of a pronoun: "I searched for *the keys* and I found *them* in my bag."
4. The members allow the syntactic modifications that characterize a free element and can therefore be said to be syntactically autonomous/

independent. For example, for *book*: "I ordered the/a/many/some *book*(s)," "the *book* that I ordered," "the *book*, I ordered it yesterday," "the *book* was ordered," "I ordered a new *book*," and so forth.

5. The meaning of the combination is compositional, that is, it can be predicted from the meaning of the single words and their syntactic arrangement (apart from such contextual adjustments of meanings as those discussed in section 3.4, for example "*long* dress (= covering the legs)," "*long* silence (= protracted)," and so on).

On this basis, free combinations can be said to be combinations of words that are compatible.

## 6.4.2. Restricted combinations

Although all word combinations can be said to be conceptually/ontologically restricted (see section 6.3.1), if we focus on linguistic constraints, it is possible to identify two main types of **restricted combinations**, depending on whether the restriction is based on a lexical solidarity (as in "breastfeed one's child," where *breastfeed* implies that the action is directed towards a baby) or on patterns of use. An example of the latter is the English expression "to guard a secret." In the context of *secret*, the meaning of *guard* would be equally well conveyed by *preserve*, but *guard* is significantly more frequent, and is felt by speakers as the usual way to express this type of action. We focus here on the first case. A detailed consideration of the second case (collocations proper) will be postponed to the next section. As we shall see, the distinction between the two cases is, however, controversial.

Regarding combinations based on a lexical solidarity, the following observations can be made:

1. Restrictions vary with respect to their level of generality/specificity with respect to the taxonomy of categories. That is, they may either target a general category, such as CONCRETE OBJECT, or a specific one, such as VEHICLE. Consider first verb–noun combinations. If the restriction targets a class which is high in the hierarchy, the verb is perceived as selecting multiple classes of objects, as in the case of *buy*, which does not co-occur with ABSTRACT OBJECTS (except in figurative uses, such as "I bought your arguments"), but selects various kinds of CONCRETE OBJECTS (solid, liquid, etc.). If the restriction is low in the hierarchy, i.e. more specific, the verb

selects a single class of objects, as in *park* (VEHICLES: a car, a bicycle, a scooter, etc.), *wear* (GARMENTS: a suit, a dress, a hat, a uniform, jeans, a helmet), *fax* (DOCUMENTS: a letter, a copy of the driver's license), *utter* (SOUNDS made with one's voice: a cry, a groan, a scream), or even a single object, as in the case of *pasteurize* (*milk*, rarely *beer* and *wine*). It should be noted that the meaning of a verb that selects more specific object classes is more specific as well, and tends to monosemy. Analogously, in noun–adjective combinations, the adjective can be said to apply to several classes of nouns ("*long* hair," "*long* day," "*long* drink"), a restricted set ("*blonde* hair," "*blonde* beer"), a single class ("*isosceles* triangle"), or a single object ("*curdled* milk"). In the latter case, the adjective can be said to be a "dedicated" word for that class.

2. The meaning of a restricted combination is compositional, that is, it can be predicted from the meaning of the single words (adjusted according to the context and from their syntactic arrangement).

3. The ability to make substitutions for the members of the combination (so-called lexical variability) is constrained because of the presence of a restriction. When the restriction is very specific, it is impossible to substitute the term on which the restriction applies, in that no other word is available that denotes an object that can, for example, undergo the action denoted by the verb (what is *pasteurized* is milk) or that can have the property expressed by the adjective (nothing besides *milk* can be *curdled*).

4. The members of the combination behave like free elements from a syntactic point of view; they undergo various kinds of syntactic operations, including passivization ("the *car* can be parked"), relativization ("the *car* that I parked"), internal modification ("park the new *car*," "park a/the/ many *cars*"), extraction ("whose *car* did he park?"), and so forth.

## 6.4.3. Collocations

A particular type of restricted word combination is collocation. Right at the start we encounter deep controversies, as there are several definitions of collocation. In the following, we shall start from a broad definition of collocation, that includes any frequent word combination, and then move on to a narrower definition, that includes all word combinations to which a restriction applies (whatever the nature of such a restriction may be), and arrive, finally, at a very narrow definition, for which collocation is an institutionalized word combination, corresponding to a conventionalized way of saying a certain thing.

A broad and therefore very neutral definition is as follows: a collocation is a frequent co-occurrence of two words in a language. For example, according to Sinclair (1991: 170), a collocation may be defined as "the occurrence of two or more words within a short space of each other in text," apt to be "frequently repeated." Similarly, Sag et al. (2002) use the term collocation for "any statistically significant co-occurrence [...] predictably frequent because of real world events or other nonlinguistic factors, such as *sell a house*." Such a broad definition of collocation is often found in lexicographic work, for example in Benson, Benson, and Ilson (1986), where the term used is *recurrent word combination*.

This is a statistical definition of collocation, based on frequency. It is interesting as a starting point but, in and of itself, it does not say much on the structure of the lexicon, because also *I* + *ate* or *the* + *people* are frequent combinations, but not collocations (at least, not as we intend them here). We will not regard frequent combinations such as *sell* + *house* as collocations, but rather as combinations between words that are compatible, i.e. free combinations in the sense outlined in 6.3.1. above.

A more precise definition of collocation is the following: a collocation is a co-occurrence of words on which one or more restrictions apply. This is the definition proposed for example in Mel'cuk and Wanner (1994), where the term used is *restricted lexical co-occurrence*. This definition is more precise, because it highlights the fact that the words that co-occur more frequently than one would expect by chance do so by virtue of the fact that a restriction applies on their combination that favors their co-occurrence and at the same time constrains their compatibility with other words. Nevertheless, it is still far from clear what type of restriction(s) we are talking about. As we have seen, there are different types.

A third definition is more technical, but more satisfying from a linguistics point of view. A collocation is a word combination on which a restriction applies, for which the choice of a particular word (the **collocate**) to express a given meaning is influenced by a second word (the **base**) to which this meaning applies. A well-known example of this kind of collocation is noun modification by magnitude adjectives, as in the English expression *heavy rain*. To express the concept of "intensity" (or *magnitude* function, in Mel'cuk and Wanner 1994's terms), *rain* (the base) is frequently found with the adjective *heavy* (the collocate), rather than with other adjectives that in principle are equally compatible from a semantic point of view (*strong*, *intense*, and so forth). Other examples of adjective–noun combinations involving magnitude are: *large* (vs. *high* or *great*) *number*; *great* (vs. *major* or *big*) *success*; *great* (vs. *major* or *high*) *import-ance*; *major* (vs. *great*) *problem*; *high* (vs. *great*) *quality*. In these examples, the first adjective appears to be the most conventional, i.e. the one that most typically expresses that property of that particular object. Another well-known example of collocation is provided by verb–noun construc-tions with "specialized" verbs such as *launch an appeal*. In this case, to express the act of "creating" an *appeal*, intended as in "launch a large scale charitable appeal for disaster relief," the base (*appeal*) combines more naturally with a specific collocate (*launch*) rather than with other compatible verbs (note that *make an appeal* would be normal for a different type of appeal—a personal or legal appeal).

The definition of collocation given above, however, can still be improved. For example, one might suppose that lexical semantic solidarities, on the one hand (such as that existing between *to wear* and *garment*), and proper collocations on the other hand (such as, for example, *pay attention*) are similar phenomena, while we can draw some distinctions between them. One of these distinctions emerges if we apply the following test:

**(6)**  Lexical semantic solidarities:

| even alone | *to park* | implies | *vehicle* |
|---|---|---|---|
| | *to wear* | implies | *garment* |
| | *aquiline* | implies | *nose* |
| | *blonde* | implies | *hair* |

**(7)**  Collocations proper:

| *even alone | *to launch* | implies | *appeal* |
|---|---|---|---|
| | *to pay* | implies | *attention* |
| | *heavy* | implies | *rain* |
| | *strong* | implies | *tea* |

The test above can be formulated as follows: can a foreign speaker, who knows the meaning of words but not the collocations of the language, guess the noun from the verb or the adjective? For example, can he/she guess *garment* from *wear* taken in isolation? Can he/she guess *attention* from *pay*?

The test shows that in lexical semantic solidarities there is a connection between the two terms, which is preserved for the collocate when it is taken individually (if taken alone, *wear* necessarily implies *garment*). By contrast, in collocations (according to the narrow definition we adopt here) the connection is present in the combination but is absent if the collocate is taken individually. For example, if taken alone, *pay* does not imply *attention*. This is because the collocate is either highly polysemous— in the sense that it describes a property or action that may apply to several classes of objects (*heavy*, *strong*)—or it is a term whose core meaning does not inherently express an activity in which the referent of the base participates (*pay*, *launch*). By contrast the collocates in (7) are words whose core meaning denotes a property or an activity that applies to the class of objects represented by the base (they are *dedicated* words for the base), and tend to monosemy.

In English, *launch*, *pay*, *heavy*, and *strong* are selected by their bases (*appeal*, *attention*, *rain*, *tea*) from a range of possible terms to express a meaning that they do not have when they are combined with other words and that they acquire in the specific combination; this is what in the literature is called **meaning by collocation** (for this terminology, see Firth 1957, 194; recall also the observations made in section 2.1). In other words, these terms establish a solidarity with the base only in the specific use; for this reason we can speak of solidarities institutionalized by use.

> Note that in the examples above, the meaning by collocation is achieved by metaphorical shift. For example, in the context of *rain* (the base) the meaning of *heavy* (the collocate) becomes 'falling with force.'

Finally, the direction of the restrictions operating in (6) and (7) differs. In semantic solidarities, the verb and the adjective impose a semantic requirement on the noun, whereas in collocations proper, the restriction can be said to operate in the opposite direction, in the sense that it is the noun that calls for a specific verb or adjective to express a certain action or property of its referent. In this view, collocation can be said to be ultimately a matter of lexical choice governed by use rather than the result of a semantic constraint.

Collocations are interesting when looked at across languages, because languages display variability in their choice of collocates. For example, Engl. *to brush one's teeth* has the following equivalents: It. *lavarsi i denti* (literally 'to wash one's teeth'); Germ. *zich die Zähne putzen* 'to clean one's teeth'; Engl. *slice of cheese/bread/pie/pineapple* is *plakje kaas* (literally, small slice of cheese), *sneetje broot* (literally, small slice of bread), *taartpunt* (literally, pie point), and *schijfje ananas* (literally, small pineapple disk) in Dutch. Yet these differences should not surprise us, especially in the case of collocations that give rise to figurative uses. After all, figurative uses are often based on metaphors that can rest on different kinds of similarities. Such metaphorical operations are "cognitively" transparent and can be easily interpreted. For example, a non-native speaker of Italian who knows the literal meaning of the word *battere* ('to hit' or 'to strike') will most likely be able to interpret the expression *pioggia battente* (lit. beating rain), even if in his/her language the same concept is expressed with a different word, that is, with another metaphor (as in Engl. *heavy rain*).

We can distinguish different types of collocations in syntactic context. Benson, Benson, and Ilson (1986) distinguish seven major types: (1) creation or activation verb + noun: *perform a task*; (2) annulment verb + noun: *revoke a license*; (3) adjective + noun: *warm greeting*; (4) noun + verb that expresses an action typical of the noun: *the alarm goes off*; (5) quantification unit + noun to which the unit refers: *wealth of details*; (6) adverb + adjective: *intimately connected*; (7) verb + adverb: *hate viscerally, pay dearly*. From a syntactic point of view, the members of a collocation cannot be substituted because of the presence of a restriction, but are in most cases fully flexible from a syntactic point of view, in the sense that they easily undergo syntactic modifications: "launch the/an/many/some appeal(s)," "the appeal that I launched," "the appeal was launched," "I launched a second appeal"; for adjective–noun combinations: "How's the tea? Strong."; "The tea is strong" (compare with "How's the disk? *Hard," *"The disk is hard" for *hard disk*).

In rare cases, the variability of the combination is partially blocked, for example in the case of *press charges*, which occurs naturally without the article. These are partially lexicalized uses and, therefore, closer to the status of complex word, to which we will return in section 6.5.

### 6.4.3.1. *Salience vs. frequency*

What counts in a collocation is not pure frequency but salience. Consider the example of *heavy rain* above. Although *heavy* is the most frequent intensifying adjective with *rain*, there appears to be at least another expression in English that sounds even more conventionalized, namely *pouring rain*. If we query the corpus (for example the British National Corpus) using a corpus query system like the Sketch Engine (Kilgarriff et al. 2004), we see that although *heavy rain* is almost four times more frequent that *pouring rain*, *pouring rain* has a higher score for saliency. This is because although *heavy* appears with *rain* more often than *pouring*, it also occurs with a large number of other words, while *pouring* combines only with a restricted set of words, one of which is *rain*. In other words, the tendency of *pouring* to appear with *rain* rather than appearing with other words is stronger than *heavy*. The difference in saliency score between the two expressions identifies this distinction.

| BNC | Frequency | Salience |
|-----|-----------|----------|
| pouring rain | 77 | 10.36 |
| heavy rain | 264 | 9.5 |

Salience, as defined above, can be established using several kinds of association measures. Commonly used measures of association applied to lexical analysis of collocations include Mutual Information (MI, Church and Hanks 1989). Mutual Information provides a measure of the degree of association of a given segment of text with others. In the example above, we have assumed the statistical measure used in the Sketch Engine query system, which is currently *logDice*. Details about logDice can be found in Rychlý (2008).

## 6.4.4. Light verb constructions

Particular types of collocation are **light verb constructions**. These are verb–noun combinations consisting of a highly polysemous verb called a *light* or *support verb* (such as *make, do, take, give, have,* and a few others; cf. Jespersen 1965) and an event noun (*decision, call, walk, proposal*) preceded by an article and/or, in a few cases, by a preposition. Standard examples of light verb constructions for English are the following: *take a walk, do (someone) a favor, make a call, have a rest, give a talk,* and *be in danger.* These verbs tend to be the same across languages; see It. *fare* 'do, make,' *dare* 'give,' *prendere* 'take'; Fr. *faire* 'do, make,' *prendre* 'take,' *donner* 'give'; Germ. *machen* 'do, make,' *geben* 'give,' *haben* 'have,' *nehmen* 'take.'

Light verb constructions share the following properties with collocations:

1. The noun imposes a restriction on the choice of the verb. Compare *\*do a mistake* with *make a mistake,* ?*take a choice* with *make a choice.*
2. The restriction appears to be conventionalized and often varies across languages. Compare Engl. *take (\*make) a photograph* with It. *fare* ('make') *una fotografia*; Engl. *have breakfast* with It. *fare (\*avere) colazione.*
3. The noun is semantically transparent, as in Engl. *give an answer* but not in *give a hand,* which is an idiomatic expression (cf. section 6.4.6).
4. The noun displays one of the meanings it has in other combinations, that is, it does not shift meaning in the construction; compare *make a decision* with *regret/announce/postpone a decision.*
5. The noun determines how the verb is interpreted in the construction; compare *give* ( = emit) *a sigh* vs. *give* (= deliver) *a presentation.*
6. The members of the construction are flexible from a syntactic point of view. This is shown by the fact that they undergo various types of

syntactic modifications, including internal modification and determination ("take good, crucial, *decisions*"); relativization ("the *decisions* we
make every day"); passivization ("their *decision* was made after...");
anaphora ("When he makes a *decision*, he makes it") and so forth (see
more on this point below).

By contrast, light verb constructions differ from other collocations in that
the contribution of the verb to the meaning of the construction is very
"light." This can be seen clearly if we compare light verb constructions
with "regular" uses of the same verbs. Consider for example *make*. Out of
context, *make* can be said to be a highly ambiguous verb, that is, a verb that
may take on a large number of different meanings depending on the context
in which it is used. For example, when it combines with entity nouns such as
*money, friend, coffee*, etc., *make* appears to acquire specific meanings largely
determined by the noun: *make money* (= 'earn'), *make a friend* (= 'acquire'),
*make tea* (= 'prepare'); *make a list* (= 'compile'), *make a hole in the ground*
(= 'dig'), and so on. With event nouns, however, the result appears to be
different. In all combinations with event nouns, *make* has somehow the
same general meaning, no matter what type of event the noun expresses. For
example, in *make a call*, *make a proposal*, and *make a mistake*, *make* has
basically the same general sense, namely that of "create N" or "bring N into
existence." Aside from the creation sense, a light verb also expresses abstract
content features such as *Aktionsart*. *Make*, for example, can be said always
to denote an activity, as opposed to *be* that denotes a state (*be in danger*).

On these grounds, from a semantic point of view, light verb constructions
may be defined as *noun-oriented* collocations, i.e. collocations whose main
semantic load is borne by the noun instead of by the verb.

Based on these considerations some scholars have proposed that light
verb constructions differ also with regard to the (main) locus of the predication. For example, according to Gross (1996b) the actual predicate of a
light verb construction is the noun, while the verb "supports" the noun in
the construction of the sentence, inasmuch as the noun, even if it plays the
role of the main predicate, is not able, by itself, to express some of the
constituent elements of the predication, such as tense or mood information.
According to this proposal, the underlying structure of a light verb construction can be represented as follows:

1. Construction where the verb coincides with the predicate:

   SUBJECT$_N$      PREDICATE$_V$      ARGUMENT$_N$

2. Light verb construction:

   SUBJECT$_N$      SUPPORT$_V$      NOMINAL PREDICATE$_N$

The proposed structure above resembles the one proposed for copular constructions in Chapter 4. This, however, does not entitle us to conclude that the two can be reduced to the same phenomenon. In fact, the two constructions differ in that in light verb constructions the noun is an *unsaturated* noun, that is, a noun which licenses arguments (*Peter's decision, Marc's advice to John, Adam's walk*) whereas in copular constructions the predicative noun is a *saturated* noun ("Marc is an engineer," etc.) (see Prandi 2004: 194, 373 on this point).

Another difference is that ordinary collocations are fully flexible from a syntactic point of view, whereas light verb constructions can be broadly divided into two classes. Members of the first class (e.g. *make a call*) are flexible and may undergo syntactic operations of various kinds, while members of the second class (e.g. *pay attention*) are fixed or semi-fixed syntactically, as shown by the fact that they do not undergo syntactic modifications easily. This distinction can be explained by looking at the referentiality of the noun. As it happens, the constructions whose members are not fully flexible syntactically are those in which the noun is non-referential.

Another feature that sets light verb constructions apart from other collocations is that the choice of the verb is obligatory in the first case but not in the second. As we saw in section 6.4.2, collocations may permit lexical variability and in this case the restriction operating on the combination might be analyzed in terms of preference rather than requirement. This variability does not characterize light verb constructions, where the verb can be substituted for other verbs which, however, appear to convey more meaning than ordinary light verbs do. These are the *supports appropriés* in Gross' terminology (lit. appropriate verbs): *pousser un cri* 'utter a cry,' *pratiquer un sport* 'practise a sport,' *exercer une pression* 'exert pressure,' and so forth. The problem of disambiguating between light verb constructions and ordinary collocations is discussed in Ježek (2004).

Finally, the lexical status of light verb constructions differs from that of ordinary collocations. To understand how, recall the distinction between analytic and synthetic lexicalization introduced in Chapter 1. Light verb constructions are, in this respect, typical examples of analytic predicates and may therefore be analyzed as lexical units in their own right. This is supported by the observation that, very often, light verb constructions have corresponding synthetic verbs: *to make a call / to call; to give an answer / to answer; to have dinner / to dine; to take a walk / to walk*, and so forth. This is not the case with ordinary collocations, nor with verbs' regular combinations: *to make a cake / *to cake, to take the car / *to car*, and so forth.

## 6.4.5. *Other constructions*

Over the past three decades, many linguists with varying backgrounds have converged on the insight that, in addition to having a lexicon and a set of rules that govern the way in which words go together to form meaningful sentences, languages are repositories of constructions. In this context (for example, Fillmore, Kay, and O'Connor 1988), a **construction** is defined as a memorized structure associated with a particular meaning, that is to say, as a "conventional form–meaning pairing" (cf. Chapter 3, Box 3.1). A linguistic expression is therefore recognized as a construction and differentiated from an ordinary syntactic structure as long as some aspect of its form or function is not strictly predictable from its component parts or from other constructions recognized to exist.

As an example of an English construction, consider the sentence "The sooner you leave, the quicker you'll get there," discussed among others in Goldberg 1995. This sentence may be regarded as an instance of a specific construction ("The X-er [...] the Y-er [...]" construction), because its syntax cannot be accounted for by the general rules of English. Specifically, the requirement that two phrases of this type be juxtaposed without a conjunction is non-predictable. Because the structure is non-predictable according to the general rules of English syntax, a construction is posited and it is assumed that it is stored in our linguistic knowledge. Other examples of the construction above are given in (8):

**(8)**  The longer you wait, the harder it will be.
     The earlier I start, the earlier I finish.

By definition, a construction involves a certain degree of internal computation, in the sense that while some slots may be fixed, at least one slot must allow for lexical variability. If this is not the case, i.e. if the construction has no such slot, there is a good chance that the expression is in fact a multiword expression, a phraseological unit, and the like (cf. section 1.4.1.). Note that in the "The X-er [...] the Y-er [...]" construction, the two open slots may potentially include any adverbial expression. However, corpus analysis shows that only a restricted set of words actually fills the construction: *earlier, sooner, quicker, longer, faster, further, harder,* and a few others.

Interestingly, in her work, Goldberg extends the notion of construction to argument structures. In a constructional perspective, argument structures such as those examined in section 4.4.1.2 are interpreted as memorized form–meaning pairings into which verbs may or may not be inserted. That is, they are not analyzed as the product of lexical projection as in standard generative accounts but rather as independent linguistic objects that must be learned and memorized. The meaning of an **argument-structure construction** is an abstract meaning, for example *caused-motion, cause-receive, resultative*, etc., and verbs in the language can be used to fill the available slots to the extent that their meaning is compatible with (or can be adjusted to be compatible with) the meaning of the construction itself. This is known as the **compatibility constraint**. In (9) we provide an example of caused-motion construction, together with its syntactic and semantic representation (an example of coerced use can be found in Box 3.1):

**(9)** Sam put the books in the bookshelf.
Subject-V-Object-Oblique
(where V is a non-stative verb and Oblique is a directional phrase)
X causes Y to move Z

The linguistic status of the heterogeneous group of entities called constructions is controversial. A large number of linguists working within the constructional paradigm today believe that the dividing line between syntax and lexicon is too clear-cut and that construction represent a level of linguistic organization which is somehow intermediate between the two. Under this view, phenomena which exhibit properties of both lexical items and syntactic structures are expected, and construction can be seen as memorized chunks with specific meanings and a certain degree of internal productivity.

## 6.4.6. Idiomatic expressions

Examples of **idiomatic expressions** (also called idioms) are Engl. *hold the floor* (= 'talk in front of an audience'), *take a stab (at something)* (= 'try'), *hit the road* (= 'start a trip'), *bark up the wrong tree* (= 'follow the wrong course'), *be born yesterday* (= 'be naïve'), *read between the lines* (= 'understand what is meant'), *backseat driver* (= 'annoying person'), *round table* (= 'assembly for discussion'), It. *alzare il gomito* (lit. raise the elbow = 'drink too much'), *vuotare il sacco* (lit. empty the bag = 'confess'), *mosca bianca* (lit. white fly = 'person with special qualities').

Idiomatic expressions differ markedly from the phenomena discussed earlier in this chapter. Basically what distinguishes idiomatic expressions from other kinds of word combinations is the different way in which their meaning is constructed. Strictly speaking, the meaning of an idiomatic expression is not "built," but rather created *en bloc* by means of cognitive processes that lie at the core of figurative language use, such as resemblance.

The following is an example: It. *vuotare il sacco* (lit. empty the bag) →
'uncover what it contains' → 'reveal something.' By contrast, the meaning of
non-idiomatic combinations—either free or restricted in the sense defined
above—can be said to be built syntagmatically by means of compositional
processes (including strong compositionality, cf. Chapter 3).

When a resemblance applies, the meaning is transferred from its original
context and fixed upon a complex linguistic expression that is consequently
blocked as regards the possibility of either substituting members or modifying them; for example, with *hold the floor* 'talk to a group of people for a
period of time', the following transformations are not acceptable: *"He is
holding the ground," *I held two/many/some floors, *The floor that I held,
*The floor, it was me who held it, *The floor was held by me, *I held a
second floor. Note that substitution is possible, but the meaning is not
preserved; "He is holding his ground" is a perfectly well-formed expression,
but a different idiom, meaning 'He is not retreating or losing his advantage'.

In short, these complex expressions end up behaving, semantically and
syntactically, as a single word (or as a **word-with-spaces**, in Sag et al.'s 2002
terminology). In their idiomatic reading Engl. *take the cake, jump the gun,*
or It. *vuotare il sacco* are one-slot verbs (that is, verbs that requires a single
argument, i.e. the subject) and mean 'exceed all others,' 'act prematurely,'
and 'confess' respectively.

---

Several scholars have observed that idioms are not a unitary category.
For example, some idioms appear to be not completely rigid in the sense
that they allow internal variability in terms of both syntactic modification and lexical substitution. Consider the English expression *get on
somebody's nerves* meaning 'irritate someone'; it may be modified by
inserting an adjective ("You are getting on my very last nerves") or it can
be manipulated syntactically in several creative ways ("I only have one
nerve left and you're getting on it"). Similarly, Engl. *touch a nerve* in its
idiomatic reading of 'refer to a sensitive topic' may be modified by
inserting an adjective ("He touched a raw, a very sensitive, an easily
activated nerve"); it may be passivized ("I do wonder what nerve might
have been touched") and relativized ("There is some nerve that he
touches in his article"; "I think the nerve Lynda touched was that I'm
lazy"). Furthermore, the verb may be substituted, as in "This really
struck a nerve with me" or "You know you have hit a nerve." We may
call this variability the degree of *internal computation* of an idiom.

The term *constructional idiom* has gained popularity especially within
the constructional framework to identify idiomatic expressions with
internal computation as those discussed above. A **constructional idiom**
can be defined as a construction with a (partially) non-compositional

meaning, of which—unlike idioms in the traditional sense—not all ter-
minal elements are fixed (Jackendoff 1997, Booij 2002). In other words,
they are partially underspecified idioms. Nunberg et al. (2004) claim that
some idioms are semantically decomposable, i.e. components of the
overall meaning can be associated with parts of the expression. For
example, in *hold the floor*, *floor* can be identified with the audience,
whereas in *lift a finger* 'help', there is no separable meaning that can be
directly associated with finger, and the idiom can be said to be non
decomposable.

Although idiomatic expressions acquire their meaning in a way which
differs from that of standard word combinations, they may enter into
broader contexts and contribute to the overall meaning of the complex
expression of which they are part, analogously to simple words.

## 6.5. Impact of combinatory phenomena on the lexicon

After discussing combinatory phenomena between words in section 6.3 and
6.4, in this section we reconsider the notion of *complex word* introduced in
Chapter 1, and review it in the light of the various types of word combinations examined in this chapter.

Recall that what characterizes complex words and distinguishes them
from ordinary word combinations is that the former are sequences whose
members can be neither substituted for other words nor undergo syntactic
operations (insertion, modification, etc.), except to a very low degree. Recall
the examples discussed in section 1.4.1: *waiting *little* room, *evening *black*
dress,*look *the baby* after, and so forth. This is not the case with ordinary
word combinations, especially free combinations, whose members can be
substituted and modified at will, provided that conceptual/ontological
restrictions that apply on the combination are observed.

Furthermore, complex words often have a meaning that is non-
compositional, such as *round table* in "an interactive round table," where
the noun does not denote the artifact table and the adjective does not refer to
its physical properties. Again, this is not the case with ordinary word
combinations, whose meaning can be predicted from the meaning of the
individual words that make up the combination, either in a straightforward
fashion (as in *heavy table*) or through contextual activation of aspects of
meaning which remain covert otherwise. An example of the latter type is
*heavy bag*, where the most natural interpretation is that *heavy* describes a
property of the content of the bag instead of the bag itself.

As we saw in Chapter 1 (sections 1.2.1 and 1.4.2), however, shifts may occur from one category (word combination) to the other (complex word) through the process of lexicalization. In what follows, we examine this point in more detail, in the light of the additional elements introduced in this chapter. In the discussion, we deliberately leave aside strictly idiomatic expressions (*lift a finger*, *hold the floor*, and so forth), which, as we have seen, display unique characteristics as to how their meaning is created.

A first comment to make is that the process of lexicalization (understood as *univerbation*, cf. section 1.2.1) originates in the tendency of words that frequently co-occur to form lexical aggregates of sorts. These aggregates may be seen as a structural reflection of the unitary character of the conceptual content that they express as a whole. That is, lexical aggregates express, together, a concept that is salient in its totality. Because of the presence of privileged links between words that form a *conceptual constituent*, not all of the words that are arranged in sequence on the chain of speaking are semantically and syntactically equidistant from each other; some are closer than others.

> Note that *closeness* (or *cohesion/cohesiveness*, see Prandi 2004: 277, note 313), when looked at as a process, operates at two levels: the semantic level, which may be seen as the "trigger" of the lexicalization process (i.e. the level at which aggregation between words originates), and the syntactic level, which is the level at which the phenomenon manifests itself, by means of constraints to the lexical and syntactic variability of the combination. Finally, from the point of view of direction in language change, consider the following observation by Tesnière (1959: 27): "On constate qu'au cours de l'histoire des langues la profondeur des coupures qui séparent les mots va toujours en diminuant, jamais en augmentant."

When the distance between two or more words that co-occur is small, the chances that a lexicalization may occur are high. In this context, lexicalization is to be understood as a reanalysis of the boundaries between words that converts a word sequence into a single word. For example, the word sequence [go] + [out] in "How often do you go out with friends?" is reinterpreted as a single word [go out] whose meaning is 'spend time in a social event.' In other words, lexicalization is a diachronic process whose output is the creation of a new (complex) word. This can be represented as follows:

word combination → lexicalization → complex word

The lexicalization process is often associated with the loss, by the word sequence, of the property of having a predictable meaning. This is the case of the English sequence *pull off*, which means 'to separate from' in (10a) and 'to get away with' or 'to execute successfully" in (10b), where it is lexicalized:

**(10)**   a.  He *pulled off* his boots.
         b.  He *pulled off* a perfect scam.

The fact that the sequence *pull off* in (10b) is lexicalized and constitutes a complex word is shown by the impossibility of separating its constituent parts:

**(11)**   *He *pulled* a perfect scam *off*.

Similarly, It. *tirare fuori* 'take out' means 'extract' in (12a) and 'say, pronounce' in (12b), where verb–object inversion is ruled out (12c):

**(12)**   a.  It. Ha *tirato fuori* i soldi.
             'He took out the money'.
         b.  It. Ha *tirato fuori* una bella scusa.
             lit. He took out a good excuse.
         c.  It. *Ha *tirato* una bella scusa *fuori*.
             lit. He took a good excuse out.

It should be noted, however, that lexicalization may also involve word sequences whose global meaning preserves the property of being, at least in part, predictable. These are word sequences that express, together, a unitary concept and for this reason display a certain degree of formal cohesiveness, which may be detected by applying the usual tests of "wordhood" we introduced in Chapter 1. For example in (13) separating the members of the combination gives an odd result, except under particular conditions of intonation:

**(13)**   ?The man looked *quickly* up.

On closer analysis, even the It. expression *tirare fuori* in its literal sense is endowed with a certain cohesiveness, because, if it is not followed by a prepositional phrase, as in (14a), it cannot be easily interrupted, as in (14b):

**(14)**   a.  It. Hai tirato i soldi fuori dalla tasca?
             'Did you take the money out of the pocket?'
         b.  It. ?Avete tirato i soldi fuori?
             lit. 'Did you take the money out?'

This appears not to be the case in English, where object–particle inversion is allowed:

**(15)**   Have you pulled the muddy boots off?

The examples above show that lexicalization, understood as a reanalysis of word boundaries can, but need not, result in a complex word the meaning of which is not compositional. In other words, the presence of a non-compositional meaning may constitute an advanced phase of the lexicalization process, or a modality through which the process manifests itself, but not a necessary condition for it to occur.

As we just saw, one of the standard methods to verify whether a word sequence is lexicalized and, if so, what stage of lexicalization the word sequence is in, is to confirm whether the words may be substituted and the structure modified. For this aim one can use the tests introduced in Chapter 1, or other tests which are specific to the combination under examination, such as those for verb–noun combinations we introduced in this chapter. A comprehensive list of tests conceived to assess the presence of lexicalization in different types of word combinations for French can be found in Gross (1996a). In general, reduced syntactic variability, as highlighted by the tests, is interpreted as a reflection of a reduced distance between the terms and, consequently, of a more advanced lexicalization stage.

While the tests highlight certain properties of word combinations which cannot be directly perceived, there are surface features that provide direct evidence that a word sequence is undergoing lexicalization. In the case of verb–noun combinations, for example, one such feature is the absence of determiner or its reduction to one single possible form. For example, *ask (for) forgiveness*, *catch fire*, *pay attention* are semi-lexicalized sequences; this is shown by the fact that we cannot say *"the house caught *the* fire," *"they asked for *the* forgiveness," etc.

The absence or constraints in the choice of the determiner is, in turn, an indicator that the referent of the noun is not fully available. In fact, when no determiner is present, the ability of the noun to identify precisely what it refers to is reduced or ruled out. For example, the expression *press charges* in "I pressed charges against him" (but not in "I withdrew the charges") has a generic reference and does not mean 'press a specific charge' but 'accuse someone formally of one or more crimes.' Recall that a noun's referent is more identifiable when the noun is countable, definite, and singular, and tends to be less identifiable when it is mass, either indefinite or with no determiner, and plural.

Unavailability of the noun's referent or reduced referentiality activates a chain of phenomena; the noun loses its status as an argument while acquiring that of modifier to the predicate; a closer link between noun and verb is created; the syntactic independence of each word decreases and, in the most advanced stage of the lexicalization process, verb and noun end up constituting a single (intransitive) verb (*press charges* = 'accuse'). The schematization below illustrates this point, where 1 and 2 represent absence and presence of lexicalization respectively:

1.  [verb] + pred   +   [noun] + arg   *deny the charge*   [− lexicalization]
2.  [[verb] + pred   +   [noun] + arg]   *press charges*   [+ lexicalization]

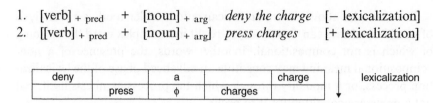

**Figure 6.1** Syntagmatic relations in two different verb–noun combinations.

Imagine examining the syntagmatic chain with a magnifying lens with the purpose of highlighting the syntagmatic relations holding between the words that make up the two combinations above. Under the lens, the difference in distance that can be said to hold between verb and noun in the two cases can be represented as in Figure 6.1.

On the one hand, a combination such as *deny the charge* is a free combination. The noun can be easily substituted for other nouns ("to deny an accusation / the responsibility / rumours / the facts," etc.) and it can undergo various kinds of syntactic operations such as relativization ("A charge the company denies"), adjectival modification ("The man denied the corruption charges"), and passivization ("The charge was initially denied by the Minister of Defence"). The combination *press charges*, on the other hand, appears to be rigid when used in contexts in which the police, for example, asks the victim of an assault whether he wants to "press charges." By rigidity we mean for example that the noun does not occur with an article or in the singular form (*"press a charge"). This can be seen as an indicator that in the context of *press*, the noun *charge* is not referential in the same way as in the context of *deny*, and that the distance between *charge* and *press* along the syntagmatic chain is smaller than the usual distance between a verb and its object, as in *charge* and *deny*. In other words, in *press charges*, *charge* tends to fuse with the verb to form a higher-order lexical unit.

Based on what we just said, it is evident that word combinations on which a restriction applies are good candidates for lexicalization processes, precisely because in this case words are "held together" by a constraint of some kind, whatever its nature.

In conclusion, our survey of combinatory phenomena from a lexical semantic perspective has established the following:

1. Word combination is a complex phenomenon. It involves the interplay of several factors of different nature, which makes it necessary to distinguish between different kinds of combination types.
2. The presence of a restriction on the combination does not correlate with a decrease of the possibility to predict its meaning. For example, *pasteurize*

*milk* is a restricted combination, from the point of view of both the verb (only certain types of things can be *pasteurized*) and the noun (only certain actions can be applied to *milk*), but the expression is fully compositional.

3. Syntactic rigidity of a combination often goes hand in hand with low predictability of its overall meaning. This correspondence, however, is not necessary; combinations such as *work in progress*, are sequences whose syntactic variability is constrained (see *\*a work in good progress*) but whose meaning is compositional.

As a consequence, the three criteria that we have considered to distinguish different types of word combinations, that is, (a) presence of a restriction on the combination, (b) predictability of meaning, and (c) syntactic and lexical variability are correlated, but not in a one-dimensional fashion.

For this reason, word combinations cannot be classified along a single continuum ranging from free combinations to restricted ones to idiomatic expressions, as is often proposed. Being idiomatic is not the result of an increase in the restrictions operating on the combination but of mechanisms of a different nature. Despite the fact that idiomaticity manifests itself by blocking our ability to substitute the members of the sequence, as in the case of *hold the floor* discussed above, the shift from literal to metaphorical meaning which characterizes idiomatic expressions does not concern, except in a peripheral way, the phenomenon of word combination.

## Further reading

As a general reference on word combinatory phenomena, see Zgusta (1971), Chapter 3—from a lexicographic perspective—and Cruse (2004), chapter 12.

On lexical combinatorics, see Heid (1994).

On collocations in a computational perspective, see Manning and Schütze (1999), chapter 5.

On directionality in selectional restrictions, see Bosque (2004a).

A pioneering work on the notion of construction and construction grammar is Fillmore, Kay and O'Connor (1988).

On idioms, Nunberg et al. (1994); Jackendoff (1997), chapter 7.

# Concluding observations

The study of the lexicon has been incredibly prolific in the last ten years. When it was first published in 2005, little bibliography was available that would gather the observations aimed at in this book; there were plenty of introductions to semantics and lexical semantics on the market, but textbooks that systematically focused on the lexicon and put words and their multifarious properties center stage, without embracing a specific theory, and were firmly based on data and its analysis were still missing. Notable exceptions were Singleton and Pinker, where, however, empirical evidence was not at the center of the discussion.

Nowadays the panorama has changed; the book on lexical analysis by Patrick Hanks, for example, provides an excellent example of such a trend, without being a textbook itself. Moreover, many introductions to morphology, such as Geert Booij's *The Grammar of Words*, go well beyond traditional morphology and devote attention to lexical matters, overcoming the strict divide between morphology and syntax, which characterized earlier production.

At present, we are witnessing a revolution not so much in the methodology but in the techniques and technology that can be used to perform lexical analysis. Distributional semantics, the major trend nowadays in lexical studies, represents a pole of attraction for many scholars dealing with lexical data. Although the framework is rooted in the work of John R. Firth, Zelig Harris, and subsequent work, it can be seen as a innovative way to look at massive data and to extract linguistic generalizations supported by empirical work informed by statistical techniques. Whether distributional semantics really represents a new paradigm in the science of language and in particular in semantic analysis, with psychological validity and cognitive adequacy, is for the years to come to confirm.

An emerging need in the field of semantics is the effort to combine two traditions of study, namely formal semantics focused on function words and aspects such as quantification and lexical inference, and distributional semantics, focusing on content words and similarities among them, to arrive at lexical representations which are both empirically grounded and theoretically informed. Many workshops organized at top conferences in linguistics, particularly computational linguistics, around the world testify to this trend.

This effort holds the promise of significantly advancing the state of the art, as it is developing a model of semantics, both lexical and compositional, that accounts for both functional and conceptual aspects of meaning. The enterprise, of course, poses great challenges from both a theoretical and an engineering point of view.

The field of lexical studies is vibrant and this book will hopefully contribute to attract new students and researchers to the area.

# References

AITCHINSON, J. (1987). *Words in the Mind: An Introduction to the Mental Lexicon*. Oxford and New York: Blackwell.

ALEXIADOU, A. (2001). *Functional Structure in Nominals*. Amsterdam and Philadelphia: John Benjamins.

ALINEI, M. (1974). *La struttura del lessico*. Bologna:1 Il Mulino.

APRESJAN, Y.D. (1973). Regular polysemy, in *Linguistics*, 142, 5–32.

APRESJAN, Y.D. (1992). *Lexical Semantics: User's Guide to Contemporary Russian Vocabulary* (2nd edn., first edn. 1974). Ann Arbor, MI.: Karoma Publishers.

ARONOFF, M. and K. FUDEMAN (2005). *What is Morphology?* Malden MA: Blackwell Publishing.

ASHER, N. (2011). *Lexical Meaning in Context: A Web of Words*. Cambridge: Cambridge University Press.

ATKINS, S. and M. RUNDELL (2008). *The Oxford Guide to Practical Lexicography*. Oxford: Oxford University Press.

BACH, E. (1986). The algebra of events, in *Linguistics and Philosophy*, 9, 5–16.

BAKER, M.C. (2003). *Lexical Categories: Verbs, Nouns and Adjectives*. Cambridge: Cambridge University Press.

BARONI, M. (2009) *Vector-based Models of Semantic Relatedness, Computational Semantics Course*, Universidad Pompeu Fabra, Barcelona, June 8–11, 2009.

BARONI, M. (2013). Composition in distributional semantics, in *Language and Linguistics Compass*, 7, 10, 511–22.

BARSALOU, L.W. (1983). Ad hoc categories, in *Memory and Cognition*, 11, 211–27.

BEAVERS, J. (2008). Scalar complexity and the structure of events, in J. Dölling, T. Heyde-Zybatow, and M. Schäfer (eds.), *Event Structures in Linguistic Form and Interpretation*. Berlin and New York: Mouton de Gruyter.

BELLETTI, A. and L. RIZZI (1981). The syntax of *ne*: some theoretical implications, in *The Linguistic Review*, 1, 117–54.

BENSON, M., E. BENSON, and R. ILSON (1986). *The BBI Combinatory Dictionary of English. A Guide to Word Combinations*. Amsterdam: Benjamins.

BERTINETTO, P.M. and M. SQUARTINI (1995). An attempt at defining the class of gradual completion verbs, in P.M. Bertinetto et al. (eds.), *Temporal Reference, Aspect and Actionality: Semantic and Syntactic Perspectives*. Torino: Rosenberg & Sellier, 11–26.

BIERWISCH, M. (1990/1991). Event nominalizations: Proposals and problems, in *Acta Linguistica Hungarica*, 40, 1–2, 19–84.

BISANG, W. (2008). Precategoriality and argument structure in Late Archaic Chinese, in J. Leino (ed.), *Constructional Reorganization*. Amsterdam and Philadelphia: John Benjamins.

BISETTO, A. and S. SCALISE (2005). The classification of compounds, in *Lingue e Linguaggio*, IV/2, 319–32.

BLACK, M. (1954). *Metaphor*, in *Proceedings of the Aristotelian Society* 55 (1954/55), 273–94.

BOAS, H.C. (2011). A frame-semantic approach to syntactic alternations with build-verbs, in P. Guerrero Medina (ed.), *Morphosyntactic Alternations in English*. London: Equinox, 207–34.

BOOIJ, G. (2002). Constructional idioms, morphology, and the Dutch lexicon, in *Journal of Germanic Linguistics*, 14(04), 301–29.

BOOIJ, G. (2007) *The Grammar of Words: An Introduction to Morphology*. Oxford: Oxford University Press (2nd edn., 1st edn. 2005).

BOSQUE, I. (ed.) (2004a). *Redes. Diccionario combinatorio del español contemporáneo*. Madrid: Ediciones SM.

BOSQUE, I. (2004b). *Sobre la redundancia y las formas de interpretarla*, en *Actas del I Simposio de Didáctica*, Río de Janeiro, junio de 2004, Instituto Cervantes, 23–49.

BOSQUE, I. and R. MAIRAL (2012). Definiciones Mínimas, in F. Rodríguez González F. (ed.), *Estudios de lingüística española. Homenaje a Manuel Seco*, Universidad de Alicante, 123–36.

BOSSONG, G. (1992). Reflections on the history of the study of universals: The example of the 'Partes Orationis', in M.Kefer and J. van de Auwera, *Meaning and Grammar. Crosslinguistic Perspectives*. Berlin and New York: Mouton de Gruyter, 3–16.

CALZOLARI, N. et al. (2002). Towards best practice for multiword expressions in computational lexicons, in *Proceedings of LREC 2002: Third International Conference on Language Resources and Evaluation*, Las Palmas de Gran Canaria, Spain, May 29, 30 and 31, 2002, vol. VI, 1934–40.

CANN, R., R. KEMPSON, and E. GREGOROMICHELAKI (2009). *Semantics: An Introduction to Meaning in Language*. Cambridge: Cambridge University Press.

CARNAP, R. (1952). *Meaning Postulates*, in *Philosophical Studies*, 3, 65–73.

CARSTON, R. (2002). *Thoughts and Utterances: The Pragmatics of Explicit Communication*. Oxford: Blackwell.

CHIERCHIA, G. (2010). Mass nouns, vagueness and semantic variation, in *Synthese*, 174, 99–149.

CHIERCHIA, G. and S. McCONNELL-GINET (1990). *Meaning and Grammar. An Introduction to Semantics*. Cambridge MA: MIT Press.

CHOMSKY, N. (1965). *Aspects of the Theory of Syntax*. Cambridge MA: MIT Press.

CHOMSKY, N. (1970). Remarks on nominalization, in Roderick Jacobs and Peter Rosenbaum (eds.), *Readings in English Transformational Grammar*. Waltham, MA: Ginn and Company, 184–221.

CHOMSKY, N. (1981). *Lectures on Government and Binding*. Dordrecht: Foris.

CHURCH, K. and P. HANKS (1989). Word association norms, mutual information, and lexicography, in *Proceedings of the 27th Annual Meeting of the Association for Computational Linguistics*.

CIMIANO, P. and J. WENDEROTH (2005). Automatically learning qualia structures from the Web, in T. Baldwin, A. Korhonen, and A. Villavicencio (eds.), *Proceedings of the ACL Workshop on Deep Lexical Acquisition*. Ann Arbor, Michigan, June 2005, ACL, 28–37.

COMRIE, B. (1976). The syntax of action nominals: A cross-language study, in *Lingua*, 40(2), 177–201.

COMRIE, B. (1981). *Language Universals and Linguistic Typology*. Oxford: Blackwell.

COSERIU, E. (1967). *Lexikalische Solidaritäten*, in *Poetica*, 1, 293–303.

CROFT, W. (2012). *Verbs: Aspectual and Causal Structure*. Oxford: Oxford University Press.

CROFT, W. and A.D. CRUSE (2004). *Cognitive Linguistics*. Cambridge: Cambridge University Press.

CRUSE, A.D. (1986). *Lexical Semantics*. Cambridge: Cambridge University Press.

CRUSE, A.D. (2004). *Meaning in Language: An Introduction to Semantics and Pragmatics*. Oxford: Oxford University Press (2nd edn., 1st edn. 1999).

CRUSE, A.D. (2011). *Meaning in Language: An introduction to Semantics and Pragmatics*. Oxford: Oxford University Press (3rd edn.).

CRUSE, A.D., F. HUNDSNURSCHER, M. JOB, and P. LUTZEIER (eds.) (2002). *Lexicology: A Handbook on the Nature and Structure of Words and Vocabularies*. Berlin-New York: Mouton de Gruyter.

DE MAURO, T. (2005). *La fabbrica delle parole: il lessico e problemi di lessicologia*. Torino: Utet.

DE SWART, H. (1998). *Introduction to Natural Language Semantics*. Stanford, CA: CSLI Publications.

DIK, S.C. (1978). *Stepwise Lexical Decomposition*. Lisse: Peter de Ridder.

DIK, S.C. (1997). *The Theory of Functional Grammar: The Structure of the Clause* (2nd edn., 1st edn. 1989), ed. by K. Hengeveld. Berlin: Mouton de Gruyter.

DIXON, R. (1977). Where have all the adjectives gone?, in *Studies in Language*, 1, 19–80.

DOWTY, D. (1979). *Word Meaning and Montague Grammar*. Dordrecht: Reidel.

DOWTY, D. (1991). Thematic proto-roles and argument selection, in *Language*, 67, 3, 547–619.

ECO, U. (1997). *Kant e l'ornitorinco*. Milano: Bompiani, 349–73.

EVANS, N. and T. OSADA (2005). Mundari: The myth of a language without word classes, in *Linguistic Typology*, 9, 351–90.

FAUCONNIER, G. (1985). *Mental Spaces: Aspects of Meaning Construction in Natural Language*. Cambridge MA: MIT Press.

FELLBAUM, C. (ed.) (1998). *Wordnet: An Electronic Lexical Database*. Cambridge MA: MIT Press.

FELLBAUM, C. (2002). On the semantics of troponymy, in R. Green, C.A. Bean, and S.H. Myaeng (eds.), *The Semantics of Relationships: An Interdisciplinary Perspective*, Dordrecht: Kluwer Academic Publishers, 23–34.

FILLMORE, C.J. (1968). The Case for Case, in E. Bach and R.T. Harms (eds.), *Universals in Linguistic Theory*, New York: Holt, Rinehart and Winston, 1–88.

FILLMORE, C.J. (1992). Frame semantics, in *Linguistics in the Morning Calm*, ed. by The Linguistic Society of Korea, Seoul, Hanshin, 111–37.

FILLMORE, C.J., P. KAY, and C. O'CONNOR (1988). Regularity and idiomaticity in grammatical constructions: The case of let alone, in *Language*, 64, 501–38.

FIRTH, J.R. (1957). Modes of meaning (1951), in id., *Papers in Linguistics, 1934–1951*, London: Oxford University Press, 190–215.

FODOR, J.A. (1987). *Psychosemantics*. Cambridge MA: MIT Press.

FODOR, J.A. (1998). *Concepts: Where Cognitive Science Went Wrong*. Oxford: Clarendon Press.

FRAWLEY, W. (1992). *Linguistic Semantics*. Hillsdale, New Jersey: L. Erlbaum Associates.

FREGE, G. (1892). Über Sinn und Bedeutung, in *Zeitschrift für Philosophie und philosophische Kritik*, 100, 25–50.

GANGEMI, A., N. GUARINO, C. MASOLO, A. OLTRAMARI, L. SCHNEIDER et al. (2002), *Sweetening Ontologies with DOLCE*, in A. Gómez-Pérez and V.R. Benjamins (eds.), *Proceedings of the 13th International Conference on Knowledge Engineering and Knowledge Management* (EKAW' 02), Ontologies and the Semantic Web, Berlin: Springer-Verlag, 166–81.

GEERAERTS, D. (2010). *Theories of Lexical Semantics*. Oxford: Oxford University Press.

GIACALONE RAMAT, A. (1993). *Italiano di stranieri*, in A. Sobrero (a cura di), *L'italiano contemporaneo: la variazione e gli usi*, Roma-Bari: Laterza, 341–410.

GIVÓN, T. (1979). *On Understanding Grammar*. New York: Academic Press.

GOLDBERG, A. (1995). *Constructions: A Construction Grammar Approach to Argument Structure*. Chicago: University of Chicago Press.

GRIMSHAW, J. (1990). *Argument Structure*. Cambridge MA: MIT Press.

GROSS, G. (1996a). *Les expressions figées en français*. Ophrys: Paris.

GROSS, G. (1996b). Prédicats nominaux et compatibilité aspectuelle, in *Langages*, 121, 54–72.

GROSS, G. and F. KIEFER (1995). La structure événementielle des substantifs, in *Folia Linguistica*, XXIX/1–2, 29–43.

GRUBER, J. (1965). *Studies in Lexical Relations*, PhD dissertation at MIT; then *Lexical Structures in Syntax and Semantics* (1976), Amsterdam: North Holland.

HAIMAN, J. (1980). Dictionaries and Encyclopaedias, in *Lingua*, 50, 329–57.

HANKS, P. (2000). Do word meanings exist?, in *Computers and the Humanities*, 34(1), 205–15.

HANKS, P. (2004). Corpus Pattern Analysis, in G. Williams and S. Vessier (eds.), *Proceedings of the Eleventh EURALEX International Congress* (EURALEX 2004), Lorient, 6–10 July, Université de Bretagne Sud, 87–98.

HANKS, P. (ed.) (2007). *Lexicology: Critical Concepts in Linguistics*. London: Routledge.

HANKS, P. (2013). *Lexical Analysis: Norms and Exploitations*. Cambridge MA: MIT Press.

HANKS, P. and J. PUSTEJOVSKY (2005). A pattern dictionary for natural language processing, in *Revue Française de Linguistique Appliquée*, 10/2, 63–82.

HARRIS, Z. (1956). Distributional Structure, in *Word*, X/2–3, 146–62.

HAY, J., C. KENNEDY, and B. LEVIN (1999). Scalar structure underlies telicity in degree achievements, in T. Matthews and D. Strolovitch (eds.), *The Proceedings of SALT IX*, Ithac: CLC Publications, 127–44.

HEID, U. (1994). On ways words work together. topics in lexical combinatorics, in Martin W. et al. (eds.). *Euralex 1994 Proceedings*, Amsterdam, Vrije Universiteit, 226–57.

HEIM, I. and A. KRATZER (1998). *Semantics in Generative Grammar* (Vol. 13). Oxford: Blackwell.

HENGEVELD, K. (1992). Parts of Speech, in *Non Verbal Predication: Theory, Typology and Diachrony*, Berlin and New York: Mouton de Gruyter, 47–72.

HENGEVELD, K., J. RIJKHOFF, and A. SIEWIERSKA, (2004). Parts-of-speech systems and word order, in *Journal of Linguistics*, 40, 527–70.

HIRST, G. (2004). Ontology and the Lexicon, in S. Staab and R. Studer (eds.), *Handbook on Ontologies* (2nd edn. 2009), Berlin: Springer, 269–92.

HJELMSLEV, L. (1959). *Essais linguistiques, Travaux du cercle linguistique de Copenhague* 12, Copenhagen: Nordisk Sprog-og Kulturforlag.

HJELMSLEV, L. (1961). *Prolegomena to a Theory of Language* (2nd edn., 1st edn. 1943), Madison: University of Wisconsin Press.

HOPPER, P. and S.A. THOMPSON (1980). Transitivity in grammar and discourse, in *Language*, 56, 251–99.

HOPPER, P. and S.A. THOMPSON (1984). The discourse basis for lexical categories in Universal Grammar, in *Language*, 60, 703–52.

HUANG, C.-R., N. CALZOLARI, A. GANGEMI, A. LENCI, A. OLTRAMARI, and L. PREVOT (eds.) (2010). *Ontology and the Lexico: A Natural Language Processing Perspective*. Cambridge: Cambridge University Press.

JACKENDOFF, R. (1988). Conceptual semantics, in U. Eco, M. Santambrogio, and P. Violi (eds.), *Meaning and Mental Representations*, Bloomington: Indiana University Press, 81–97.

JACKENDOFF, R. (1990). *Semantic Structures*. Cambridge MA: MIT Press.

JACKENDOFF, R. (1996). Conceptual Semantics and Cognitive Linguistics, in *Cognitive Linguistics*, 7–1, 93–9.

JACKENDOFF, R. (1997). *The Architecture of the Language Faculty*. Cambridge MA: MIT Press.

JACKENDOFF, R. (2002). *Foundations of Language*. Oxford: Oxford University Press.

JACKSON, H. (2002). *Lexicography: An Introduction*. London: Routledge.

JESPERSEN, O. (1965). *A Modern English Grammar on Historical Principles*, Part VI, *Morphology*, London: George Allen and Unwin.

JEŽEK, E. (2003). *Classi di verbi tra semantica e sintassi*. Pisa: ETS edizioni.

JEŽEK, E. (2004). Types et degrés de verbes supports en italien, in *Linguisticae Investigationes*, 27, 269–85.

Ježek, E. and P. Ramat (2009). On parts-of-speech transcategorizations, in *Folia Linguistica*, 43, 391–416.

Ježek, E. and P. Hanks (2010). What lexical sets tell us about conceptual categories, in *Corpus Linguistics and the Lexicon*, special issue of *Lexis*, 4, 7–22.

Ježek, E., B. Magnini, A. Feltracco, A. Blanchini, and O. Popescu (2014). T-PAS: A Resource of Typed Predicate Argument Structure for Linguistic Analysis and Semantic Processing, in N. Calzolari et al., *Proceedings of the Ninth International Conference on Language Resources and Evaluation (LREC' 14)* Paris: ELRA, 890–5.

Johnson, W. E. (1924). *Logic: Part III* (Cambridge: Cambridge University Press).

Johnston, M. and F. Busa (1999). Qualia structure and the compositional interpretation of compounds, in E. Viegas (ed.), *Breadth and Depth of Semantics Lexicons*. Dordrecht: Kluwer Academic Publisher, 167–87.

Katz, J.J. and J.A. Fodor (1963). The structure of a semantic theory, in *Language*, 39, 2, 170–210.

Kearns, K. (2007). Telic senses of adjectival verbs, in *Lingua*, 117, 1, 26–66.

Kennedy, C. and B. Levin (2008). Measure of change: The adjectival core of degree achievements, in L. McNally and C. Kennedy (eds.), *Adjectives and Adverbs: Syntax, Semantics and Discourse*. Oxford: Oxford University Press, 156–82.

Kilgarriff, A. (1997). I don't believe in word senses, in *Computers and the Humanities*, 31(2), 91–113.

Kilgarriff, A., P. Rychlý, P. Smrz, and D. Tugwell (2004). The sketch engine, in G. Williams and S. Vessier (eds.), *Proceedings of the XI Euralex International Congress*, July 6–10, 2004, Lorient, France, 105–16.

Kipper Schuler, K. (2005). *VerbNet: A Broad-coverage, Comprehensive Verb Lexicon*, PhD thesis, University of Pennsylvania, Philadelphia, PA.

Kleiber, G. (1999a). Associative anaphora and part–whole relationship: The condition of alienation and the principle of ontological congruence, in *Journal of Pragmatics*, 31, 339–62.

Kleiber, G. (1999b). *Problèmes de sémantique. La polysémie en question*. Villeneuve d'Asq: Presses Universitaires du Septentrion.

Koptjevskaja-Tamm, M. (2008). Approaching lexical typology, in M. Vanhove (ed.), *From Polysemy to Semantic Change: A Typology of Lexical Semantic Associations*. Amsterdam and Philadelphia: John Benjamins, 3–52.

Lakoff, G. (1987). *Women, Fire and Dangerous Things*. Chicago: University of Chicago Press.

Lakoff, G., J. Espenson, and A. Schwartz (1991). *The Master Metaphor List*. Technical report, University of California at Berkeley.

Landau, S.I. (2001). *Dictionaries: The Art and Craft of Lexicography*, Cambridge: Cambridge University Press (2nd edn.).

Lauwers, P. and D. Willems (2011). Coercion: definition and challenges, current approaches and new trends, in *Linguistics*, 49, 6, 1219–35.

Lazard, G. (1994). *L'actance*. Paris: Presses Universitaires de France.

Lenci, A. et al. (2000). *SIMPLE:* A general framework for the development of multilingual lexicons, in *International Journal of Lexicography*, XIII/4, 249–63.

LEVI, J.N. (1978). *The Syntax and Semantics of Complex Nominals*. Academic Press: New York.

LEVIN, B. (1993). *English Verb Classes and Alternations: A Preliminary Investigation*. Chicago: University of Chicago Press.

LEVIN, B. and M. RAPPAPORT HOVAV (1995). *Unaccusativity: At the Syntax–Lexical Semantics Interface*. Cambridge MA: MIT Press.

LEVIN, B. and M. RAPPAPORT HOVAV (2005). *Argument Realization*. Cambridge: Cambridge University Press.

LEWIS, D. (1986). *On the Plurality of Words*. Oxford: Blackwell.

LI, C.N. and S.A. THOMPSON (1981). *Mandarin Chinese: A Functional Reference Grammar*. Berkeley: University of California Press.

LIEBER, R. (2010). *Introducing Morphology*. Cambridge: Cambridge University Press.

LIEBER, R. and P. ŠTEKAUER (eds.). *The Oxford Handbook of Compounding*. Oxford: Oxford University Press.

LO CASCIO, V. and DE MAURO, T. (a cura di) (1997). *Lessico e Grammatica. Teorie linguistiche e applicazioni lessicografiche*. Roma: Bulzoni.

LYONS, J. (1966). Towards a 'notional' theory of the 'parts of speech', in *Journal of Linguistics*, 2, 2, 209–36.

LYONS, J. (1968). *Introduction to Theoretical Linguistics*. Cambridge: Cambridge University Press.

LYONS, J. (1977). *Semantics*. Cambridge: Cambridge University Press.

LÖBNER, S. (2013). *Understanding Semantics*. London: Routledge (2nd edn., 1st edn. 2002).

LÖBNER, S. (2011). Concept types and determination, in *Journal of Semantics* 28, 3, 279–333.

MANNING, C. and H. SCHÜTZE (1999). *Foundations of Statistical Natural Language Processing*. Cambridge MA: MIT Press.

MARCONI, D. (1997). *Lexical Competence*. Cambridge MA: MIT Press.

MASOLO, C., S. BORGO, A. GANGEMI, N. GUARINO, and A. OLTRAMARI (2003). WonderWeb Deliverable D18. *Laboratory for Applied Ontology, ISTC-CNR, Trento*.

MEL'CUK, I.A. and L. WANNER (1994). Towards an efficient representation of restricted lexical cooccurrence, in W. Martin et al., *Euralex 1994 Proceedings*, Amsterdam: Vrije Universiteit, 325–38.

MELLONI, C. (2012). *Event and Result Nominals: A Morpho-semantic Approach*, Bern: Peter Lang.

MENNECIER, P. (1995). *Le tunumiisut, dialecte inuit du Groenland oriental: description et analyse*, Paris: Klincksieck.

MICHAELIS, L. (2004). Type shifting in construction grammar: An integrated approach to aspectual coercion, in *Cognitive Linguistics*, 15, 1–67.

MILLER, G., R. BECKWIDTH, C. FELLBAUM, D. GROSS, and K.J. MILLER (1990). Introduction to WordNet: An on-line lexical database, in *International Journal of Lexicography*, 3, 4, 235–44.

MITHUN, M. (1984). The evolution of noun incorporation, in *Language*, 60, 847–94.

MITHUN, M. (1999). *The Languages of Native North America.* Cambridge: Cambridge University Press.

MOENS, M. and M. STEEDMAN (1988). Temporal ontology and temporal reference, in *Computational Linguistics*, 14, 15–38.

MURPHY, G.L. (2002). *The Big Book of Concepts.* Cambridge MA: MIT Press.

MURPHY, M.L. (2010). *Lexical Meaning.* Cambridge: Cambridge University Press.

NERLICH, B. (2003). *Polysemy: Flexible Patterns of Meaning in Mind and Language.* Berlin and New York: Walter de Gruyter.

NUNBERG, G. (1995). Transfers of meaning, in *Journal of Semantics*, 12,109–32.

NUNBERG, G., I.A. SAG, and T. WASOW (1994). Idioms, in *Language*, 70, 491–538.

OGDEN, C.K. and I.A. RICHARDS (1923). *The Meaning of Meaning.* London: Routledge & Kegan Paul.

OSSWALD, R. (2014). *Syntax and Lexicography*, in T. Kiss and A. Alexiadou (eds.), *Syntax—An International Handbook of Contemporary Research*, 2nd edn., Handbücher zur Sprach- und Kommunikationswissenschaft. Berlin: de Gruyter.

PALMER, M. and N. XUE (2010). Linguistic annotation, in A. Clark, C. Fox, and S. Lappin (eds.), *The Handbook of Computational Linguistics and Natural Language Processing.* Wiley-Blackwell, 238–70.

PARSONS, T. (1990). *Events in the Semantics of English: A Study in Subatomic Semantics.* Cambridge MA: MIT Press.

PARTEE, B., and M. ROOTH (1983). Generalized conjunction and type ambiguity, in *Formal Semantics: The Essential Readings*, 334–56.

PETUKHOVA, V. and H. BUNT (2008). Semantic role annotation: Design and evaluation of a set of data categories, in *Proceedings of the Sixth International Conference on Language Resources and Evaluation* (LREC 2008). Marrakech, Morocco, 28–30.

PINKER, S. (1999). *Words and Rules: The Ingredients of Language.* London: Phoenix.

POESIO, M. and A. ALMUHAREB (2008). Extracting concept descriptions from the Web; the importance of attributes and values, in P. Buitelaar and P. Cimiano (eds.), *Ontology Learning and Population: Bridging the Gap between Text and Knowledge.* Amsterdam: IOS Press, 29–44.

PORZIG, W. (1934). Wesenhafte Bedeu-tungsbeziehungen, in *Beiträge zur Geschichte der deutchen Sprache und Literatur*, 58, 70–97.

PRANDI, M. (2004). *The Building Blocks of Meaning.* Amsterdam and Philadelphia: John Benjamins.

PUSTEJOVSKY, J. (1991). The syntax of event structure, in *Cognition*, 41(1), 47–81.

PUSTEJOVSKY, J. (1995). *The Generative Lexicon.* Cambridge MA: MIT Press.

PUSTEJOVSKY, J. (2001). Type structure and the logic of concepts, in P. Bouillon and F. Busa (eds.), *The Language of Word Meaning.* Cambridge: Cambridge University Press, 109–45.

PUSTEJOVSKY, J. (2002). Syntagmatic processes, in Cruse et al. (eds.), 565–70.

PUSTEJOVSKY, J. (2008). From concepts to meaning. The Role of Lexical Knowledge, in P.G.J. Sterkenburg (ed.), *Unity and Diversity of Languages.* Amsterdam and Philadelphia: John Benjamins, 73–84.

PUSTEJOVSKY, J. and B. BOGURAEV (1993). Lexical knowledge representation and natural language processing, in *Artificial Intelligence*, 63, 193–223; reprinted in P. Hanks (ed.) (2007).

PUSTEJOVSKY, J., B. BOGURAEV, and E. JEŽEK (2008). Semantic coercion in language: Beyond distributional analysis, in *Italian Journal of Linguistics*, 20, 1, 181–214.

PUSTEJOVSKY, J. and E. JEŽEK (forthcoming). *Generative Lexicon Theory: A Guide.* Oxford: Oxford University Press.

QUILLIAN, M.R. (1968). Semantic memory, in N. Minsky (ed.), *Semantic Information Processing.* Cambridge MA: MIT Press.

RAMAT, P. (2005). *Pagine Linguistiche.* Rome and Bari: Laterza.

RAPPAPORT HOVAV, M. (2008). Lexicalized meaning and the internal temporal structure of events, in S. Rothstein (ed.), *Crosslinguistic and Theoretical Approaches to the Semantics of Aspect*, Amsterdam and Philadelphia: John Benjamins, 13–42.

RAPPAPORT HOVAV, M. and B. LEVIN (1998). Building verb meanings, in M. Butt and W. Geuder (eds.), *The Projection of Arguments: Lexical and Compositional Factors*, Stanford, CA: CSLI Publications, 97–134.

RAVIN, Y. and C. LEACOCK (eds.) (2000). *Polysemy.* Oxford: Oxford University Press.

RECANATI, F. (2004). *Literal Meaning.* Cambridge: Cambridge University Press.

RECANATI, F. (2012). Compositionality, flexibility and context-dependence, in M. Werning, W. Hinzen, and E. Machery (eds.), *The Oxford Handbook of Compositionality*, Oxford: Oxford University Press, 175–91.

RIEMER, N. (2010). *Introducing Semantics.* Cambridge: Cambridge University Press.

RIJKHOFF, J. (1991). Nominal aspect, in *Journal of Semantics*, 8, 291–309.

RUPPENHOFER, J., M. ELLSWORTH, M.R. PETRUCK, C.R. JOHNSON, and J. SCHEFFCZYK (2010). *FrameNet II: Extended Theory and Practice*, International Computer Science Institute, University of Berkeley (manuscript).

RYCHLÝ, P.A. (2008). A lexicographer-friendly association score, in P. Sojka and A. Horák (eds.), *Proceedings of Recent Advances in Slavonic Natural Language Processing* 2008 (RASLAN), Brno: Masaryk University.

SAEED, J.I. (2003). *Semantics.* Malden: Blackwell Publishing.

SAG, I.A., T. BALDWIN, F. BOND, A. COPESTAKE, and D. FLICKINGER (2002), Multiword expressions: A pain in the neck for NLP, in *Proceedings of CICLing 2002, Computational Linguistics and Intelligent Text Processing.* Berlin: Springer, 1–15.

SAHLGREN, M. (2006). *The Word-Space Model*, PhD thesis, Stockholm University.

SAPIR, E. (1921). *Language: An Introduction to the Study of Speech.* New York: Harcourt, Brace and World.

SASSE, H.J. (1993). Das Nomen—eine universale Kategorie?, in *Sprachtypologie und Univer-salienforschung*, 46, 3, 187–221.

SAUSSURE, F. DE (1916). *Cours de linguistique générale.* Paris: Edition Payot.

SCALISE, S. and A. BISETTO (2009). The classification of compounds, in R. Lieber and P. Štekauer (eds), 49–82.

SCHACHTER, P. (1985). Parts-of-speech systems, in T. Shopen (ed.), *Language Typology and Syntactic Description*, vol. I. Cambridge: Cambridge University Press, 1–61.

SCHWARZE, C. (1997). Strutture semantiche e concettuali nella formazione delle parole, in V. Lo Cascio and T. De Mauro (a cura di), 311–29.

SEARLE, J. (1969). *Speech Acts: An Essay in the Philosophy of Language*. Cambridge: Cambridge University Press.

SEILER, H.J. (1975). Die Prinzipien der deskriptiven und der etikettierenden Benennung, in id., *Linguistic Workshop III*, München, Fink, 2–57.

SIMONE, R. (1990). *Fondamenti di Linguistica*. Roma and Bari: Laterza.

SIMONE, R. (1997). *Esistono verbi sintagmatici in italiano?*, in V. Lo Cascio and T. De Mauro (a cura di), 155–169.

SIMONE, R. (2003). *Masdar, 'ismu al-marrati et la frontière verbe/nom*, in J.M. Girón Alconchel (ed.), *Estudios ofrecidos al profesor J. Bustos de Tovar*, Madrid: Universidad Complutense de Madrid, 901–18.

SIMONS, P. (1987). *Parts: A Study in Ontology*. Oxford: Clarendon Press.

SINCLAIR, J. (1991). *Corpus, Concordance, Collocation*. Oxford: Oxford University Press.

SINGLETON, D. (2000). *Language and the Lexicon: An Introduction*. London: Arnold.

SMITH, C. (1991). *The Parameter of Aspect*. Dordrecht: Kluwer Academic Publishers.

SPEER, R. (2007). Open mind commons: An inquisitive approach to learning common sense, in *Proceedings of the Workshop on Common Sense and Intelligent User Interfaces*.

TALMY, L. (1985). Lexicalization patterns: semantic structure in lexical forms, in T. Shopen (ed.), *Language Typology and Syntactic Description*, Cambridge: Cambridge University Press, vol. I, 56–149; reprinted in L. Talmy, *Toward a Cognitive Semantics*. Cambridge MA: MIT Press, 2000, vol. II, 21–212.

TENNY, C. (1992). The aspectual interface hypothesis, in I. Sag and A. Szabolsci (eds.), *Lexical Matters*. Stanford, CA: CSLI Publications, 1–27.

TESNIÈRE, L. (1959). *Eléments de syntaxe structurale*. Paris: Klincksieck.

TONHAUSER, J. (2007). Nominal tense? The meaning of Guaraní nominal temporal markers, in *Language*, 83, 4, 831–69.

TRIER, J. (1931). *Der Deutsche Wortschats im Sinnbezirk des Verstandes*. Heidelberg: Winter.

VAN VALIN JR, R.D. (1990). Semantic parameters of split intransitivity, in *Language*, 66, 221–60.

VAN VALIN, R.D. (2005). *Exploring the Syntax–Semantics Interface*. Cambridge: Cambridge University Press.

VAN VALIN, R.D. and R.J. LAPOLLA (1997). *Syntax, Structure, Meaning and Function*. Cambridge: Cambridge University Press.

VAN VALIN, R.D. and DAVID P. WILKINS (1996). The case for 'effector': Case roles, agents, and agency revisited, in M. Shibatani and A. Thompson (eds.), *Grammatical Constructions: Their Form and Meaning*. Oxford: Clarendon Press, 289–322.

VENDLER, Z. (1967). Verbs and times, in *Linguistics in Philosophy*, Ithaca (NY): Cornell University Press, 97–121.

VIBERG, Å. (1984). The verbs of perception: A typological study, in *Linguistics*, 21, 123–62.

VOSSEN, P. (eds.) (1998). *Eurowordnet: A Multilingual Database with Lexical Semantic Networks*. Dordrecht: Kluwer.

WEINREICH, U. (1964). Webster's Third: A critique of its semantics, in *International Journal of American Linguistics*, 30, 405–9.

WERNING, M., W. HINZEN, and E. MACHERY (eds.) (2012). *The Oxford Handbook of Compositionality*. Oxford: Oxford University Press.

WHORF, B. (1956). *Language, Thought and Reality: Selected Writings by Benjamin Lee Whorf*, ed. by J.B. Carroll. Cambridge MA: MIT Press.

WIERZBICKA, A. (1996). *Semantics: Primes and Universals*. Oxford and New York: Oxford University Press.

WILKS, Y. (1975). A preferential, pattern-seeking semantics for natural language interference, in *Artificial Intelligence*, 6, 1, 53–74.

WITTGENSTEIN, L. (1953). *Philosophical investigations*. New York: Macmillan.

WYNNE, M. (ed.) (2005). *Developing Linguistic Corpora: A Guide to Good Practice*. Oxford: Oxbow Books; available online at <http://ahds.ac.uk/linguisticcorpora/>.

ZAENEN, A. (2006). Unaccusativity, in K. Brown (editor-in-chief), *The Encyclopedia of Language and Linguistics*, 2nd edn. Cambridge: Cambridge University Press.

ZGUSTA, L. (1967). Multiword lexical units, in *Word*, 23, 578–87.

ZGUSTA, L. (1971). *Manual of Lexicography*. Prague, The Hague and Paris: Academia-Mouton.

ZIPF, G.K. (1945). The meaning–frequency relationship of words, in *Journal of General Psychology*, 33, 251–6.

ZIPF, G.K. (1949). *Human Behavior and the Principle of Least Effort*. New York: Addison-Wesley.

# Index